BOOKS BY

ROBERT HASS

Field Guide

Praise

Human Wishes

Twentieth Century Pleasures

First published by The Ecco Press in 1984
100 West Broad Street, Hopewell, NJ 08525
Printed in the United States of America
Second Edition, 1987

Cover design by Cynthia Krupat

Library of Congress Cataloging in Publication Data
Hass, Robert.
Twentieth century pleasures.
1. Poetry, Modern—20th century—History and criticism—
Addresses, essays, lectures. I. Title.
II. Title: 20th century pleasures.
PN1271.H35 1984 809.1′04 83-16394
ISBN 0-88001-046-0 (paper)

TWENTIETH CENTURY PLEASURES

Prose on Poetry /

Robert Hass

The Ecco Press

New York

Acknowledgments

These essays were written for editors who asked for them. They would probably not have been written otherwise or perhaps I would have found myself writing about other poets. In any case, grateful acknowledgment, which is customary, is in this case heartfelt, because I learned about my art by writing about it and was glad both for the encouragement to write and places to publish.
So thanks to Michael Cuddihy of *Ironwood*, Dan Halpern of *Antaeus*, Robert Boyers of *Salmagundi*, Jonathan Galassi at Random House, Phil Dow who edited *Golden Gate Watershed*, Harvey Shapiro of *The New York Times Book Review*, Ann Hulbert at *The New Republic*, and Wendy Lesser of *The Threepenny Review*. Thanks also for the support of the Guggenheim Foundation during a time when I did some of this writing.

Contents

Twentieth Century Pleasures

Lowell's Graveyard

It's probably a hopeless matter, writing about favorite poems. I came across "The Lost Son," "The Quaker Graveyard in Nantucket" and "Howl" at about the same time. Some of the lines are still married in my head and they still have talismanic power: *snail, snail, glister me forward; Mohammedan angels staggering on tenement roofs illuminated; this is the end of running on the waves.* I see now that they are all three lost son poems, but at the time I didn't see much of anything. I heard, and it was the incantatory power of the poems that moved me. Enchantment, literally. I wandered around San Francisco demolishing the twentieth century by mumbling to myself, *blue-lunged combers lumbered to the kill* and managed to mix up Roethke's *ordnung! ordnung! papa's coming* with the Lord who survived the rainbow of his will.

You can analyze the music of poetry but it's difficult to conduct an argument about its value, especially when it's gotten into the blood. It becomes autobiography there. The other night in a pub in Cambridgeshire (named The Prince Regent and built just before the regency in the year when the first man who tried to organize a craft union among weavers was whipped, drawn, quartered and disemboweled in a public ceremony in London) the subject of favorite poems came up and a mild-looking man who taught high school geology treated us to this:

For it's Din! Din! Din!
You limpin' lump o' brick dust, Gunga Din!
Though I've belted you and flayed you,
By the livin' Gawd that made you,
You're a better man than I am, Gunga Din!

And he began to talk about his father's library in a summer cottage in Devon. I thought of how my older brother had loved that poem, how we had taken turns reading Vachel Lindsay and Kipling aloud on summer nights in California, in our upstairs room that looked out on a dusty fig orchard and grapevines spilling over the wooden fence.

Poems take place in your life, or some of them do, like the day your younger sister arrives and replaces you as the bon enfant in the bosom of the family; or the day the trucks came and the men began to tear up the wooden sidewalks and the cobblestone gutters outside your house and laid down new cement curbs and asphalt streets. We put paper bags on our feet to walk back and forth across the road which glistened with hot oil. That was just after the war. The town was about to become a suburb in the postwar boom. The fig orchard went just after the old road. I must have been six. Robert Lowell had just published in the *Partisan Review* a first version of "The Quaker Graveyard in Nantucket."

•

Thinking about this a long time later made me realize that "The Quaker Graveyard" is not a political poem. I had assumed that it was, that its rage against the war and Puritan will and the Quakers of Nantucket who financed the butchery of whales was an attack on American capitalism. But a political criticism of any social order implies both that a saner one can be imagined and the hope or conviction that it can be achieved. I had by then begun to have a way of describing such an order, got out of a melange of Paul Goodman, Camus and *To the Finland Station*, but what lay behind it was an imagination of early childhood, dusty fig leaves and sun and fields of wild fennel. Nostalgia locates desire in the past where it suffers no active conflict and can be yearned toward pleasantly. History is the antidote to this. When I saw that my paradise was Lowell's hell, I was forced to see that it was not a place in time I was thinking of, but a place in imagination. The fury of conflict is in "The Quaker Graveyard" but I went back to the poem looking for the vision of an alternative world. There is none. There's grief and moral rage but the poem imagines the whole of human life as sterile violence:

> All you recovered from Poseidon died
> With you, my cousin, and the harrowed brine
> Is fruitless on the blue beard of the god . . .

and it identifies finally with the inhuman justice of God:

> You could cut the brakish waters with a knife
> Here in Nantucket, and cast up the time
> When the Lord God formed man from the sea's slime
> And breathed into his face the breath of life,
> And blue-lunged combers lumbered to the kill.
> The Lord survives the rainbow of his will.

There are no choices in this history of the experiment of evolution and so there can be no politics. "The Lost Son," all inward animal alertness and numbed panic, contains the possibility of a social order by imagining return. And "Howl" wants to imagine a fifth international of angels.

It struck me then that the poem was closer in sensibility to someone like Robinson Jeffers than to most of the poets whom I had come to associate with Lowell. Both poets are forced to step outside the human process and claim the vision of some imperturbable godhead in which the long violence of human history looks small. But in "The Quaker Graveyard" it is important to say that is the position the poem *finally* arrives at because it is a poem of process, and of anguish. Warren Winslow drowns, the Quakers drown, the wounded whale churns in an imagination of suffering and violence which it is the imperative of the poem to find release from, and each successive section of the poem is an attempt to discover a way out. When I was beginning to read poetry to learn what it was and what it could be, this seemed the originality of the poem and its greatness.

•

And it's still hard for me to dissociate it from the excitement of that first reading. The poem leapt off the page. Its music, its fury and grief, haunted me:

> where the bones
> Cry out in the long night for the hurt beast
> Bobbing by Ahab's whaleboats in the East

By that time Lowell was writing in the later, more influential style, then controversial, now egregious orthodoxy:

> These are the tranquilized fifties
> and I am forty . . .

But I didn't know that, and I still find myself blinking incredulously when I read—in almost anything written about the poetry—that those early poems "clearly reflect the dictates of the new criticism," while the later ones are "less consciously wrought and extremely intimate." This is the view in which it is "more intimate" and "less conscious" to say "my mind's not right" than to imagine the moment when

> The death-lance churns into the sanctuary, tears
> The gun-blue swingle, heaving like a flail,
> And hacks the coiling life out . . .

which is to get things appallingly wrong.

•

Years later I heard a part of this judgment echoed in a curious way. I was listening to Yvor Winters, just before his death, lecturing on George Herbert. He was talking about Herbert's enjambments and, in one of his rare excursions into the present, he said in a bass grumble, "Young Lowell has got a bad enjambment which he got from Allen Tate who probably got it from Herbert." I thought of "The Quaker Graveyard":

> Light
> Flashed from his matted head and marble feet
>
> Seagulls blink their heavy lids
> Seaward

It lit up the poem all over again. Lowell had just published this in one of the fashionable journals:

> Only man thinning out his kind
> sounds through the Sabbath noon, the blind
> swipe of the pruner and his knife
> busy about the tree of life . . .

Non est species, but plenty of *decor*. I'm still not sure what I think about these lines. There is enormous, ironic skill in the octosyllabic couplets, and terrible self-laceration in their poise. It is probably great writing in the sense that the state of mind couldn't be rendered more exactly. But I wondered about the state of mind and said a small prayer to the small gods—hilarity and carnality—that I could escape it. The writer, among other things, is getting a certain magisterial pleasure from seeming to be outside the picture. The writer of these lines is in it:

And rips the sperm-whale's midriff into rags,
Gobbets of blubber spill to wind and weather,
Sailor, and gulls go round the stoven timbers
Where the morning stars sing out together . . .

•

It is possible, I suppose, to object to the brilliance of the writing. Charles Olson is said to have complained that Lowell lacquered each of his poems and hung it in a museum. But this judgment, like the "confessional" revolution envisaged by the professoriat, seems to be based on the sociology of Kenyon College or the fact of meter or Lowell's early models, on everything but a reading of the poems. Finish in poetry is, as Olson insisted, a question of form following function. "The Quaker Graveyard" is brilliantly written, and in a decade of amazing poetry: the *Pisan Cantos*, the first books of *Paterson, Four Quartets*, HD's *War Trilogy*, Stevens' "Credences of Summer," Roethke's "The Lost Son." But its brilliance seems neither dictated nor wrought; it is headlong, furious, and casual. There are moments that hover near grandiloquence—"Ask for no Orphean lute . . ." but they didn't bother me then and don't much now.

Everything about the sound of the poem seemed gorgeous on first reading. "A brakish reach of shoal off . . ." sounded like an impossible Russian word, sluggish and turbulent; the Indian-Yankee "Madaket" bit it off with wonderful abruptness. I still like to say it:

A brakish reach of shoal off Madaket, —

In the second line, the oddness of the sound, which is a substitution in the third foot, has a slightly startling effect:

The sea was still breaking violently . . .

The rhythm breaks "breaking," makes a violence out of slackness in a way that I had never seen before, and it was clearly intended because *still* is an extra syllable:

> The sea was still breaking violently and night

From here to the end of the stanza, the energy of the poem allows no rest—

> Had steamed into our North Atlantic fleet,
> When the drowned sailor clutched the drag-net. Light
> Flashed from his matted head and marble feet,
> He grappled at the net
> With the coiled hurdling muscles of his thighs:

I loved the nervous restlessness of the rhyming, the way you accept "net" as the rhyme for "fleet" and "Madaket," then get the off-rhyme "light," so that when you arrive at "feet" it is hardly an arrival and you are pushed toward "net" again. It's like a man shooting at a target with such random desperation that the hits count for no more than the misses. This effect, together with "young Lowell's bad enjambment," transmute an acquired skill into articulate rage. And the colon after "thighs" is not a rest; it insists on the forward hurtle of the lines:

> The corpse was bloodless . . .

•

Warren Winslow or not, it has always seemed to me that Lowell himself was the drowned sailor, just as Roethke is the lost son. Otherwise the sudden moments of direct address make no sense:

> Sailor, will your sword
> Whistle and fall and sink into the fat?

In the great ash-pit of Jehoshaphat
The bones cry for the blood of the white whale,
The fat flukes arch and whack about its ears,
The death-lance churns into the sanctuary . . .

It is having it both ways to be the young man drowned in the "slush," in the "bilge and backwash," "the greased wash," "the sea's slime" where "the whale's viscera go and the roll of its corruption overruns the world" and to be at the same time the young poet who identifies with the vengeance of the earth-shaker, "green, unwearied, chaste" whose power outlasts the merely phallic brutality of the guns of the steeled fleet, but the impacted writing permits this and it is psychologically true. Distrust of birth is the beginning of one kind of religious emotion.

In the speed of the writing, the syntax comes apart; it dissolves into emotion, into music and the subterranean connections among images. Throughout the poem it is characteristic that the important associations occur in subordinate clauses or compounds so breathless that you have to sort your way back quite consciously to the starting point. This resembles the syntactical strategies of the French surrealists, particularly Desnos and Peret. The main clause is a pushing off place and the poem makes its meaning out of its momentum. It's a way of coming to terms with experience under pressure and not some extrinsic decision about style. Even the lines about the shark—

Where the heelheaded dogfish barks its nose
On Ahab's void and forehead

are not Clevelandizing; they are not even—in the period phrase—a metaphysical image because their force is not intellectual. The lines depend on our willingness to let barking dogs marry scavenging sharks in the deep places where men void and are voided. To complain about this is not to launch an attack on "consciously wrought" but the reverse.

The current taste is for the explicit, however weird. Surrealism comes to mean the manufacture of peculiar imagery and not something in the sinews of a poem. The fish in "For the Union Dead" are a midpoint in this leveling process. They are transformed into sharks and then into cars as "a savage servility slides by on grease," but the delivery is slower, the context narrative and topographical. It is pretty much the same image as in "The Quaker Graveyard," but it has been clarified like broth, a fish stock served up as clam chowder to the peremptory gentleman in the cartoon who likes to see what he's eating.

And this won't do for Lowell because the power of his imagery has always been subliminal; it exists as the nervous underside of the thing said. Look at this, for example, from "Fourth of July in Maine." The poet is addressing Harriet Winslow:

Dear Cousin, life is much the same,
though only fossils know your name
here since you left this solitude,
gone, as the Christians say, for good.
Your house, still outwardly in form
lasts, though no emissary comes
to watch the garden running down,
or photograph the propped-up barn.

If memory is genius, you
had Homer's, enough gossip to
repeople Trollope's Barchester,
nurses, Negro, diplomat, down-easter,
cousins kept up with, nipped, corrected,
kindly, majorfully directed,
though family furniture, decor,
and rooms redone meant almost more.

How often when the telephone
brought you to us from Washington,
we had to look around the room

to find the objects you would name —
lying there, ten years paralyzed,
half-blind, no voice unrecognized,
not trusting in the afterlife,
teasing us for a carving knife.

High New England summer, warm
and fortified against the storm
by nightly nips you once adored,
though never going overboard,
Harriet, when you used to play
your chosen Nadia Boulanger
Monteverdi, Purcell, and Bach's
precursors on the Magnavox.

This is affectionate, even cozy. And beneath that first sensation is deep pathos; and beneath that is something like terror, so that the force of the phrase "life is much the same" keeps changing—for the worse—as you read. The imagery of a life with fossil memory, a run-down garden, a propped-up barn, a devastated Troy and cursed Mycenae, a Barchester that needs repeopling, people who need to be nipped and corrected, or redone, a half-blind paralyzed woman (the syntax has a way of paralyzing her objects as well), the need to be fortified against summer (with nips: the carving knife lying suddenly across both the cozy drinking and the corrected behavior) all issue in, among time's other wreckage, a Magnavox, the great voice which reproduces a great religious passion in the form of a performer's art. Everything dwindles, is rendered. Boulanger's Monteverdi. Lowell's Harriet. It's easy to explicate poems and hard to get their tone. The tone here has one moment of extraordinary pathos which is deeper than the catlike movement through entropy and corrosion:

half-blind, no voice unrecognized,
not trusting in the afterlife,
teasing us for a carving knife.

High New England summer . . .

But in the end the tone has to do with rendering; the whole passage is majorfully directed. It is not the experience but a way of handling the experience. The imagery accumulates its desolating evidence, but in such a way that the terror in the poetry is perceived while the novelistic pathos is felt. The subterranean images, whether "consciously wrought" or not, are intellectual. In this way, it is exactly a metaphysical poem as nothing in *Lord Weary's Castle* is.

•

In the second section of "The Quaker Graveyard" there's not much that could be called development. Four sentences, three of which use syntax only as a line of energy, do little more than elaborate an instance of what used to be called the pathetic fallacy, but they confront the experience of grief, of terror at the violence of things, directly:

Whenever winds are moving and their breath
Heaves at the roped-in bulwarks of this pier,
The terns and seagulls tremble at your death
In these home waters. Sailor, can you hear
The Pequod's sea-wings, beating landward, fall
Headlong and break on our Atlantic wall
Off 'Sconset, where the yawing S-boats splash
As the entangled screeching mainsheet clears
The blocks: off Madaket, where lubbers lash
The heavy surf and throw their long lead squids
For blue-fish? Seagulls blink their heavy lids
Seaward. The wind's wings beat upon the stones,
Cousin, and scream for you and the claws rush
At the sea's throat and wring it in the slush
Of this old Quaker Graveyard where the bones
Cry out in the long night for the hurt beast
Bobbing by Ahab's whaleboats in the East.

The effect here is not simple, but for me it is the most beautiful moment in the poem. The whole of that first sentence relaxes. The lines break deliberately as if they were trying to hold the emotion in place. But the content is terrible and the perception is extraordinarily intense. The feathers of the gulls ruffling in the wind are made to hurt. And it's such an ordinary perception. "Whenever winds are moving," to my Pacific grounding, is almost always, so that the image registers the steady pain of merely seeing. For some reason this connected in my mind with a thing Lévi-Strauss says near the end of *Tristes Tropiques*: "What I see is an affliction to me, what I cannot see a reproach." The power of this image connects all the description in the poem with the eyes of the dead sailor and the gulls' eyes and the profoundly becalmed eyes of the Virgin of Walsingham. It connects the wind's breath with the breath of the poet which accelerates into violence again in the next sentence. And that sentence is a good example of the expressive power of syntax in the poem. In its fierce accumulation of images, you lose any sense that it began, rather gently, as a rhetorical question. This is a way of being lost, of drowning in the dissolution of syntax. Surrealism, I'm tempted to say, is syntax: not weird images but the way the mind connects them. Here they swell and gather toward violence, toward a continuous breaking like the breaking of waves on the shore, and the effort of control is conveyed by the way "the entangled screeching mainsheet clears the blocks."

So the poem must slow down again: "Seagulls blink their heavy lids / Seaward." This fixity, the imperturbable consciousness of the gull whose feathers a moment before were trembling in "home waters," is an enormous relief. It is not the dead staring eyes of the drowned sailor and it is not yet the seeing of Our Lady of Walsingham. That heavy-lidded blinking of gulls seems to have a wonderful Buddhalike somnolent alertness when you look at it. It accepts things as they are. It's when gulls are perched on piers, heads tucked in a little, eyes blinking matter-of-factly, that I'm suddenly aware they have no arms, no hands. Even if they don't like what they see, they're not going to do anything about it. And this is a relief. But gulls are also scavengers. Their seeing doesn't hope for much, but it belongs to the world of appetite and their appetites are not very ambitious. That is why the sailors, grasping at straws in section IV, are only three-quarters fools. They want something, have heard news "of IS, the whited monster." So the lines accelerate again. The sea, godly in the first section, is consumed in the general violence in this one and the section ends in a long wail for Moby Dick, the object of desire, monster and victim.

Almost all of "The Quaker Graveyard" works in this way. It's hard to get at without a lot of tedious explication, but look at the third section of the poem. If you ask yourself how the language or the thought proceeds, it's not easy to say. First sentence: All you recovered died with you. Second sentence: Guns blast the eelgrass. Third sentence: They died . . . ; only bones abide. Characteristically, the Quaker sailors appear at the extremity of a dependent clause; then their fate is seized on, midway through the section, as a subject, and the stanza unravels again into violence as the sailors drown proclaiming their justification. And it does not seem arbitrary. It seems inevitable, because this hopelessly repeated unraveling into violence is both the poem's theme and the source of its momentum. Hell is repetition and the structure of anger is repetition. In this poem history is also repetition, as it is the structure of religious incantation. They are all married here, desperately, and the grace of the poem has to exist in modulation of tone. This modulation, like the different textures of an abstract expressionist painting or like the very different modulations that create the texture of Whitman's poems—"Song of Myself" comes to mind—is the grandeur and originality of "The Quaker Graveyard." Not theme, not irony or intimacy or the consciously wrought, but absolute attention to feeling at that moment in the poem's process.

•

"They died / When time was open-eyed, / Wooden and childish." It takes a while—or took me a while—to see that this is the one moment in the poem that reaches back into childhood. The image has about it the helplessness of childhood. Time here must be the wooden, open-eyed figureheads on old whaling ships, probably seen in books or a maritime museum. The look of the eyes on those old sculptures, their startled and hopeful innocence, dawns on you and it creates the state of mind of the child looking up at them. *Was,* not *seemed.* The verb makes the child's seeing sovereign and irrecoverable. Lost innocence is not the subject of the poem. There is a kind of pleading between the poet and the innocence of his cousin, the ensign who went to the war and did his duty. "All you recovered . . . died with you." But the innocence of the child, of the ensign, of the figureheads is only one syntactical leap away from the stupidity and self-righteousness of the Quaker sailors —"If God himself had not been on our side"—who are swallowed up without understanding a thing. Their eyes are "cabin-windows on a stranded hulk / Heavy with sand."

•

Sections IV and V continue this riding out of violence but the conclusions of both take a turn that brings us to the religious issue in the poem. It didn't puzzle me much in that first excited reading because I ignored it. I was living down a Catholic childhood, and religious reference in poetry seemed to me not so much reactionary as fossilized and uninteresting. But it was surely there in a lot of what I was reading. Robert Duncan's work was thick with religious imagery, and the "Footnote to Howl" exclaimed, "Holy! Holy! Holy!" I didn't know Lowell was a convert to Catholicism or that this was a momentous rejection of his heritage. For that matter, I didn't know what a Lowell was. But I could see that the poem was not Catholic in any sense that I understood. It is true that the implicit answer to the question "Who will dance the mast-lashed master of Leviathans / Up . . ." is Christ. Orpheus, the way of art, is explicitly dismissed at the beginning of the poem. And the fifth section, the most terrible, the one in which the whale receives the sexual wound of all human violence, ends with a prayer: "Hide / Our steel, Jonas Messias, in thy side."

But the first of these passages is a question and the second is a supplication, not a statement of faith. Insofar as the poem is Christian, it seemed to me to be a very peculiar Christianity. I was prepared to grant that the killing of the whale was also an image of the crucifixion of Christ, but in the poem this act is the source and culmination of evil. "When the whale's viscera go . . . its corruption overruns this world." There is no sense here of the crucifixion as a redemption. I can imagine that three or four pages of theological explication could put it there, but it isn't in the poem. Typologically the legal torture and murder of the man-god is not the fall; in the Christian myth it was not cruelty and violence but pride and disobedience through which men fell. One can make a series of arguments, threading back through the blasphemous pride of Ahab to the dominion given man by God in the epigraph to the poem, and emerge with a case for cruelty as a form of pride, but cruelty is not pride. They're different things, and it is cruelty and death, not pride and the fall, that preoccupy the poet, no matter how much of Melville or theology we haul in to square this vision with orthodoxy.

Reading Robert Duncan has given me a way to think about this issue in Lowell:

There was no law of Jesus then.
                                                There was
    only a desire of savior . . .

Somewhere in his prose at about the same time Duncan had written that the mistake of Christianity was to think that the soul's salvation was the only human adventure. That was an enormously liberating perception. It put Christ on equal footing with the other gods. And the gods, Pound had said in a phrasing that seems now late Victorian, were "eternal moods," forms of consciousness which men through learning, art and contemplation could inhabit. They were not efficacious. We were not Mycenaean warlords, burning bulls and hoping the good scent of roast beef found its way to attentive nostrils; and the Mother of Perpetual Help did not, as my aunts seemed to believe, repair carburetors or turn up lost purses. But the gods were real, forms of imagination in which we could dwell and through which we could see. "The verb," Pound had said with the wreckage of his life around him, "is 'to see' not 'walk on.' "

I got my Catholicism from my mother's side, Foleys from Cork by way of Vermont who drank and taught school and practiced law on the frontiers of respectability until they landed in San Francisco at the turn of the century. My father's side was Protestant and every once in a while, weary probably with the catechisms of his children, he would try to teach us one of his childhood prayers. But he could never get past the first line: "In my father's house there are many mansions . . ." He would frown, squint, shake his head, but that was as far as he ever got and we children who were willing to believe Protestants capable of any stupidity including the idea that you could fit a lot of mansions into a house, would return to memorizing the four marks of the true church. (It was one, holy, catholic, and apostolic.) But that phrase came back to me as a way through the door of polytheism and into myth. If Pound could resurrect the goddesses, there was a place for a temple of Christ, god of sorrows, desire of savior, restingplace of violence. I could have the memory of incense and the flickering candles and the battered figure on the cross with the infinitely sad and gentle face and have Aphrodite as well, "the fauns chiding Proteus / in the smell of hay under olive trees" and the intoning of Latin with which we began the mass: "*Introibo ad altare Dei.*" On these terms, Lowell's prayer moved me: "Hide our steel, Jonas Messias, in thy side." And I could accept cruelty as the first fall; it was truer to my experience than pride or disobedience, which the violence of the state has made to seem, on the whole, sane and virtuous. Not the old dogma, but a piece of the unborn myth which American poetry was making. And this is the sense of things in the poem. There is no redemption promised in the prayer at the end of section V. There is only the god of sorrows and the receiving of the wound.

Sexual wounding: it is certainly there in section V, both in the imagery and in the way the section functions, literally, as a climax to the poem. This is the fall, the moment when corruption overruns the world. And the rhetorical question, "Sailor, will your sword / Whistle and fall and sink into the fat?" wants to make us all complicit. The passage is Calvinist in feeling; every day is judgment day:

> In the great ash-pit of Jehoshaphat
> The bones cry for the blood of the white whale

In sexual imagery, not only the penetration by the death lance but the singing of stars, the dismemberment of the masthead, we are all judged:

> The fat flukes arch and whack about its ears,
> The death-lance churns into the sanctuary, tears
> The gun-blue swingle, heaving like a flail,
> And hacks the coiling life out: it works and drags
> And rips the sperm-whale's midriff into rags,
> Gobbets of blubber spill to wind and weather,

Sailor, and gulls go round the stoven timbers
Where the morning stars sing out together
And thunder shakes the white surf and dismembers
The red flag hammered in the masthead . . .

This needs to be seen straight on, so that we look at the sickening cruelty it actually describes. It's a relief and much easier to talk about myth or symbolic sexuality. This is an image of killing written by a pacifist who was willing to go to prison. It makes death horrifying; it makes the war horrifying, and the commerce of the Nantucket Quakers whom Melville reminded his readers to think of when they lit their cozy whale-oil lamps. "Light is where the landed blood of Cain . . ."

But, just as there is disgust with the mothering sea in the bilge and backwash throughout the poem, there is a deep abhorrence of sexual violence, of sexuality as violence. I'm not sure how to talk about it. There is Freud's gruesome little phrase, as gruesome in German as in English but lacking the pun: the sadistic conception of coitus. But calling it that doesn't take us very far. The fact is that there is an element of cruelty in human sexuality, though that isn't the reason for the Puritan distrust of sex. The Puritans distrusted sexuality because the sexual act dissolved human will for a moment, because—for a moment—men fell into the roots of their mammal nature. You can't have an orgasm and be a soldier of Christ. Thus *Samson Agonistes*. And the Puritan solution, hidden but real in the history of imagination whether in Rome or the Enlightenment, was to turn sex into an instrument of will, of the conscious cruelty which flowered in the writings of Sade. It is there in our history and Lowell is right to connect it with the annihilative rage of capitalism. Flesh is languor ("All of life's grandeur / is something with a girl in summer . . .") but it is also rage. It marries us to the world and the world is full of violence and cruelty. This is part of the bind of the poem which is also the Calvinist bind of determinism and free will.

The way out is not-world, an identification at the end of the poem with the "unmarried" Atlantic and the Lord who survives the rainbow-covenant of evolution.

•

All of which would be pretty grim if it were not for "Our Lady of Walsingham." It's a remarkable moment in the poem, the most surprising of its modulations, a little tranquil island in all the fury. I imagine that for a lot of younger writers it was the place where they learned how far you could go away from the poem and still be in it. Pound says somewhere, sounding like a surly Matthew Arnold, that a history of poetry that's worth anything ought to be able to point to specific poems and passages in poems and say here, here and here are inventions that made something new possible in poetry. This is one of those places.

Its occurrence makes emotional sense because it follows section V. It is the peace of the satisfaction of the body's rage, a landscape of streams and country lanes. The nineteenth century would have described the writing as chaste or exquisite and I'm not sure we have better words to praise it with. It's wonderfully plain and exact:

> Our Lady, too small for her canopy,
> Sits near the altar. There's no comeliness
> At all or charm in that expressionless
> Face with its heavy eyelids. As before,
> This face, for centuries a memory,
> *Non est species, neque decor,*
> Expressionless, expresses God: it goes
> Past castled Sion. She knows what God knows,
> Not Calvary's cross nor the crib at Bethlehem
> Now, and the world shall come to Walsingham.

This is another temple, not the god of sorrows but the goddess of an almost incomprehensible peace. It appears to be the emphatically Catholic moment in the poem (which adds a peculiar comedy to the idea that "Lycidas" was somehow its model; I've just visited the cathedral at Ely where Milton's friend Thomas Cromwell personally beheaded all the statues in the Lady Chapel. If the set-piece digressions of Alexandrian pastoral taken over by Milton to scourge a Popish clergy have really become a hymn to the Virgin Mary, it is the kind of irony—funny, too elaborately bookish—that would please the author of *History*). But I don't think it is Catholic, or not especially Catholic, and that is its interest.

The crucial phrase is "past castled Sion." Lowell is not after sacramental mediation but a contemplative peace beyond any manifestation in the flesh, beyond thought or understanding, and—most especially—beyond desire. This isn't incompatible with Catholic theology, but it's not central to its spirit which is embodiment: the Orphean lute and the crib at Bethlehem. This apprehension of God, of a pure, calm and utterly clear consciousness, belongs equally to all mysticisms, Christian or otherwise, and it has always seemed to me that the figure of Our Lady here looks a lot like Gautama Buddha. It is the embodiment of what can't be embodied. This is a contradiction, but it is one that belongs to any intellectual pointing toward mystical apprehension. It is the contradiction that made the world-denial of Buddhists and Cathars at the same time utterly compassionate toward and alert to the world and the flesh and makes the Buddhist Gary Snyder our best poet of nature. This is not the rejection of the world which the last lines of the poem suggest; it's something else and for me it's something much more attractive as a possibility of imagination.

But how does it square with the last lines? I don't think it does. Nor does it contradict them. That's the aesthetic daring of this section. What the Lady of Walsingham represents is past contention. She's just there. The method of the poem simply includes her among its elements, past argument, as a possibility through which all the painful seeing in the poem can be transformed and granted peace. She floats; everything else in the poem rises and breaks, relentlessly, like waves.

•

I finally got to hear Robert Lowell read a couple of years ago in Charlottesville, Virginia—in Jefferson country where the road signs read like a rollcall of plump Hanoverian dowagers and America comes as close as it ever will to a munching English lane. The setting made me feel truculent anyway, and when he began by murmuring an apology for the earlier poems —"rather apocalyptic," "one felt so intense"—I found myself on the poems' side. And the voice startled me, probably because I'd been hearing the work in my own for so long. I thought it sounded bizarrely like an imitation of Lionel Barrymore. It was not a voice that could say "Face of snow, / You are the flowers that country girls have caught, / A wild bee-pillaged honeysuckle brought / To the returning bridegroom—the design / Has not yet left it, and the petals shine" without sounding like a disenchanted English actor reading an Elizabethan sonnet on American television.

I had felt vaguely hostile toward Lowell's later work, though I admired it. I thought, for one thing, that the brilliant invention of "The Quaker Graveyard" had come about because he had nothing to go on but nerve and that, when the form cloyed in *The Mills of the Kavanaughs*, he had traded in those formal risks for the sculpted anecdote and the Puritan autobiography, a form about as original as John Bunyan's *Grace Abounding*. There is something new in it. Lowell found a way to accommodate realistic detail and narrative structures out of Chekhov and the short story tradition to his own resonant version of the free verse of William Carlos Williams, but out of that manner had come, not so much in Lowell himself as in the slough of poetry *Life Studies* engendered, a lot of narrative beginning "Father, you . . ." or "The corn died in the field that summer, Mother / when . . ." It struck stances toward experience, as if Williams had said "No attitudes but in things!" I wanted the clarity that "Our Lady of Walsingham" looked toward and in "Waking Early Sunday Morning" I thought he had come to something like that earlier insight and abandoned it too easily:

I watch a glass of water wet
with a fine fuzz of icy sweat,
silvery colours touched with sky,
serene in their neutrality—
yet if I shift, or change my mood,
I see some object made of wood,
background behind it of brown grain,
to darken it, but not to stain.

O that the spirit could remain
tinged but untarnished by its strain!
Better dressed and stacking birch . . .

As if you had to choose between them or tarnishing were the issue. That glass of water interested me a lot more than the ironies about electric bells ringing "Faith of our fathers."

Anyway, when he began to read, all this buzzing of the head stopped. There was the sense, for one thing, of a body of work faithful to itself through all its phases (early, middle and ceaseless revision). And there was the reading of "Near the Ocean." Hearing it, I began to understand the risks attendant on backing away from the drama and self-drama of *Lord Weary's Castle*. Pain has its own grandeur. This disenchanted seeing was not serene neutrality—it was not serene at all; it had the clarity of a diminished sense of things not flinched at. I thought it was a brave piece of writing and it revisits the territory of "The Quaker Graveyard," so it seems like a place to end:

Sand built the lost Atlantis . . . sand,
Atlantic ocean, condoms, sand.

Sleep, sleep. The ocean, grinding stones,
can only speak the present tense;
nothing will age, nothing will last,
or take corruption from the past.
A hand, your hand then! I'm afraid
to touch the crisp hair on your head—

James Wright

Young boys read verses to help themselves express or know their feelings, as if the dim intuited features of love, heroism, or sensuality could only be clearly contemplated in a poem.
—OCTAVIO PAZ

The kind of poetry I want to write is
The poetry of a grown man.
—JAMES WRIGHT

1/

I have been worrying the bone of this essay for days because, in an issue of *Ironwood* honoring James Wright, I want to say some things against his poems. The first of his books that I read was *The Branch Will Not Break.* It is supposed to have broken ground by translating the imagery of surrealist and expressionist poetics into American verse. That was not what I responded to. What mattered to me in those poems was that their lean, clear, plain language had the absolute freshness of sensibility. They made sensibility into something as lucid and alert as intelligence. We speak of animal intelligence, of the intelligence of the body, but my experience is that when we are most possessed by it, we are least aware of it, or least self-conscious about it. The part of the mind that needs to learn from it, to be able to reflect on it, is absorbed by it. And the only other way it is available to us is through art. Not all art, either, but the work of some few artists. It is rare enough, I think, and hard to talk about, but it involves a special kind of alertness. I can give you an example from *Shall We Gather at the River*:

Along the sprawled body of the derailed
   Great Northern freight car,
I strike a match slowly and lift it slowly.
No wind.

Beyond town, three heavy white horses
Wade all the way to their shoulders
In a silo shadow.

Suddenly the freight car lurches.
The door slams back, a man with a flashlight
Calls me good evening.
I nod as I write good evening, lonely
And sick for home.

Those last two lines are what I mean. They were not written by the poet who is lonely and sick for home, they were written by the man who noticed that the poet, sitting in his room alone, recalling a scene outside Fargo, North Dakota, nods when he writes down the greeting of his imagined yardman, and catches in that moment not the poet's loneliness but a gesture that reveals the aboriginal loneliness of being—of the being of the freight cars, silos, horses, shadows, matches, poets, flashlights. And that man, the man who wrote those lines, is not lonely. At least that is not quite the word for it. There is a poem by Basho that gets at this:

   Not my human
sadness, cuckoo,
   but your solitary cry.

The cuckoo, or hototogisu, is the nightingale of Japanese poetry. Its evening song has all the automatic associations with loneliness and beauty, and Basho is correcting that tradition. He is not, he says, talking about our plangent human loneliness but about the solitariness of being, of beings going about their business. The business of singing, if you are a bird, of feeling lonely, if you are a human. This is a distinction and it is the function of intelligence to make distinctions, but this one has been felt toward, with an absolute clarity of feeling, and that is what I mean by sensibility. It is a quality that flashes out from time to time in Wright's poems and it made *The Branch Will Not Break* an enormously important book for me. So I should probably rephrase my first sentence in the manner of *Two Citizens*: I want to say some things against James Wright's poems, which I love.

A brief might begin with what he has to say about "a grown man":

> The long body of his dream is the beginning of a dark
> Hair under an illiterate
> Girl's ear.

It's hard to know whether to complain first about the fabricated ingenuity of the image or the preciousness of the diction. Or about the fact that it is so sculpted as to be memorable anyway. Or the fact that Wright's characteristic tenderness almost redeems it. What bothers me, finally, is the familiar celebration of whatever is not mind, of everything unformed, unconscious, and suffused, therefore, with yearning. The important thing about the image is scale; it has the scale of body knowledge. It is as sharply focused as the body is in lovemaking or in pain. It is also predictable. The hair is dark, not light. The person is a girl, not a woman or a man. And just to make sure we are in the dark of sex or the dark of nature or the spirit's darkness, the girl is illiterate. This from a man who loves Goethe, for whom Horace is "a good secret," whose work has been an exemplary struggle with the difficult and specifically human possibilities of the lyric poem.

I think of Truffaut's severe and beautiful *Wild Child*, of the mixed feelings with which I watched, in grainy black and white, while the wolf boy of Aveyron struggled with language —which I wanted him to acquire, which I did not want him to have to acquire. In a very quiet way Truffaut makes us feel the cost of the struggle to perform those symbolic operations which turn body knowledge into symbol and make thought and feeling available to us, in the way that they are available to us. The best and hardest moment of the film occurs when the boy finally rebels and runs out of the house into the field where he sits in the high grass in the rain, rocking slowly back and forth in a state of mute, warm, fetal peace that shuts out his fear and confusion. The heart goes out to him completely and everything conspires against the heart, because so much of what moves us about the image belongs to culture, including the fact that it is an image: the French doors through which the boy is photographed, the espaliered trees in the background, the fact that the slanting rain looks like rain in Kurosawa, that the antic, melancholy music on the sound track is Mozart. So much light, so many centuries of the evolution of light, to render the pathos and beauty of that darkness.

Someone has calculated that the words *dark*, *darkness*, and *darkening* appear over forty times in the twenty-six pages *The Branch Will Not Break* occupies in the *Collected Poems*. *Green* must appear at least as often. And the book is full of those Wordsworthian words that no one is supposed to be able to get away with: *lovely*, *terrible*, *beautiful*; *body* and *lonely* run like a threnody through all his books. I don't care how often James Wright uses any word, but I do care how he uses them and why. The early poems have helped me to think about this, particularly "On Minding One's Own Business" in *Saint Judas*. It's about a couple gliding on a lake after sundown:

All evening fins have drowned
Back in the summer dark.
Above us, up the bank,

Obscure on lonely ground,
A shack receives the night.

The speaker goes wide and quiet past the place. He is not going to interfere with whoever is inside, but he describes the kind of people who would, people who use "will," who have "force" and "weight":

We will not land to bear
Our will upon that house,
Nor force on any place
Our dull offensive weight.

This is an American poem and an American place, so the people who have will and force are Puritans, the hard-sleepers, enviers of pleasure:

Long may the lovers hide
In viny shacks from those
Who thrash among the trees,
Who curse, who have no peace,
Who pitch and moan all night
For fear of someone's joys,
Deploring the human face.

The poem ends, like many of Wright's poems, with a prayer:

From prudes and muddying fools,
Kind Aphrodite, spare
All hunted criminals,
Hoboes, and whip-poor-wills,
And girls with rumpled hair,
All, all of whom might hide
Within that darkening shack.
Lovers may live, and abide.

Maybe the worst thing about American Puritanism is the position it forces its opponents into. If the Puritan can't distinguish a hobo from a hunted criminal, a little nighthawk from a girl who does the sorts of things that rumple hair, the poet won't. Hunted criminal, in fact, equals hobo equals bird equals girl. The Puritan can't tell one from another and knows they are all bad; the poet can't tell either, only he knows they belong to the dark and are good. When he agrees to disagree with the Puritan on his own terms, he gives away will, force, power, weight because they are bad American qualities and he settles for passivity and darkness. This explains why the grown man's dream is the beginning of a dark hair under an illiterate girl's ear. It explains why another early poem is called "All the Beautiful Are Blameless."

It glosses these lines from the poem about President Harding:

"Warren lacks mentality," one of his friends said.
Yet he was beautiful, he was the snowfall
Turned to white stallions
Under dark elm trees.

And it is the only thing that can explain the puzzling and repellent lines that end one of the poems about the rapist, George Doty. Wright has been meditating on the execution of this man who "stopped his car and found / A girl on the darkening ground, / And killed her in the snow." He says this:

. . . I mourn no soul but his
Not even the bums who die
Nor the homely girl whose cry
Crumbled his pleading kiss.

Wright has often been praised, to use the curious language of *The Norton Anthology of Modern Poetry,* for his "compassionate interest in social outcasts." That has never seemed to me to be the way to say it. What has always been a remarkable, almost singular, fact about his poetry is the way in which the suffering of other people, particularly the lost and the derelict, is actually a part of his own emotional life. It is what he writes from, not what he writes about. He has a feeling in his own bones for what a cold and unforgiving place the social world is. More than that, he has a feeling, almost Calvinist, for how unforgiving the universe is, so that he can make poetry of Warren Harding who claimed "the secret right to be ashamed," of Judas "flayed without hope." He is fascinated by defeat the way some men are fascinated by money, as the intelligible currency of our lives. His poems return and return to this theme, to the unformed hopes growing in the warm dark and the cold dark to which they return, until loneliness and death seem like the price exacted for living.

In the poem about George Doty, he is thinking hard about these issues, however mindless and uncanny those last lines seem. The bums, for example, whom he doesn't mourn, appear in an earlier stanza:

> Beside his cell, I am told,
> Hardy perennial bums
> Complain till twilight comes
> For hunger and for cold.
>
> They hardly know of a day
> That saw their hunger pass.
> Bred to the dark, their flesh
> Peacefully withers away.

I don't believe this (and neither does Wright in "The Minneapolis Poem"), but it explains what the bums mean to him and why he doesn't mourn them. They live and die in the dark, more or less contented with complaining. It also explains why he does mourn George Doty:

> Sick of the dark, he rose
> For love, and now he goes
> Back to the broken ground.

There are things to doubt here, too. But if it is true that the man raped and murdered in a dark channel of the impulse to love, then it is not hard to see why he is a crucial figure. It still doesn't explain why Wright uses the conclusion of the poem to say so explicitly that he mourns the killer but not the victim. What I think is that he is trying to speak as intensely as he can the depth of his identification with the criminal and the criminal sin of rising.

Rise. Rise and *gather.* They must be the most important active verbs in Wright's work. A dream of transcendence and a dream of community. This theme of rising is echoed later and very richly in *Two Citizens:*

> The last time I tried to escape from my body,
> You threw me down into a tangle of roots.
> Out of them I clambered up into the elbows
> Of a sycamore tree . . .
>
> . . . .
>
> I rose out of my body so high into
> That sycamore tree that it became
> The only tree that ever loved me.

And again:

> There used to be a sycamore just
> Outside Martins Ferry,
> Where I used to go.
> I had no friends there.
> Maybe that tree was no woman
> But when I sat there, I gathered
> That branch into my arms.
> It was the first time I ever rose.

And again, in a daffy, ecstatic love poem:

> Oh tree.
> We climbed into the branches

Of the lady's tree.
We birds sang.

We might add to this, for the imagery of light and dark, sick and cold, his account of how, one summer, he came to steal crabapples:

I don't know why,
One evening in August something illuminated my body
And I got sick of laying my cold
Hands on myself.
I lied to my family I was going for a walk uptown.

Having no language to explain rising, illumination, in the ordinary world, he invents.

I come back to that remark by Octavio Paz. All these lines by the older man remember the young man's discovery of his own inwardness, of his consciousness of himself, some passion in him akin to love and sexuality and prayer. In the early poem he is thinking about George Doty and the crime of rape and the crime, less intelligible, of state execution, but he is also thinking about himself and about poetry which is in himself and beautiful and lonely and some kind of sexual crime. So another early poem is a sonnet about a fugitive. It begins:

The night you got away, I dreamed you rose
Out of the earth to lean on a young tree.

The sestet owes something to Robinson and something to old Warner Brothers movies:

Hurry, Maguire, hammer the body down,
Crouch to the wall again, shackle the cold
Machine guns and the sheriff and the cars;
Divide the bright bars of the cornered bone,
Strip, run for it, break the last law, unfold,
Dart down the alley, race between the stars.

Hopeless, this melodramatic grandeur. You could not tell the qualities of the poet who wrote it except for that one phrase, "the cornered bone." It is what Wright knows and what makes his poems, so often, tense with the impulse to escape.

"We Americans," the older man writes, "loneliness of body, / Puritans sick at the beauty of the body." "Ugliness," he writes. "What is it? A bitter / Taste of one body."

Over and over again in American writing, this theme or discovery, that the inner life has no place, that it makes outlaws of us. Whether it is Huck deciding to go to hell or the hell of West's *Miss Lonelyhearts,* or Gatsby thinking the rich with their good teeth and fast cars can transform the ugly Midwestern body of the world, or poor Clyde Griffith who rises from the squalor of his childhood when he glimpses velvet curtains in a Kansas City hotel, or Robinson's loyalty to Luke Havergal and the boozy moon, there is always this sense of a radical division between the inner and outer worlds and the hunger for a magic which will heal it, a sanctification or election. It gives a kind of drama to Wright's search for a style, but it also gives me the uneasy feeling that the way of posing the problem is the problem.

These themes persist through all the later work: a poetry that aims at beauty of feeling, a continuous bone-aching loneliness, a continuous return to and caressing of the dark, a terror of the cold dark, a compassion for whoever suffers it, a desire to escape from the body. The new manner of *The Branch Will Not Break* doesn't signal a change in theme, but a different rhetorical strategy. The more relaxed rhythms, with pauses at line end, feel like a man taking a deep breath:

> Po Chu-i, balding old politician,
> What's the use?

And the playfulness of the titles insists on the fact of imagination. So do the plain words from romantic poetry, *lovely, beautiful, terrible,* that don't describe anything but tell you that someone is feeling something. And the images let go of the known configurations so that they can look inward and try to name the agency of transformation:

> Tiller of waves or whatever, woman or man,
> Mother of roots or father of diamonds,
> Look: I am nothing.

This is the freshness of the book and it helps me to understand why I responded to it so deeply and why I end by gnashing my teeth over so many of the poems:

> . . . Only two boys
> Trailed by the shadow of rooted police,
> Turn aimlessly in the lashing elderberries.
> One cries for his father's death,
> And the other, the silent one,
> Listens into the hallway
> Of a dark leaf.

The means, this style that is to make transformation possible, keeps wanting to be the end, the transformation itself, the beauty by which we are justified. There is no ground in these lines between the violent outer world and the kid listening poetically down the hallway of a dark leaf. There must be a Yiddish joke somewhere or a story by Peretz in which the poet appears before the recording angel who asks him what he's done and he says I listened down the hallway of a dark leaf or the long dream of my body was the beginning of a dark hair, etc. And one of the angels, maybe Raphael whom Rilke called the terrible one, says, this guy has got to be kidding.

Wright knows this most of the time, that the "one wing" of beauty won't take him very far. But again and again in *The Branch Will Not Break* he tries to see what can be made to happen by saying beautiful things, by repeating his talismanic nouns and adjectives of the discovery of the inner world:

Two athletes
Are dancing in the cathedral
Of the wind

Small antelope
Fall asleep in the ashes
Of the moon

. . . I am lost in the beautiful white ruins
Of America

The sad bones of my hands descend into a valley
Of strange rocks

The secret shelters of sparrow feathers fallen in the snow

. . . if I stepped out of my body I would break
Into blossom

                    At a touch of my hand
The air fills with delicate creatures
From another world

Only after nightfall
Little boys lie still, awake,
Wondering, wondering,
Delicate little boxes of dust.

This last is from a poem called "The Undermining of the Defense Economy." Many of the poems make political reference and it was very exciting to me to see a poetry that brought sensibility to political issues, that could confront the utilitarian spirit—which *is* a way of feeling, an admiration for efficiency and coolness—with what is fuller and stronger and clearer in human feeling. But these lines don't do that. Against the active man who despises the world in the light, there is the passive man who loves it in the dark:

I want to lie down under a tree.
This is the only duty that is not death.

The poem is called "A Prayer to Escape from the Market Place." The fugitive again.

In 1963, the year in which *The Branch Will Not Break* appeared, Robert Bly printed in *Choice* a passionate, ragged, very contradictory and very important essay called "A Wrong Turning in American Poetry." He attacked the modernist movement, especially imagism, as a kind of pictorialism, mesmerized by things, frightened of the spirit, preoccupied with technique, a replica of American culture. A great deal of what Bly had to say is true. He wanted a poetry that was inward, fresh, alive to its own impulse. "When the senses die, the sense within us that delights in poetry dies." "In a poem, as in the human body, what is invisible makes all the difference." But much of it reads like an Evangelical tract. It distrusts the mind and it insists on the radical and permanent division between the inner and the outer, believing only in the election of inward illumination: "A man cannot turn his face at the same moment toward the inward world and the outer world: he cannot face both north and south." Imagination is the source of election and, as in Wright, the world is its enemy. "The imagination *out of its own resources* creates a poem as strong as the world which it faces." And, as in Wright, the world is a jail in which the soul is imprisoned. Bly translates Rilke's "die Befreiung der dichterisch Figur" as "the releasing of the image from jail," and adds, "the poet is thinking of a poem in which the image is released from its imprisonment among objects." But what is an object? A horse? The round white stone on my desk? The old curled postcard of a still life by Georgia O'Keeffe? It is when the imagination withdraws from things that they become objects, when it lets the world go. This is a Calvinist and solipsistic doctrine. No wonder that the poetry of the deep image is preoccupied with loneliness.

Here is Bly's account of the role intelligence plays in the life of imagination: "The intelligence knocks at the door, demanding some imagination to put between a flat statement and a piece of glass and rushes out with the gift. Then it hurries back to get a little more imagination to prevent two subway cars from rubbing together. The imagination is continually disturbed, torn away, bit by bit, consumed like a bin of corn eaten gradually by mice. The imagination does not want these constant knockings on the door. It prefers to remain in its chamber, undisturbed, until it can create the poem all of one substance—itself." This is polemical and funny and it gets at certain kinds of deadness in poetry. But it has to be fundamentally wrong about the relationship between imagination and intelligence because, as everyone knows, the imagination is luminously intelligent. Imagination cannot be without intelligence, any more than it can be without feeling. This description, which is contradicted anyway by Bly's best poems and by other, more plausible things he says in the same pages, is typical of the hatred of intelligence that pervades the evangelical side of American culture. Regarding imagination as a kind of ruminative wombat denies that perceptive and apprehensive cooperation between ourselves and the world, between imagination and things, which makes the world a place to live in and makes poetry communicable, gives it its active force. It leaves the poet isolated and the world dead. "Great poets," he says, "are merely sensitive."

Galway Kinnell has said some of these things with less polemical distortion. "We have to feel our own evolutionary roots and to know that we belong to life in the same way that other animals do and the plants and the stones. . . . The real nature poem will not exclude man and deal only with animals and plants and stones, but it will reach for a connection deeper than personality, a connection that resembles the attachment one animal has for another." This seems to me to say many of the things that are valuable in Bly's essay without hauling in a

Manichean dualism,—if we add to it that the poem has to be made out of one's whole being and not out of assent to the idea.

Wright is both a more literary and less theoretical poet than Bly or Kinnell. If Bly seems sometimes to apply his ideas about imagination to the activity of writing, Wright suffers the tenor of a style as if it were the temperament of a lover. He lives inside it, feels through it. That's why his poems reflect, with desperate force, the lameness of the isolated inner world, "the sight of my blind man," its mere sensitivity which issues so often in the same nouns and adjectives, the same verbal constructions, the same will to be beautiful. Against the defense economy, we place—as plea and touchstone—little boys wondering, wondering. Against Moloch, as Allen Ginsberg said in a moment of lovely impatience, the whole boatload of sensitive bullshit.

Aestheticism is what I am talking about, decadence. It's a cultural disease and it flourishes when the life of the spirit, especially the clear power of imagination and intelligence, retreats or is driven from public life, where it ought, naturally, to manifest itself. The artists of decadence turn away from a degraded social world and what they cling to, in their privacy, is beauty or pleasure. The pleasures are esoteric; the beauty is almost always gentle, melancholy, tinged with the erotic, tinged with self-pity. Pound and Eliot, Joyce and Lawrence grew up in a period of decadence in poetry. They did not put down the aesthetes who ought to have been their fathering generation; they honored them. Pound was especially alert to their courage and "Hugh Selwyn Mauberly," whatever else it is, is both a tribute to them and a measure of the trap.

The issue seems to me urgent and I want to say the whole thing against these poems, this tone, in Wright because his struggle with it belongs so much to our culture, to American ugliness, to every kid who wanders into every public library Carnegie built in every devastated American town and, glimpsing the dim intuited features of his own inwardness in some book of poems he has picked up, is, when he emerges into the sunlight of drugstore, liquor store, gas station, an outcast and a fugitive. *The Branch Will Not Break* is a book vivid with inward alertness, but it also brings us up against the limitations behind the aesthetic that informs it.

Wright's subject, like Wordsworth's, is the discovery of his own inwardness and the problem of what it can mean, what form it can take in the world. A large part of Wordsworth's struggle had to do with the fact that, in his time, there was no coherent psychological or philosophical accounting for the intensity and reality of his own experience, so he labored in *The Prelude* both to make it visible and to find a form for it in thought. Wright's problem is different in crucial ways. For one thing, he was born a convicted sinner in southern Ohio. For another, his experience is closer to the erotic. For that reason, it seems to me, by some measure, truer because it is through the erotic that one body turns to another and social life, in which the intensity of human inwardness has to find a form, begins.

2 /

> *As far as life, spontaneity, sorrow and darkness are concerned, I have enough of my own; it flows through my veins. I have enough with my own flesh and my bones and in the flameless fire of my conscience. What I need now is clarity, a dawn above my life.*
>
> —JOSÉ ORTEGA Y GASSET

"Autumn Begins in Martins Ferry, Ohio" is about a form the inner life takes in the world. Everyone knows the poem, but let me quote it so we can have it here on the page:

> In the Shreve High football stadium,
> I think of Polacks nursing long beers in Tiltonsville,

And grey faces of Negroes in the blast furnace at Benwood,
And the ruptured nightwatchman of Wheeling Steel,
Dreaming of heroes.

All the proud fathers are ashamed to go home.
Their wives cluck like starved pullets,
Dying for love.

Therefore,
Their sons grow suicidally beautiful
At the beginning of October
And gallop terribly against each other's bodies.

In the first version of Blake's "London" the opening lines went like this:

I wander'd thro' each dirty street,
Down where the dirty Thames does flow.

Raymond Williams in *The City and the Country* talks about the kind of difference the revision made. *Dirty* is a protest; *charter'd* is a seeing: it confronts not squalor but an order that men have made. It meets power with power, the power of poetry to illuminate and clarify, to speak out of its whole being. Wright's poem does the same, I think, but with important differences. These Friday night football games are in one way a deeper order than either the political or the economic systems of which Blake is thinking, because their necessity is entirely imaginative. This is a harvest festival and a ritual. Ritual form is allied to magic, as it is in every community, and magic is allied to the seasons and the sexual potency of the earth.

Because this festival is American and Puritan, it is an efficient transmutation of lovelessness into stylized violence. "Gallop terribly": or changing chickens into horses. It is a way of describing and evoking the animal beauty in the violence of the dying year, the explosive beauty of boys who are heroes because they imagine they are heroes and whose cells know that it will be their turn to be ashamed to go home. Even the stanzaic structure of the poem participates in the ritual. The first two stanzas separate the bodies of the men from the bodies of the women and the third stanza gives us the boys pounding against each other, as if they could, out of their wills, effect a merging. Insofar as this is a political poem, it is not about the way that industrial capitalism keeps us apart, but the way it brings us together.

This is, in other words, the poem Wright has always been writing:

> Sick of the dark, he rose
> For love, and now he goes
> Back to the broken ground.

Everything about those fall nights is brought to bear here, even the harsh artificial light in which they occur and the cold and darkness that surround them. The poet knows—and tells us in "The Minneapolis Poem"—what happens when the season is over:

> The Chippewa young men
> Stab one another shrieking
> Jesus Christ.
> Split-lipped homosexuals limp in terror of assault.
> High school backfields search under benches
> Near the Post Office. Their faces are the rich
> Raw bacon without eyes.

Later again, in "A Mad Fight Song for William S. Carpenter," he will make the connection between this ritual and war—between the beauty of football and the beauty of war. Saying that, we are in the territory of *The Iliad* and the territory of tragedy. Beyond any social considerations, what the fall of the year tells us is that we are all going down to the dark, one way or another. It is Homer who describes battle as the winds of autumn sweeping the leaves, terribly, from the trees and it is Homer's Apollo who watches the battle and says, with a god's luminous contempt, "Men, they are like leaves, they flourish a little and grow warm with life, and feed on what the ground gives, and then they fade away." Suicidally beautiful: that adverb is not there to nudge us into feeling. It means what it says. It tries to describe what happens when the inner life can't find its way out of the dark and it also describes, illuminates that tendency in James Wright's art.

One of the things that has always moved me most about this poem is the situation of the speaker. There is an awful uprooting here. The man who sees this clearly is not any longer a part of the community he is seeing and it is unlikely that he could see so clearly if he had not been part of it. So, one of the things the poem records is a recognition; and another thing it records is an estrangement. The poet is alone, but not with the loneliness of the defeated fathers; present, but not with the immersion of the sons. If you ask whether this is a poem of the inner world or the outer world, the distinction seems meaningless. What there is here is an adult clarity which sees and feels with great affection and compassion and sees each thing as it is. I suppose that is why the completely plain opening lines have such resonance: *In the Shreve High football stadium, I think . . .*

That is a distinction the poem does enforce, the one between *dreaming* and *I think*. This vision is not given to the defeated fathers or to the animal brilliance of the sons. Nor does it come from delicate boxes of dust wondering. And the words don't fall as they do when we are filling that emptiness in us that is starved for love. It is given to the man who thinks. That's why that *therefore* explodes on the page, though there are formal reasons for this as well. The poem does not at first feel as if it will have the force of a logical inference and a leap of imagination, because each of the first two stanzas ends with the hemistich of a Latin elegiac poem. Dreaming of heroes, dying for love; a liquid, quantitative dying fall so that you think melancholy grace and not the power of seeing is what the poem is about and then wham! something happens. The word *therefore* is what isolates the speaker, but it is also what gathers the people of Martins Ferry to the poet and his readers, makes them known and felt. The poet does not rise into suicidal light; he brings himself and them and all of us up into the different kind of light that poetry is, so that, even though what he sees is tragic, that he sees is a consolation.

3 /

Maybe Jehovah was drowsing, and Eros heard the prayer and figured that love after all was love, no matter what language a man sang it in, so what the hell.
—JAMES WRIGHT

Suicidally beautiful: the poems have suffered from that temptation and the poems from this point on, the best of them I think, reflect a determination to face "the black ditch of the Ohio" and not be killed by it. This is announced—in another place by another river—in "The Minneapolis Poem," the second poem in *Shall We Gather at the River*, that utterly painful book:

I wonder how many old men last winter
Hungry and frightened by namelessness prowled
The Mississippi shore
Lashed blind by the wind, dreaming
Of suicide in the river.
The police remove their cadavers by daybreak
And turn them in somewhere.
Where?

How does the city keep lists of its fathers
Who have no names?
By Nicollet Island I gaze down at the dark water
So beautifully slow.

His response to this suicidal beauty matters to me because it introduces that odd comic tone which will continue into some very desperate poems:

And nobody would commit suicide, only
To find beyond death
Bridgeport, Ohio

and because what he places over against that death is the life of the imagination:

. . . I could not bear
To allow my poor brother the body to die
In Minneapolis.
The old man Walt Whitman our countryman
Is now in America our country
Dead.
But he was not buried in Minneapolis
At least.
And no more may I be
Please God.

The poem almost ends in a familiar pathos of yearning, but there is also some note of skepticism, of self-mockery in the explicit specifications of the last stanza which suggests Wright has begun to distrust that verbal magic:

I want to be lifted up
By some great white bird unknown to the police,
And soar for a thousand miles and be carefully hidden
Modest and golden as one last corn grain,

Stored with the secrets of the wheat and the mysterious lives
Of the unnamed poor.

The poem doesn't take us to that place. It reminds us that the sentence is about wanting; and whatever the poet wants, what he does is turn back to Ohio. A strange thing, a wonderful and strange act of imagination occurs in *Shall We Gather at the River*. It is the appearance of Jenny. She is the secret inside the word *secret* which appears so often in the book: the discovery of his spirit and of the beauty of the body and of the desire for love which grew up in Ohio and was maimed there. She is probably also the young girl in the earlier poem "Beginning" who lifts up the lovely shadow of her face and disappears wholly in the air. *Shall We Gather at the River* is dedicated to her and, in the hells of that book, she is glimpsed first through the fractured ballad rhythms of Robinson:

And Jenny, oh my Jenny
Whom I love, rhyme be damned,
Has broken her spare beauty
In a whorehouse old.
She left her new baby
In a bus-station can,
And sprightly danced away
Through Jacksontown.

Her next appearance is an arrival and a remembering:

I am home again.
Yes: I lived here, and here, and my name
That I carved young, with a girl's, is healed over, now,
And lies sleeping beneath the inward sky
Of a tree's skin, close to the quick.

And finally she appears in the last, desperate, lonely poem in the book where the title, "To the Muse," identifies her:

It is all right. All they do
Is go in by dividing
One rib from another. I wouldn't
Lie to you. It hurts
Like nothing. I know. All they do
Is burn their way in with a wire.
It forks in and out like the tongue
Of that frightened garter snake we caught
At Cloverfield, you and me, Jenny,
So long ago.

I would lie to you
If I could.
But the only way I can get you to come up
Out of that suckhole, the south face
Of the Powhatan pit, is to tell you
What you know.

That suckhole is the one in "The River Down Home":

Under the enormous pier-shadow,
Hobie Johnson drowned in a suckhole.
I cannot even remember
His obliterated face.
Outside my window, now, Minneapolis
Drowns, dark.
It is dark.
I have no life.

And it is the ghostly one in "Miners":

The police are probing tonight for the bodies
Of children in the black waters
Of the suburbs.

It is probably even "the shifting hole where the slow swimmer fell aground" all the way back in "To a Defeated Savior" in *The*

Green Wall. We come to a point in these later books where Wright's poetry is so compressed with self-reference, with recurrent meditation on these images and themes, that tracing them belongs to long reading and not the ten thumbs of criticism. But the whole body of Wright's work lies behind "To the Muse" and gives terrifying pathos to this struggle to get the soul up into the light, the soul that is also the poor flesh:

> Oh Jenny
> I wish to God I had made this world, this scurvy
> And disastrous place. I
> Didn't, I can't bear it
> Either.

This nightmare poem is everybody's hospital nightmare, the bad long dream of the body, of how it ends up, of the mechanical heart and the draining lung, of what work can do to you and life can do to you, and the three fates, the one who unwinds and the one who spins and the one who cuts the thread:

> Three lady doctors in Wheeling open
> Their offices at night.
> I don't have to call them, they are always there.
> But they only have to put the knife once
> Under your breast.
> Then they hang their contraption
> And you bear it.
>
> It's awkward a while. Still, it lets you
> Walk about on tiptoe if you don't
> Jiggle the needle.
> It might stab your heart, you see.
> The blade hangs in your lung and the tube
> Keeps it draining.
> That way they only have to stab you
> Once.

This is the least bearable of Wright's poems to me, as wrenching as anything in Sylvia Plath, worse in some ways because it glints with so many more tones, with the will to live. And when it ends, this book that began with the waters of the Mississippi ends:

Come up to me, love,
Out of the river, or I will
Come down to you.

In the new poems at the end of the *Collected Poems*, Jenny is "The Idea of the Good," and as she emerges, her name echoing all those sentimental Midwestern songs, Wright returns again and again to the terror of the river down home:

THE OHIO RIVER

Has flown by me twice, the dark jubilating
Isaiah of mill and smoke marrow. Blind son
Of a meadow of huge horses, lover of drowned islands
Above Steubenville, blind father
Of my halt grey wing

and:

That black ditch
Of river

and:

. . . into the
Tar and chemical strangled tomb,
The strange water, the
Ohio River, that is no tomb to
Rise from the dead
From.

And, quoting the old poet H. Phelps Putnam:

> "That reeking slit, wide, soft and lecherous
> From which we bleed and into which we drown."

What emerges from this birth and death was not possible in the diction of the early poems or in the willful beauty of *The Branch Will Not Break*—the poems about Uncle Willie, Uncle Shortie, Emerson Buchanan, Aunt Agnes, Wright's teacher Charles Coffin, the poems of the people of Ohio, his own Winesburg. Much of this is in *Two Citizens*, where Jenny is identified as "the Jenny sycamore" who had been "the one wing, the only wing." But it isn't only Ohio that emerges in these poems. There is also a more open insistence by Wright on his art and the traditions of his art. And this has required him, once again, to find a new language, a style that can accommodate what he has learned and gather it to the spoken language of his childhood. The way he has achieved this is, I think, intensely artificial, even a little weird, and I think it is meant to be. At its best it's very funny and playful:

> The one tongue I can write in
> Is my Ohioan.

This is based, presumably, on the well-known Ohio habit of speaking in off-rhymed couplets; the lines come from a poem that moves in and out of a grave iambic trimeter, like that of Yeats, and contains some of the most powerful writing in the book:

> This poem frightens me
> So secretly, so much,
> It makes me hard to touch
> Your body's secret places.
> We are each other's faces

and:

The sky is shattering.
The plain sky grows so blue,
Some day I have to die,
As everyone must do,
Alone, alone, alone,
Peaceful as peaceful as stone.

At other times its artfulness consists in rendering peculiarities of diction exactly. The first poem is called "Ars Poetica," which sounds solemn enough. It begins:

I loved my country
When I was a little boy.
Agnes is my aunt,
And she doesn't even know
If I love anything
On this God's
Green little apple.

The *even* is what delights me. And "God's green little apple" is full of guile: one of the best poems in the book is about licking the sweetness from very tart green apples and having the sense not to eat them.

Here and there in the artifice is something like boozy insistence, that strange pride that dares you to contradict:

I was a good child,
So I am
A good man. Put that
In your pipe.

It makes me feel vaguely like Raskolnikov being collared by Marmeladov in a bar: "Pardon me, sir, but may I inquire whether you have ever spent a night on a haybarge in the

Neva?" And it's not clear who is being addressed, though one guesses Jehovah, since the passages tend, like this one, to call off original sin.

Sometimes the manner blusters through difficulty, but at their best these poems do make a wholeness. Especially "Prayer to the Good Poet" in which he links his own father to Horace, one of his fathers in poetry, and the poems to his Ohio teacher, and the unmannered fluidity and assurance (and amazed gratitude) of some of the love poems. And here, in the lines I have already quoted, Jenny becomes the sycamore, his first rising and discovery of poetry. That is why "October Ghosts" is the most crucial poem in the book, for me. It's a poem in which Wright makes a kind of peace with the terror and loneliness of "To the Muse":

> Jenny cold, Jenny darkness,
> They are coming back again.
> We came so early,
> But now we are shovelled
> Down the long slide.
> We carry a blackened crocus
> In either hand.

And then these lines in which Wright seems to have, at last, two wings. One of them is Jenny who is beauty, loneliness, death, the muse, the idea of the good, a sexual shadow, a whore, the grandmother of the dead, the lecherous slit of the Ohio, an abandoner of her child, a "savage woman with two heads . . . the one / Face broken and savage, the other, the face dead," the name carved under a tree in childhood close to the quick, a sycamore tree, a lover, the first time he ever rose. The other wing is his art, and with both of them he returns to his native place. The lines are a four-verse summary of "The Heights of Machu Picchu" and, because they gather—at the river—the whole struggle of James Wright's poetry, I think they are among the most beautiful lines he has written:

I will walk with you and Callimachus
Into the gorges
Of Ohio, where the miners
Are dead with us.

This is the poem that ends, "Now I know nothing, I can die alone." Which is what has to be, and did not seem supportable before.

4 /

I had mostly finished writing these notes before I came upon the little book called *Moments of the Italian Summer.* I had thought I would end by saying that James Wright was writing the poetry of a grown man and that I expected it would be sometimes a poetry of light. And that I was grateful for it. But in this book of prose poems, he is saying a good deal of this for himself:

> It is all right with me to know that my life is only one life. I feel like the light of the river Adige.

Especially in "The Lambs on the Boulder," he says it. The poem deals with the legend of Giotto, that Cimabue found him a shepherd boy drawing lambs on a stone with a sharp rock and saw that he had genius and took him home and taught him to draw. It is a little like the story of the wild boy of Aveyron. Here is how he treats it:

> One of my idle wishes is to find the field where Cimabue stood in the shade and watched the boy Giotto scratching his stone with his pebble.
>
> I would not be so foolish as to prefer the faces of the boy's lambs to the faces of his angels. One has to act his age sooner or later.

> Still, this little planet of rocks and grass is all we have to start with. How pretty it would be, the sweet faces of the boy Giotto's lambs gouged, with infinite and still uncertain and painful care, on the side of a boulder at the edge of a country field.

This is a poem about his own art. It ends this way:

> In one of the mature Giotto's greatest glories, a huge choir of his unutterably beautiful angels are lifting their faces and are becoming the sons of the morning, singing out of pure happiness the praises of God.
>
> Far back in the angelic choir, a slightly smaller angel has folded his wings. He has turned slightly away from the light and lifted hands. You cannot even see his face. I don't know why he is weeping but I love him best.
>
> I think he must be wondering how long it will take Giotto to remember him, give him a drink of water, and take him back to the fold before it gets dark and shepherd and sheep alike lose their way in the darkness of the countryside.

I don't see how this could be any better. It has that stubborn preference for animals and angels, that wish to cut out the middleman, but it is about the mature artist Giotto who must, if anyone is going to, lead both the shepherd and the sheep out of the dark. That is what makes the poem feel intricate with thought.

One Body: Some Notes on Form

I've been trying to think about form in poetry and my mind keeps returning to a time in the country in New York when I was puzzled that my son Leif was getting up a little earlier every morning. I had to get up with him, so it exasperated me. I wondered about it until I slept in his bed one night. His window faced east. At six-thirty I woke to brilliant sunlight. The sun had risen.

Wonder and repetition. Another morning I was walking Kristin to her bus stop—a light blanket of snow after thaw, the air thick with the rusty croaking of blackbirds so that I remembered, in the interminable winter, the windy feel of June on that hill. Kristin, standing on a snowbank in the cold air, her eyes alert, her face rosy with cold and with some purity of expectation, was looking down the road. It was eight-fifteen. Her bus always arrived at eight-fifteen. She looked down the road and it was coming.

The first fact of the world is that it repeats itself. I had been taught to believe that the freshness of children lay in their capacity for wonder at the vividness and strangeness of the particular, but what is fresh in them is that they still experience the power of repetition, from which our first sense of the power of mastery comes. Though *predictable* is an ugly little word in daily life, in our first experience of it we are clued to the hope of a shapeliness in things. To see that power working on adults, you have to catch them out: the look of foolish happiness on the faces of people who have just sat down to dinner is their knowledge that dinner will be served.

Probably, that is the psychological basis for the power and the necessity of artistic form. I think of our children when they first came home from the hospital, wide, staring eyes, wet mouths, fat, uncontrollable tongues. I thought they responded when I bent over their cribs because they were beginning to recognize me. Now I think it was because they were coming to recognize themselves. They were experiencing in the fluidity of things a certain orderliness: footsteps, a face, the smell of hair and tobacco, cooing syllables. One would gradually have the sense that looking-out-of-the-eyes was a point around which phenomena organized themselves; thinking *this is going to happen* and having it happen might be, then, the authentic source of the experience of being, of identity, that word which implies that a lot of different things are the same thing.

Being and being seen. R. D. Laing says somewhere that small children don't get up at night to see if you're there, they get up to see if *they're* there. It helps me to understand that my first delighted mistaking of the situation—they know who I am!—was natural because I had the same experience as my children. Maybe our first experience of form is the experience of our own formation.

And we have that experience mainly with our mothers. Its roots are in hunger. The infant wants to know that his hunger is going to be satisfied. He cries out, there is a stirring of sensations that begin to be a pattern, and he is fed. The lovely greed of babies: so that the later experience of cognition, of the apprehension of form, carries within it the experience of animal pleasure and the first caressing experience of human affection.

This is clearest in poems of disintegration and return. In Rimbaud's "The Drunken Boat" there is the power of the moment when, in the exhaustion of the impulse of flight, he says: "I dream of Europe and her ancient quays." And Roethke in "The Lost Son"—

The weeds whined,
The snakes cried,
The cows and briars
Said to me: Die.

What a small song. What slow clouds. What dark water.
Hath the rain a father? All the caves are ice . . .

—returns: "A lively understandable spirit once entertained you." It feels like the first moment after a hard rain. And Pound: "Soshu churned in the sea." The return is so powerful we are cradled entirely in the form of things, as in that poem when Gary Snyder's mind leaps from his small fire in the mountains to the little fires of the summer stars:

Burning the small dead
            branches
broke from beneath
    thick spreading
                    whitebark pine
                    a hundred summers
snowmelt   rock   and air
hiss in a twisted bough
    sierra granite:
                    Mt. Ritter—
                    black rock twice as old
Deneb, Altair
windy fire

But I am not thinking mainly of poems about form; I'm thinking of the form of a poem, the shape of its understanding. The presence of that shaping constitutes the presence of poetry. Not tone, not imagery, however deep or subtle, not particular qualities of content. It is easiest to say what I mean by way of example, but almost all the bad examples seem unfair. This, from last night's reading, "The Sphinx's Riddle to Oedipus" by Randall Jarrell:

Not to have guessed is better: what is, ends,
But among fellows, with reluctance,
Clasped by the Woman-Breasted, Lion-Pawed.

To have clasped in one's own arms a mother,
To have killed with one's own hands a father
—Is not this, Lame One, to have been alone?

The seer is doomed for seeing; and to understand
Is to pluck out one's own eyes with one's own hands.
But speak: what has a woman's breasts, a lion's paws?

You stand at midday in the marketplace
Before your life: to see is to have spoken.
—Yet to see, Blind One, is to be alone.

The intentions of this poem are completely real. And I learn things from it: learn from its verbs why Oedipus blinds himself with Jocasta's clasp, for example. And I see that the sphinx is herself death. But the poem never quite occurs. It can't find its way to its rhythm. In the first line, in the fourth, in the sixth, in the seventh, in the ninth, Jarrell tries, each time in a different way, to find a rhythm. You can feel the poem groping for it, like someone trying to gain admittance to a dance and being each time rebuffed by centrifugal force because he has not got the feel of the center. The last stanza, in his craftsman's hands, gives the poem a structure, but I do not feel the presence of form. That's why the last line sounds portentous and hollow. He has not entered the dance. My guesses about the reasons for this have to do with my reading of the rest of Jarrell's work. He is *sympathizing* with Oedipus and that is a characteristic stance of his poems, to be slightly outside the process sympathizing with someone else, soldiers in the early work, lonely women in the later work. In this poem, he has found an interesting perception, an important perception, but the stance has thrown him off himself. He has not found for himself the form of being in the idea.

Criticism is not especially alert to this matter. It talks about a poet's ideas or themes or imagery and so it treats all the poems of Stevens or Williams equally when they are not equally poems. The result is the curiosity of a huge body of commentary which has very little to do with the art of poetry. And this spills over into university instruction—where, whether we like it or not, an awful lot of the reading and buying of poetry goes on. Students are trained to come away from that poem of Jarrell's thinking they have had an experience of poetry if they can write a four-page essay answering the question, "What has a woman's breasts, a lion's paws?" What gets lost is just the thing that makes art as humanly necessary as bread. Art is an activity of the spirit and when we lose track of what makes an art an art, we lose track of the spirit. It is the form of "Western Wind"—

Western wind, when wilt thou blow,
The small rain down can rain.
Christ, if my love were in my arms
And I in my bed again!

—that makes life seem lucky, and intense. It is the form of "The White Horse"—

The youth walks up to the white horse, to put its halter on,
and the horse looks at him in silence.
They are so silent they are in another world.

—that makes it seem wonderful and solemn.

The connection between gazing and grazing in the Lawrence poem brings us back to the connection between form, being and looking. The best account of this that I know is in the 1805 *Prelude*. Wordsworth writes:

Blessed the infant babe
(For with my best conjectures I would trace
The progress of our being), blest the babe,

Nurs'd in his mother's arms, the babe who sleeps
Upon his mother's breast, who, when his soul
Claims manifest kindred with an earthly soul,
Doth gather passion from his mother's eye!
Such feelings pass into his torpid life
Like an awakening breeze, and hence his mind
Even in the first trial of its powers
Is prompt and watchful, eager to combine
In one appearance, all the elements
And parts of the same object, else detached
And loth to coalesce.

Loth to coalesce. The phrase seems to speak particularly to the twentieth century, to our experience of fragmentation, of making form against all odds. It explains something of Picasso's cubist nudes which come to form in the insistence of some previous and violent dismemberment; it glosses Bergman's borrowings from Picasso in the haunting visualizations of films like *Persona* and the savage dismemberments of Sylvia Plath, the strange rachitic birds Charles Simic is likely to see arising from the shape of a fork. We have been obsessed with the difficulty of form, of any coherent sense of being, so one of the values of this passage is that it takes us back to a source:

Thus, day by day,
Subjected to the discipline of love,
His organs and recipient faculties
Are quickened, are more vigorous, his mind spreads,
Tenacious of the forms which it receives,
In one beloved presence, nay and more,
In that most apprehensive habitude
And those sensations which have been derived
From this beloved presence, there exists
A virtue which irradiates and exalts
All objects through all intercourse of sense.
No outcast he, bewilder'd and depressed;
Along his infant veins are interfused

The gravitation and the filial bond
Of nature, that connects him with the world.
Emphatically, such a being lives,
an inmate of this *active* universe . . .

It is this forming, this coming into existence of imagination as a shaping power, that "irradiates and exalts all objects" and makes the forms of nature both an echo of that experience and a clue to the larger rhythms of a possible order in which the human mind shares or which it can make. This is also the force of that passage, early in the *Cantos*, when Pound reaches back through a scrap of Chaucer to the origins of poetry in European consciousness:

Betuene Aprile and Merche
                    with sap new in the bough
With plum flowers above them
                    with almond on the black bough
With jasmine and olive leaf
To the beat of the measure
From star up to the half-dark
From half-dark to half-dark
                    Unceasing the measure
Flank by flank on the headland
                    with the Goddess' eyes to seaward
By Circeo, by Terracina, with the stone eyes
                    white toward the sea
With one measure, unceasing:
                    "Fac deum!" "Est factus."
Ver novum!
               ver novum!
Thus made the spring . . .

And I might just as well summon Stevens on "our old dependency of day and night," on the power of the knowledge that the world is out there:

Deer walk upon our mountains, and the quail
Whistle about us their spontaneous cries;
Sweet berries ripen in the wilderness . . .

It amazes me, the way Wordsworth has come to it:

From nature largely he receives; nor so
Is satisfied, but largely gives again,
For feeling has to him imparted strength,
And powerful in all sentiments of grief,
Of exultation, fear and joy, his mind,
Even as the agent of the one great mind,
Creates, creator and receiver both,
Working but in alliance with the works
Which it beholds—Such, verily, is the first
Poetic spirit of our human life . . .

though I have none of this assurance, either about the sources of the order of nature or about the absolute continuity between that first nurturing and the form-making activity of the mind. It seems to me, rather, that we make our forms because there is no absolute continuity, because those first assurances are broken. The mind, in the act of recovery, creates.

Louise Glück's "To My Mother" explores this territory and it registers a shock that Wordsworth doesn't:

It was better when we were
together in one body.
Thirty years. Screened
through the green glass
of your eye, moonlight
filtered into my bones
as we lay
in the big bed, in the dark,
waiting for my father.

Thirty years. He closed
your eyelids with
two kisses. And then spring
came and withdrew from me
the absolute
knowledge of the unborn,
leaving the brick stoop
where you stand, shading
your eyes, but it is
night, the moon
is stationed in the beech tree
round and white among
the small tin markers of the stars:
Thirty years. A marsh
grows up around the house.
Schools of spores circulate
behind the shades, drift through
gauze flutterings of vegetation.

The power of this poem has to do with the intensity of the sense of loss, the breaking of myth. The fabulous mother has become an ordinary woman on a brick stoop, squinting into the sun. And the assurance of natural process breaks down: day becomes night, the moon is stationed in the beech, the stars are tin. There is a strange veering definiteness to the syntax which moves us from a world of romance to a lost, Chagall-like memory of it. The repeated phrase does not have the magic of recurrence; it is spoken with a kind of wonder, but it has the relentlessness of time, of the ways in which time excludes our own lives and deaths from the magic of recurrence. "It is spring!" she says, in another poem, "We are going to die!" But already something else is at work in the movement; the deliberate writing and the articulation of the syntax are making a form. When we come to the phrase "A marsh grows up around the house," we feel both house and marsh, the formed and the unformed thing, with equal intensity. In the title of the book from which the poem comes, the nouns have been reversed to make an aesthetic commitment: *The House on Marshland.* The marsh, the shifting ground, gives the image a terrible pathos. This is a poem about growing up and it is the marsh, not the house, that grows up. *The mind creates,* Wordsworth says. The final image is a creation. It makes a form from all the pathos of loss and dispersal. Spores, gauze curtains, window, the vegetable world beyond the window are gathered into a seeing, into the one body of the poem.

One body: it's an illuminating metaphor, and so is the house, the human indwelling which art makes possible when it makes forms the imagination can inhabit. I don't think we have thought about the issue very well. What passes for discussion of it among younger poets has been an orgy of self-congratulation because they are not writing metrical poems. A marginal achievement, since many of us, not having worked at it, couldn't write them competently if we wanted to. The nature of the music of poetry has become an open question and music, the rhythm of poetry, is crucial to its form. Thinking about poetic form has also been complicated by the way we use the word. We speak of the sonnet as "a form," when no two sonnets, however similar their structures, have the same form.

The form of a poem exists in the relation between its music and its seeing; form is not the number or kind of restrictions, conscious or unconscious, many or few, with which a piece of writing begins. A sonnet imposes one set of restrictions and a poem by Robert Creeley with relatively short lines and three- or four-line stanzas imposes another. There are always restrictions because, as Creeley says, quoting Pound, "Verse consists of a constant and a variant." That is, the music of the poem as it develops imposes its own restrictions. That is how it comes to form. When Robert Duncan, in "A Poem Beginning with a Line from Pindar," comes upon all those trochees and dactyls in the names of the presidents—

> Hoover, Roosevelt, Truman, Eisenhower—
> where among these does the power reside
> that moves the heart? What flower of the nation
> bride-sweet broke to the whole rapture?
> Hoover, Coolidge, Harding, Wilson
> hear the factories of human misery turning out commodities

—he has to go with it and then find his way out of that music, which he does, beautifully:

> Garfield, Hayes, Grant, Johnson
> dwell in the roots of the heart's rancor.
> How sad "amid lanes and through old woods"
>   echoes Whitman's love for Lincoln!

This is a matter of bodily rhythm and the mind's hunger for intelligible recurrence. It applies equally to all verbal music.

I don't think we are in a position yet to understand the reaction against metrical poetry that began in the middle of the nineteenth century. It's an astonishing psychological fact, as if a huge underpinning in the order of things had given way and, where men had heard the power of incantatory repetition before, they now heard its monotony. Or worse. Frost's rhythms use meter in a way that is full of dark, uneasy irony:

> And I keep hearing from the cellar bin
> The rumbling sound
> Of load on load of apples coming in.

And irony, the stresses falling like chains clanking, is very often Robert Lowell's way with meter:

> Our fathers made their world with sticks and stones
> And fenced their gardens with the red man's bones.

The writing seems to accuse not only the fathers but the culture that produced meter and rhyme.

It has always interested me that, if you define meter as the constant, and the rhythmic play of different sounds through meter as the variant, then meter itself can never be heard. Every embodiment is a variation on the meter. One-TWO is a rhythmic variant on the pure iamb and three-FOUR is another. The pure iamb in fact can't be rendered; it only exists as a felt principle of order, beneath all possible embodiments, in the mind of the listener. It exists in silence, is invisible, unspeakable. An imagination of order. A music of the spheres.

Which is how the Renaissance conceived it. All through the Elizabethan period the dance of the order of things is associated with music. And this was the period of the other momentous event in the history of the sound of English-language poetry, the invention of the printing press. In the course of about a hundred years, the printing press tore the lyric poem away from music and left the poet with the sound of his own voice. I think that's why, in the freshness of those writers, in the satires of Wyatt, for example—

> My mother's maids when they do sew and spin,
> They sing a song made of the fieldish mouse . . .

or in a prayer by Ben Jonson—

> Good and great God, can I not think on thee,
> But it must straight my melancholy be . . .

—meter has the authority of a profound formal order. I think the human voice without music required it; otherwise it was just individual noise in the universe.

Herrick is a fascinating figure in this way. He seems to be a maker of Elizabethan songs, but really he was living by himself fifty years past that time in a country priory in Devonshire, making that music out of his own head. The public occasions of Campion—

When to her lute Corinna sings

—have become a private music in the mind, a small imagined ordering dance of things. Meter has replaced the lute and become a way of imagining experience, a private artistic vision. It has become form:

Whenas in silks my Julia goes,
Then, then, methinks . . .

And meanwhile in London, Denham and Waller were tuning up the new, print-conscious and social sounds of the heroic couplet.

Another clue is the response to Wordsworth's poetry. When he sent one of his books to Charles James Fox, the leader of the liberal faction in Parliament, Fox wrote him a note saying he loved "Goody Blake and Harry Gill" but that he didn't like "Michael" and "The Brothers" because he felt "blank verse inappropriate for such simple subjects." You could write about working people in ballad meters, but not in the lofty riverrun sound of blank verse. That was what bothered people about those poems. They democratized the imagination of spiritual order inside meter.

That's why it's a short leap from Wordsworth to Whitman—or one of the reasons why. It is why free verse appears as part of a consciously democratic poetic program. As long as the feudal class system was a series of mutual obligations, a viable economy, it seemed a natural principle of order. By the time of the French Revolution, it had stopped working and society seemed class-ridden. So meter seemed class-ridden. Only it took someone as stubborn as Wordsworth to demonstrate it by introducing the Cumberland beggar to his readers in the spiritual dress of blank verse:

In the sun,
Upon the second step of that small pile,
Surrounded by those wild unpeopled hills,

He sat, and ate his food in solitude:
And ever, scattered from his palsied hands,
That, still attempting to prevent the waste,
Was baffled still, the crumbs in little showers
Fell on the ground; and the small mountain birds,
Not venturing yet to peck the destined meal,
Approached within the length of half his staff.

Once this gesture, or the swollen ankles of a shepherd, was included in the music of the spheres, that music had ceased to have the same function and the ear was prepared for the explosion of "Crossing Brooklyn Ferry":

I too lived, Brooklyn of ample hills was mine,
I too walked the streets of Manhattan Island, and
  bathed in the waters around it,
I too felt the curious abrupt questionings stir
  within me,
In my walks home late at night or as I lay in my
  bed they came upon me,
I too had been struck from the float held forever
  in solution,
I too received identity by my body

And after this moment in the history of the race, in the history of the race's relation to the magic of language, the godhead was scattered and we were its fragments.

So Frost was wrong to say that free verse was like playing tennis without a net. The net was the resisting of the iamb. A lot of William Carlos Williams's individual perceptions are a form of iambic music, but he has rearranged them so that the eye breaks the iambic habit. The phrase—"a dust of snow in the wheeltracks"—becomes

a dust of
snow in
the wheeltracks

and people must have felt: "yes, that is what it is like; not one-TWO, one-TWO. A dust of / snow in / the wheeltracks. That is how perception is. It is that light and quick." The effect depends largely on traditional expectation. The reader had to be able to hear what he was not hearing.

That's probably why Eliot and Pound were so alarmed when Amy Lowell moved in on imagism. Pound records the moment in one of his essays: "At a particular date in a particular room, two authors, neither engaged in picking one another's pocket, decided that the dilution of *vers libre*, Amygism, Lee Masterism, general floppiness, had gone too far and that some countercurrent must be set going. Parallel situation centuries ago in China. Remedy prescribed *Emaux et Camées*. (or the Bay State Hymnbook). Rhyme and regular strophes. Results: poems in Mr. Eliot's *second* volume . . . also 'H. S. Mauberly.' Divergence later."

It does seem to be the case that the power of free verse has had something to do with its revolt against some alternative formal principle that feels fictitious. That was certainly part of the excitement of first reading Creeley and Ginsberg, Duncan and Dorn. They had come back, passionately, to the task of discovering forms of perception. In what Gary Snyder describes as "the spiritual loneliness of the nineteen-fifties," there were all these voices finding their way. And a decade later, when I read them, they still had that intensity.

Now, I think, free verse has lost its edge, become neutral, the given instrument. An analogy occurs to me. Maybe it is a little farfetched. I'm thinking of balloon frame construction in housing. According to Gideon, it was invented by a man named George Washington Snow in the 1850s and 1860s, about the same time as *Leaves of Grass*. "In America materials were plentiful and skilled labor scarce; in Europe skilled labor was plentiful and materials scarce. It is this difference which accounts for the differences in the structure of American and European industry from the fifties on." The principle of the balloon frame was simply to replace the ancient method of mortise and tenon—heavy framing timbers carved at the joints so that they locked heavily together—with construction of a frame by using thin studs and nails. It made possible a light, quick, elegant construction with great formal variability and suppleness. For better or worse. "If it had not been for the balloon frame, Chicago and San Francisco could never have arisen, as they did, from little villages to great cities in a single year." The balloon frame, the clapboard house, and the Windsor chair. American forms, and *Leaves of Grass* which abandoned the mortise and tenon of meter and rhyme. Suburban tracts and the proliferation of poetry magazines. The difference between a democratic society and a consumer society.

Stanley Plumly has written a very shrewd essay in which he argues that, in contemporary verse, tone has become important in the way that it is important in the dramatic monologues of Browning. Only the poems aren't dramatic monologues, they are spoken by the poets out of their own lives. That is, instead of being an instrument to establish person, tone has become an instrument to establish personality. And the establishment of distinctions of personality by peripheral means is just what consumer society is about. Instead of real differences emanating from the life of the spirit, we are offered specious symbols of it, fantasies of our separateness by way of brands of cigarettes, jogging shoes, exotic food. Once free verse has become neutral, there must be an enormous impulse to use it in this way, to establish tone rather than to make form. Because it has no specific character, we make a character in it. And metrical poetry is used in the same way. When it is strong, it becomes, as it did for Eliot and Pound in the twenties, a personal reaction against cultural formlessness. When it is graceful and elegant, it becomes, as it was in Herrick, a private fiction of civility with no particular relation to the actual social life we live.

Tranströmer's *Baltics*: Making A Form of Time

Thinking about Tranströmer's *Baltics* in midwinter and mid-Vermont; lots of snow: white, grey, smoke blue; dark green pines, windrows of snow-burned cedar. I had hardly seen snow until I was eighteen and so the intensity and neutrality of the New England landscape is permanently strange and vivid to me. And present. Because it does not belong to childhood, it calls up no longing, is the after-image of nothing lost; and it makes me completely happy, except for a small sensation of wonder which is like an itch. The happiness is like an experience of pure being; the itch is wondering what it means or what to do with it. This seems like a huge question and it reminds me of what I had first valued in Tranströmer's poems, or in the translations of them I've seen:

> 2 A.M.: moonlight. The train has stopped
> out in a field. Far off sparks of light from a town,
> flickering coldly on the horizon.
>
> As when a man goes so deep into his dream
> he will never remember that he was there
> when he returns again to his room.
>
> Or when a person goes so deep into a sickness
> that his days all become flickering sparks, a swarm,
> feeble and cold on the horizon.

The train is entirely motionless.
2 o'clock: strong moonlight, few stars.

This poem feels like it is about the social man waking up to the fact of his being. It feels very austere. In the translation there is—or I imagine there is—a secondary drama in watching the poem discipline Robert Bly's hunger for excited states of mind. The middle stanzas are a kind of war between the Whitmanic possibilities of the long, enjambed line and Tranströmer's quiet precision. The result is a very strong poem in English. The stanzas breathe long and then freeze in place. What holds them, and what haunts me, is the metaphor or fact of the stopped train. The poem is called "Track," and the track becomes a figure for time, for the preordination with which our social life glistens pointlessly into the future, while the train in a moment of clarity—like an eye opening suddenly—is stopped. The moonlight is a figure for that; for pure consciousness, without object. Because it is pure, because it just is, it means nothing special; and its not meaning anything is what fascinates me about Tranströmer.

When I look across the page, with edified ignorance, at the Swedish, I see that the main musical device of the poem seems to be the repeated vowel rhyme on *flimrande* and *synranden,* flickering and horizon. At the end of the first stanza,

flimrande kallt vid synranden

and at the end of the third

att allt som var hans dagar blir några flimrande
punkter, en svärm,
kall och ringa vid synranden

make an insistence. *Synranden,* I have been told, means "horizon," but it is not exactly the same word. Something more powerful than the English word is buried in the Germanic root of the Swedish: *syn*=vision, *randen*=border. I find that etymology, in the context of the poem, wrenching and mysterious. The held, vivid moment and life flickering out there at the vision-border. It is not lonely exactly, but it's so pure I don't know what to do with it. I don't know what its relation to the track is. And Tranströmer's early poems call up this feeling in me again and again.

I have said to myself that it has something to do with the epistemology of the lyric poem. Novels and narrative and discursive forms of the poem imitate life in time. They move and accumulate, ripen; some things fall away and other things come up. But the lyric imitates insight, or being, or consciousness without object, or waking up to oneself on the stopped train, or my two-week stint at Goddard College in the New England snow that has for me no past or future. This morning, walking to breakfast—trying to think about Tranströmer, about a lecture the poet Stephen Dobyns had given yesterday on metaphor, about a note I had written in my journal for no apparent reason which went "The *Cantos* are a long struggle between image and discourse"—I passed a bird feeder under pine trees and saw suddenly against the snow twin flashes of pure yellow and bright blue, a jay and an evening grosbeak swooping up fast to perch at a safe distance, and the color and surprise made my heart leap in my chest, and there it was again.

This is the way I come at *Baltics* which I like to read. I can't know how good a poem it is because I know it only in Samuel Charters' translation, but it is very interesting to me. Tranströmer is one of the most remarkable European poets of his generation, and I had thought of him as a deeply private writer. That he had written a poem called *Baltics* surprised me. Though my paternal great-grandfather had emigrated from a small village outside the Baltic port of Stettin, now Polish and Szczecin, no stories survived in my family and all I knew of that part of the world was Günter Grass' novels about Danzig, now Polish and Gdansk. I was also struck by the fact that the Irish poet Seamus Heaney had just addressed the North Sea region in *North*. Maybe something was up. And this curiosity re-awakened wonderings I have had about Tranströmer's politics and about the relation between image and discourse or, to make a long jump, between history and pure moment, story and song. The political question enters in this way: in a poem like "Track," Tranströmer seems to feel that the social man is not quite real and, if that is true, the social relations between men cannot be quite real either. He doesn't say that in the poem; he doesn't say anything quite like that in any of the poems that I know but in all the poems, including *Baltics*, which explores the relation of people to a place, it does seem to be something that he feels at least some of the time. Look, for example, at the metaphor he develops from the baptismal font at the beginning of the third section. It looks like a gloss on "Track":

In the half dark corner of the Gotland church, in the
    mildewed daylight
stands a sandstone baptismal font—12th century—the stone
    cutter's name
still there, shining
like a row of teeth in a mass grave:
                                        HEGWALDR
                                            the name still there. And his scenes
here and on the sides of the vessels crowded with people,
    figures on their way out of the stone.
The eyes' kernels of good and evil bursting there.
Herod at the table: the roasted cock flying up and
    crowing "Christus natus est"—the servant executed—
close by the child born, under clumps of faces as worthy
    and helpless as young monkeys.
And the fleeing steps of the pious
drumming over the dragon scales of sewer mouths.

(The scenes stronger in memory than when you stand in
front of them,
strongest when the font spins like a slow, rumbling carousel
in the memory.)
Nowhere the lee-side. Everywhere risk.
As it was. As it is.
Only inside there is peace, in the water of the vessel
that no one sees,
but on the outer walls the struggle rages.
And peace can come drop by drop, perhaps at night
when we don't know anything,
or as when we're taped to a drip in a hospital ward.

"And peace can come drop by drop": I don't know what the resonances of this line are in Swedish; in English it echoes a famous poem so directly that it seems to refer to it:

And I shall have some peace there, for peace comes
dropping slow,
Dropping from the veils of the morning . . .

Tranströmer's lines may not be a "better" poem than "The Lake Isle of Innisfree," but the translation is certainly a more interesting poem, because there is nothing in Yeats that has the power of "nowhere the lee-side." And "Track" is also a more interesting poem to me because it renders an awakening which has no form but itself; it is not the fantasy of a paradisal form that exists elsewhere.

It is easy to see how this raises political questions. The figure is so completely and exactly realized that the self seems to be separated from the world by eight inches of old sandstone. It has made a wall of the body, with social life outside in a stylized medieval frieze and inside the held, blessed water, and this is achieved through the unarguableness of metaphor. It is typical of the power of Tranströmer's poetry and almost a perfect embodiment of the hermetic attitude toward art and experience. There can be no picking and choosing. If you want to object to it, you have to dismiss it outright, saying, as the social poet will say about the hermetic poet, that it's very well done but all wrong, that the figures for inwardness in "Track" are dream and sickness, that there must be some other solution than a gnostic one to this long European disease of alienation and solipsism. And I would say all of this about Tranströmer, and say more, that the poems reek existentialism, reek the ambiance of Tranströmer's youth in the late forties and early fifties, which I was already sick of at second hand in my youth in the late fifties and early sixties, when my teachers tried to persuade me that the dead, affectless voices of *Nausea* and *The Stranger* were the very form of freedom.

Only my experience tells me that, tone and period feeling aside, there is something about what Tranströmer is saying that is permanently true, and especially true to the form of the lyric poem. That clean sense of wonder in "Track" is something I have heard in Sappho and Tu Fu. Besides, another disconcerting fact about Tranströmer's poetry is that it always seems to be the work of a deeply rooted man. Friends have told me about his Swedishness, in "Evening—Morning" for example, where the image of the dock and the half-suffocated summer gods seem inseparable from the paradisiacal long days of the short Swedish summer, and in "Sailor's Tale," how the *barvinterdagar*, the dark winter days without snow in November and December are so central to the poem that it can almost not be felt without knowledge of that experience. It is this completely local and rooted sense conveyed in a poetry that always wakes stunned from the rooted and local into a place where the self throbs with itself and the world seems elsewhere that makes me inclined not to mount arguments but to shut up and listen.

And it is what fascinates me most about *Baltics*. Partly because of its length, partly because of its subject, this poem focuses Tranströmer's themes more intensely than anything else of his I have read. Samuel Charters describes its shape and occasion in his introduction: "The poem is largely about his family and the island in the archipelago off the east coast of Sweden where they lived for many years, and where he returns each summer with his wife and his own children. The poem is in some ways almost like taking a summer walk with Tomas across the island's stretches of forest and overgrown fields." Another fact of its occasion is the death of his mother after a long illness. If you look back at the final image in the passage I have already quoted, you can see some of the ways in which the fact of death refocuses the whole passage. The mystery of the solitary self, because it is the mystery of any human being's last hours, becomes already a social thing; it aches with a question about the ways in which we can and cannot reach out to others.

The poem is in six sections, framed by an account of his grandfather in the first and an account of his grandmother in the last. There is no apparent progression; it wanders, as Charters says, and it seems to wander partly through the island and partly through a sequence of Tranströmer poems and fragments of Tranströmer poems. The connections among the sections and among the parts of the individual sections are rarely logical or discursive. And yet everything in it tugs against everything else. Fact has the pull of metaphor and one metaphor pulls against another. Here, for example, is the whole first section of the poem:

> It was before the time of radio masts.
>
> My grandfather was a newly licensed pilot. In the almanac he
> wrote down the vessels he piloted—
> name, destination, draft:
> Examples from 1884:
> Steamer Tiger Capt Rowan 16 feet Hull Gefle Furusund
> Brig Ocean Capt Andersen 8 feet Sandofjord Hernosand

Furusund
Steamer St. Petersburg Capt Libenberg 11 feet Stettin Libau
Sandhamn

He took them out to the Baltic, through that wonderful labyrinth
of islands and water.
And those that met on board, and were carried by the same hull
for a few hours or a few days,
how well did they get to know each other?
Talking in misspelled English, understanding and misunderstanding, but very little conscious lying.
How well did they get to know each other?

When it was thick fog: half speed, almost blind. The head-
land coming out of the invisibility with a single stride,
it was right on them.
Foghorn blasting every other minute. His eyes reading straight
into the invisible.
(Did he have the labyrinth in his head?)
The minutes went by.
Lands and reefs memorized like hymn verses.
And the feeling of we're-right-here that you have to keep,
like carrying a pail filled to the brim without spilling a drop.

A glance down into the engine room.
The compound engine, as long-lived as a human heart, worked
with great soft recoiling movements, steel acrobatics, and
the smells rising from it as from a kitchen.

When I first started reading *Baltics*, I wanted to make a joke to someone about the influence of Charles Olson, whom I am quite sure Tranströmer has never read: "Hmm, Steamer Tiger Capt Rowan 16 feet Hull Gefle Furusund. Where have I heard that rhythm before?" But Tranströmer is right, as Olson was right in his insistence on it, that we know the man through the specifics of his trade. If this were Olson, it would send us reeling back from this first laconic fidelity of the written word to its origin in Phoenicia and, although Tranströmer is free from the majesty of that imperialist ambition of American poetry, the transcription does circle back profoundly for me to all the unvarnished records of half-lettered men that called writing into being. And rightly: the poem patently becomes a metaphor for the connection between poetry and navigation, grandson and grandfather. *Did he have the labyrinth in his head?* All of this is fairly obvious. His curiosity about the men raises the theme of communication. The "pail filled to the brim" looks forward to the baptismal font. The knowledge secure as "hymn verses" looks longingly to the secure pieties of another age. And the final metaphor of the engine is packed in enough ways that I won't insult it with explication. The passage does not become allegory; the facts stay solidly facts, but the pull of metaphor almost overwhelms it at the outset. So much so that, if this were a poem by itself, however surprising as a Tranströmer poem, it would seem finally nostalgic and familiar, full of easy longing.

Instead, it introduces us to a labyrinth of islands and water which seems to be absolutely the terrain of modern poetry. It explains to me why, in the middle of thinking about it, I made a note to myself about Pound. One of the impulses of the modernist poem is to leap out of time, or to record those moments in which we seem to. In English poetry the process began as soon as Wordsworth tried to make an account for himself of the way, when he was a boy skating, the heavens spun when he pulled up abruptly and silence fell all around him. It was intensified as soon as Baudelaire started reading Swedenborg. Imagism was its surest expression. Pound makes a joke of it in one poem by including a date in the title, "Pagani's, November 8": "Suddenly discovering in the eyes of the very beautiful Normande cocotte / The eyes of the very learned British Museum assistant." Not *déjà vu* exactly, but the way resemblance empties time of time. If there was ever an inappropriate method for embarking on a long poem which must somehow make a shape over time, imagism is that method. And it is no accident that *The Cantos* begins with a mariner and a navigator: "And then went down to the ship." Or: "It was before the time of radio masts."

I don't know how much of this bears on the traditions of Swedish poetry. What does seem clear is that the proposal of this poem, the haunting presence of the grandparents, the death of the poet's mother, his love of the island, compels Tranströmer in a new way, to struggle with the materials of his art. *Baltics*, as I've said, is an anthology of Tranströmer poems, an archipelago. The baptismal font passage in the third section is an instance. So is section one. Here, randomly, are some others:

The strategic planetarium rotates. The lenses stare into
        the darkness.
The night sky is full of numbers, and they're fed into
a blinking cupboard,
a piece of furniture,
inside it the energy of a grasshopper swarm that devours the acres
        of Somalia in half an hour.

*

Bullhead. The fish that's a toad that wanted to be a butterfly and made it a third of the way, hiding himself in the seaweed, but pulled up in the net, hooked fast by his pathetic spikes and warts—when you untangle him from the mesh of the net your hands shine with slime.

*

Sometimes you wake at night
and quickly throw some words down
on the nearest paper, on the margin of a newspaper
(the words glowing with meaning!)
but in the morning: the same words don't say anything anymore,
        scrawls, mis-speakings.
Or fragments of a great nightly style that dragged past?

*

I don't know if we're in the beginning or in the final stage.
No conclusion can be made, no conclusion is possible.
The conclusion is the mandrake—
(see the encyclopedia of superstitions:
MANDRAKE

miracle working plant
that gave such a dreadful shriek when it was torn from the earth
that the person fell dead. A dog had to do it . . .)

*

The wind that blew so carefully all day—
all the blades of grass are counted on the furthest islets—
has lain down in the middle of the island. The matchstick's
flame stands up straight.
The sea painting and the forest painting darken together.
Also the foliage of the five-story trees is turning black.
"Every summer is the last." These are empty words
for the creatures at late summer midnight
where the crickets sew on their machines as if possessed
and the Baltic's near
and the lonely water tap stands among the wild rose bushes
like an equestrian statue. The water tastes of iron.

Each of these is wonderful in its way. They have the carefulness and surprise and sardonic tenderness and despair and sheer intelligence that make Tranströmer always worth reading. There is not a false note, and I even had that fatuous feeling of the exhilaration of creation that sometimes overtakes literary criticism, when I typed them out. If I have a criticism of them, it is that they have for me the aftertaste of *17 Dikter*, the sensation that they could be engraved in stone under the superscription "Twentieth Century Sentiments" and survive for centuries as an emblem of our mortal weariness with living in our time.

The first passage makes an emblem of alienation by physics. The second figures despair in the face of evolutionary theory, saved somehow by the shiny slime of the sculpin which is like the mystery of the stuff of the spirit but feels like semen. The third is our haunting by the unconscious and by the fragmentation of our speech. The fourth is our literal rootlessness, our having been hauled, half-dead and half-alive, out of traditional and organic forms of society by industrial and technological revolution. The fifth is that Tranströmer poem of the self which is like water; it is almost too beautiful, too deft, the poet and the poem, each man on the edge of his own Baltic, a "lonely water tap" standing "among the wild rose bushes like an equestrian statue." By themselves, they become an irritation, and Tranströmer's striking talent doubles back on him, as if the style were the face of a man who appeared to have answers and had instead a stunning repertoire of methods for describing the predicament.

But the passages don't occur by themselves. They are parts of a longer poem which take their central weight—at least I have chosen to believe Charters when he says they take their central weight—from the fact of his mother's death, which draws the whole sequence downward toward a place where there can be no satisfaction in the iterated revelation of a self without meaning in a world that is busy, admirable, terrible and pointless. The reference to his mother's death is the most opaque passage in the poem and I don't know if I could have seen it if Charters had not pointed it out:

> The Death lectures went on for several terms. I was present
> together with classmates I didn't know
> (who are you?)
> —afterwards everyone went off on his own, profiles.
>
> I looked at the sky and the earth and straight ahead
> and since then I've been writing a long letter to the dead
> on a typewriter that doesn't have a ribbon, only a horizon line
> so the words beat in vain and nothing stays.

It is one thing to wake up to the solitariness of one's own being, to recognize that solitariness as a fact about each of us, and to contemplate its extinction in oneself; it is another to experience it happening to someone you love. The figure of "the Death lectures" gets the relentlessness and desperation of it. And it recurs in the meditation on his grandfather's death, which leads him in turn to wonder about the fate of a stranger in a nineteenth-century photograph, some anonymous human whose life must mean whatever the idea of a *Baltics* means:

> But in the next brown photo
> someone I don't know—
> by the clothes from the middle of the last century.
> A man about thirty, the powerful eyebrows,
> the face that looks me right in the eye
> whispering: "Here I am."
> but who "I" am
> is something no one remembers anymore. No one.
>
> TB? Isolation?
>
> Once he stopped
> on the stony, grass streaming slope coming up from the sea
> and felt the black blindfold in front of his eyes.

This perilousness of our individual lives is what makes the insight of the isolated lyric poem untenable. It creates the need in the wandering fragments or islands of *Baltics* to somehow transform image into discourse, into a form of time, as the terse notations of the poet's grandfather had turned the isolated towns his ship visited into a rudimentary culture: "Steamer St. Petersburg Capt Libenberg 11 feet Stettin Libau Sandhamn". It makes the form of the poem its deepest and most urgent subject.

There are metaphors for this throughout the poem, metaphors of writing, speech, mis-speech, communication. The men on shipboard in section one prefigure it, "talking in misspelled English, understanding and misunderstanding, but very little conscious lying / How well did they get to know each other?" It appears in the second section in what seems to be a reference to the Soviet Union: "where a conversation between friends is a test of what friendship means," but could be a reference to America in the late sixties, or to any repressive society. In section four, it appears in an image that is particularly crucial because it calls up our distrust of abstract thought which is the traditional method or form of discourse: "the seaweed holding themselves up with air bladders, as we hold ourselves up with ideas." In section five, he speaks of the problem directly:

> August 2. Something wants to be said, but the words don't agree.
> Something that can't be said,
> *aphasia*,
> there aren't any words but maybe a style . . .

The style is, simply, the attentive, loose wandering of *Baltics*, a sort of slowly turning mobile of mind and island, in which discourse occurs because the separate parts tug at one another and everything seems metaphorically related to everything else. I had better pause over that phrase: metaphorically related. In the lecture I heard yesterday, Stephen Dobyns began by talking about the wonder he felt at the swiftness of the mind's perception of metaphorical connection, the speed with which it takes in, connects, and generalizes that perception. The example he used was taken from W. S. Merwin's *Asian Figures*:

> Spits straight up
> learns something

Almost before he had finished saying it, the audience laughed —as if to illustrate his point. He used this to demonstrate that metaphor is a participatory act; it surprises the hearer into self-knowledge. It heightens his relationship to himself. I loved his saying that, because I had always thought more or less naïvely that a metaphor connected two things; in fact, in metaphor, *we* connect two things, or have connected things, and metaphor calls up the work already done. Dobyns quoted this to the audience: "When he draws a tiger, it's a dog"; and asked us to feel our whole minds drawn to its solution, so that we experienced what the natural and incessant work of the imagination was. Art, he concluded, allowed the reader to establish an intimate relationship with himself and to become aware of how relationship formed his own sense of the world.

What happens quickly in the Merwin aphorisms is what happens slowly as the mind moves through the parts of *Baltics*. It is not a wisdom poem; it does not try to arrive at some healed knowledge, comic or tragic. And it is not a political poem, though its themes include community and isolation. But it enacts the qualities of a consciousness that knows it has been outside of time and is going to die, two thousand miles below words like *socialism* and *intentional anarchism* and *bankbook*, and it knows that the discovery and enactment of those qualities in our art are the spiritual precondition for a viable politics. That last sentence sounds so grand, I have scared myself a little. The proof, finally, is in the poem, for which I don't mean to advance these propositions as claims of complete success, but as an indication of Tranströmer's compelling seriousness as an artist. The reader should really apply the Dobyns test for himself by watching himself read section five of *Baltics* with a whole mind.

July 30. The channel has become eccentric—today it's teeming
with jellyfish for the first time in years, they pump
themselves along with calm consideration, they belong to the same shipping company: AURELIA,
they drift like flowers after a burial at sea, if you

take them out of the water all of their shape disappears, as when an indescribable truth is lifted out of the silence and formulated into a lifeless mass, yes, they're untranslatable, they have to stay in their element.

August 2. Something wants to be said, but the words don't agree.
Something that can't be said,
aphasia.
there aren't any words but maybe a style . . .

Sometimes you wake up at night
and quickly throw some words down
on the nearest paper, on the margin of a newspaper
(the words glowing with meaning!)
but in the morning: the same words don't say anything anymore,
scrawls, mis-speakings.
Or fragments of a great nightly style that dragged past?

Music comes to a person, he's a composer, he's played, has a
career, becomes director of the conservatory.
The trend turns downward, he's blamed by the authorities.
They put up his pupil K*** as chief prosecutor.
He's threatened, demoted, sent away.
After some years the disgrace diminishes, he's rehabilitated.
Then comes the stroke: right side paralysis, and aphasia,
can only grasp short phrases, says wrong words.
Can, as a result of this, not be touched by advancement or blame.
But the music's still there, he still composes in his own style,
he becomes a medical sensation for the time he has left to live.

He wrote music to texts he no longer understood—
in the same way
we express something with our lives
in that humming chorus of misspeech.

The Death lectures went on for several terms. I was present
together with classmates I didn't know

(who are you?)
—afterwards everyone went off on his own, profiles.

I looked at the sky and the earth and straight ahead
and since then I've been writing a long letter to the dead
on a typewriter that doesn't have a ribbon, only a horizon line
so the words beat in vain and nothing stays.

I stand with my hand on the door handle, take the pulse
 of the house.
The walls so full of life
(the children won't dare sleep alone up in the attic—what
 makes me feel safe makes them uneasy.)

August 3. Out there in the damp grass
slithers a greeting from the Middle Ages: Helix pomatia
the subtly grey-gold shining snail with its jaunty house,
introduced by some monk who liked *escargots*—yes, the
 Franciscans were here,
broke stone and burnt lime, the island was theirs in 1288,
 a donation from King Magnus
("Thes almes and othres he hath yeven / Thei meteth hym nu
 he entreth hevene.")
the forest fell, the ovens burned, the lime taken by sail
to the building of the monastery . . .
 Sister snail
stands almost still in the grass, feelers sucked in
and rolled out, disturbance and hesitation . . .
How like myself in my searching!

The wind that blew so carefully all day—
all the blades of grass are counted on the furthest islets—
has lain down in the middle of the island. The matchstick's
 flame stands straight up.
The sea painting and the forest painting darken together.
Also the foliage of the five-story trees is turning black.
"Every summer is the last." These are empty words

for the creatures at late summer midnight
where the crickets sew on their machines as if possessed
and the Baltic's near
and the lonely water tap stands among the wild rose bushes
like an equestrian statue. The water tastes of iron.

I think I like especially the crickets sewing on their machines as if possessed. It is what the stitching of Tranströmer's writing in this passage feels like to me.

In speaking about long poems, Charles Olson often quoted Whitehead: "The process of creation is the form of unity." This has been, more or less, the justification for most poems of any length since *The Cantos*, and it has always seemed to me to be a question-begging formulation. Because, by not saying how the process of creation comes to closure, it tells us nothing about either form or unity. It doesn't tell us the difference between a thing coming to form and those experiments in pure seriality which seem to end either in exhaustion or the death of their author. *Baltics* ends because the poem arrives, in the sixth section, at a figure for itself. I have read the poem many, many times, and I guess I should say that I don't think its conclusion is entirely achieved. That is, I don't feel, haven't yet felt, that its circling movement through many dark places to this last bright leap is accomplished rather than wished into being. I can't think of many places in literature where it is. *The Tempest*, the end of *The Cantos*. But the conclusion for which it reaches is surprisingly similar to Pound's, the place where the light of intelligence, of metaphor, discourse, and relation becomes indistinguishable from love, that word Pound avoided by plugging in a scrap of Italian neo-Platonism: *intelleto d'amore*.

Tranströmer comes at it in his own way when he focuses the poem at the end on the family house, a two-hundred-year-old fisherman's house, and discovers the pattern of his own mind in the tiles which ornament and encircle its roof:

So much crouching wood. And on the roof the ancient tiles
that collapsed across and on top of each other
(the original pattern erased by the earth's rotation through
the years)
it reminds me of something . . . I was there . . . wait: it's the old
Jewish cemetery in Prague
where the dead live closer together than they did in life,
the stones jammed in, jammed in.
So much encircled love! The tiles with the lichen's letters
in an unknown language
are the stones in the archipelago people's ghetto cemetery,
the stones erected and fallen down—

The ramshackle hut shines
with the light of all the people carried by a certain wave,
a certain wind,
out here to their fates.

I don't know if he has brought it off. I don't think that anyone without a knowledge of Swedish could know for sure, even in the mis-speech of Samuel Charters' clear, strong translation, but it is hard not to feel that those last lines—"a certain wave, a certain wind"—have deeply touched the mystery of place and of the shape of the poem.

What Furies

A wonderful thing about the trajectory of Stanley Kunitz's work is the way the poems alter without changing. Early and late, they have an unrepentant hunger for intensity and grandeur. It's fascinating to compare Wallace Stevens at seventy with Kunitz. Even titles: Stevens, "Of Mere Being," Kunitz, "The Knot." At the end as at the beginning, Stevens' poems have that startling becalmed clarity that's like taking deep breaths in brisk air:

The palm at the end of the mind,
Beyond the last thought, rises
In the bronze distance,

A gold-feathered bird
Sings in the palm, without human meaning,
Without human feeling, a foreign song.

You know then that it is not the reason
That makes us happy or unhappy.
The bird sings. The feathers shine.

The palm stands on the edge of space.
The wind moves slowly in the branches.
The bird's fire-fangled feathers dangle down.

(Except for the last line. Stevens has his own way of being unrepentant. "The suspect," some metaphysical Chief Inspector of Poetry might write, closing the file, "was last seen doing magic tricks and disappearing into pure, clear air.") And Kunitz:

I've tried to seal it in,
that cross-grained knot
on the opposite wall,
scored in the lintel of my door,
but it keeps bleeding through
into the world we share.
Mornings when I wake,
curled in my web,
I hear it come
with a rush of resin
out of the trauma
of its lopping off.
Obstinate bud,
sticky with life,
mad for the rain again,
it racks itself with shoots
that crackle overhead,
dividing as they grow.
Let be! Let be!
I shake my wings
and fly into its boughs.

What different summings-up. "Of Mere Being" is the last piece in Stevens' collected poems. "The Knot" is the first (or last) in the recently collected poems of Kunitz. And what different birds. Stevens' is both an alien being and the one true resident; it sings its song without human meaning at the edge of space, its feathers shining. And Kunitz—his bird sings (or croaks, you hear in the rasp of "rack," "shoot," "crackle") in a tree that blossoms from the wound of this world.

The music of the two poems gets the difference. Stevens is calm, stately, measured:

The PALM at the END of the MIND

Kunitz begins in a furious rush:

I've TRIED to SEAL-it-IN

You can almost not say "seal it in" as if they were three words. They want to run together in a single strong stress, intensified by the beat of the next few lines:

that CROSS-GRAINED KNOT
on the OPposite WALL,
SCORED in the LINtel of my DOOR,
but it KEEPS BLEEDing THROUGH
into the WORLD we SHARE.

The feeling of opposition, of contrariety, comes in the sound echoes: "opposite wall" and "world we share," "seal it in" and "bleeding through." Compare this with Stevens' ground beat of three stresses:

The PALM at the END of the MIND,
BeYOND the LAST THOUGHT, RISes
In the BRONZE DIStance,

The pattern of stresses and pauses looks like this:

3
3/1
2

and the pattern by phrase is simply 3/3/3. That one asymmetrical word in the second line keeps it from monotonous regularity, and the stresses at line-end, "RISes," "DIStance," fall off to keep things subdued. Very simple and elegant. If you read the Stevens poem, hitting the stressed syllables as hard as you can, trying to give it the thickness and writhing heaviness of Kunitz's rhythm, it doesn't alter its behavior even slightly. The bird sings. The feathers shine. And look at the diction of "The Knot": cross-grained, opposite, scored, bleed, trauma, obstinate, sticky, mad. *Beyond, beyond,* Stevens says. *Into, into,* says Kunitz. Both of them, blessedly, mean *here,* but what different ways of not going anywhere!

Stevens was a meditative poet. Kunitz has practiced the dramatic lyric all his life. The meditative poem can step a little to the side and let the world speak through it, and the world has no need to cry "Let be! Let be!" because it is. It has a mind of winter or, as the Zen teacher Robert Aitken has said, a mind of white paper. In the dramatic poem, the I, the romantic I, places itself in the center of the vast, packed (tiny, finite) stage of the poem and suffers itself to be transformed. It goes into the crucible over and over again, goes into desire, not past it, and it's anything but non-attached. Much of the original work done in the twentieth century has been in the meditative vein, partly because it is freer from the echoes of poems in the English tradition, and partly because it suggests a territory for the long poem. The dramatic lyric is a peculiarly Western form, I think. Yeats was its great modern practitioner, and in this he was Kunitz's master.

That bird of the spirit which appears in "Of Mere Being" and "The Knot" as a final transformation of the maker of poems has a long history which includes the gorgeous bird in Marvell's "The Garden" and Keats' nightingale, but its immediate ancestor is the golden bird at the end of "Sailing to Byzantium," which was written, not coincidentally, in 1928, the year Kunitz's first poems were published. Yeats was in his sixties, Kunitz in his early twenties writing furious, dense, involuted poems in which the poet, as Christ or Hamlet or Lucifer, transforms the rot of things into the pure crystal of poetry. It's not hard to see how riveting Yeats' poem might have been to a young writer or how deep the example went:

Consume my heart away; sick with desire
And fastened to a dying animal
It knows not what it is; and gather me
Into the artifice of eternity.

Once out of nature I shall never take
My bodily form from any natural thing,
But such a form as Grecian goldsmiths make
Of hammered gold and gold enamelling
To keep a drowsy Emperor awake;
Or set upon a golden bough to sing
To lords and ladies of Byzantium
Of what is past, or passing, or to come.

Many of Yeats' poems present a man suddenly shaken and then transformed. This one begins, you remember, with what could be the poet musing in a public park:

That is no country for old men. The young
In one another's arms, birds in the trees,
—Those dying generations—at their song,

The poem wants out of nature, out of time and sex and change. To get there, it has to pass through fire:

O sages standing in God's holy fire
As in the gold mosaic of a wall,
Come from the holy fire, perne in a gyre,
And be the singing-masters of my soul.
Consume my heart away . . .

That pattern—a man in a given situation often of painful memory or insight, a transforming passage through fire, and then the situation transformed—is common to Yeats' poems, and to the dramatic lyric. Death and rebirth: the subject of these poems, what the form expresses, is the shudder of becoming.

In Kunitz's work, the transforming event is very often a

wound or a wounding. Here is a very early poem, "Twilight." The source of its style is probably turn-of-the-century Yeats, moony and silvery but about to turn into something savage and unexpected:

I wait. I deepen in the room.
Fed lions, glowing, congregate
In corners, sleep and fade. For whom
It may concern I, tawny, wait.

Time flowing through the window; day
Spilling on the board its bright
Last blood. Folding (big, gauzy, gray)
A moth sits on the western light.

Sits on my heart that, darkened, drips
No honey from its punctured core,
Yet feeds my hands and feeds my lips.
The Moon, the Moon, is at my door!

There are things I love here: the dazzling music of the second stanza; the way the shadow-lions register the slowed-down body of six o'clock; the fact that the unfed lion of the spirit is still awake; the moth which is both death's-head and the delicate creature-world; that spirit is erotic in this poem. But there are also things I wonder about, mainly the melodrama of that punctured heart. I think when I first read the poem I was appalled by it. Now I waver, feeling lots of affection for the grandness of the young poet's bad literary manners. But in neither case do I feel the wounding—it's there as a romantic given.

Both *Intellectual Things* and *Passport to the War* seem to grope for an understanding of this pain. It is one of the things that accounts for the artifice and the fury of those poems. Usually the wound is in the heart or in the side. It is, often, worn as a badge of defiance, proudly. "The banner of my blood," the young poet cries, flaunting, "will not be love, only the pity and the pride of it. . . ." (The older poet will remember this when he sees his daughter in an antiwar demonstration, carrying a misspelled sign: *"Don't tred on me."*) And often it is connected to an explosive wounding pressure on the brain or the brow which occurs in the poems very often in the metaphors of doorway, lintel, threshold. In the Rousseau-like setting of "Twilight" we are not sure whether that moon at the door is the muse, or madness, or the light of the poem, or all three.

The early work is full of this theme, explored in a ransacking of possible literary styles. In "Mens Creatrix":

> Mental womb,
> Intelligence of tight
> Precision: He comes, the sudden Lord,
> A rhythmic Spike of Light
> To cleave you with that Spike:
> Himself, His flowing Word.
> Strike, O Poem, Strike!

In "Beyond Reason," he prays that he can "teach his mind to love its thoughtless crack." In "Organic Bloom," the brain swells "Till, bursting like a fruit, it scatters doom." In "Prophecy on Lethe," carrion on the beach is "a pod of silence, bursting when the sun clings to the forehead." The dead, in "In a Strange House," threaten to "part the fiery lips of thought." This tangle of sexual and intellectual woundings persists into the later poems—into "Father and Son" where the poet runs through the sleeping country of his youth, "the night nailed like an orange to my brow," and into poems like "Robin Redbreast" where the speaker picks up a living bird from the lawn and sees, with a flash of horror, that its brains have been blown out by a hunter.

Whatever the source of the wound, it seems clear that it is both desired and feared because it makes poetry possible. In the early poems, he imagines, like Yeats, that it will be his agency of transformation, that it will take him out of this world, into crystal or Byzantium or some place of pure light, radiant as Blake. When he takes it into himself, when the wound becomes a way of entering life and therefore of entering art, I think Kunitz finds himself as a poet. That happens in *Passport to the War*, a book full of oblique, tormented poems about guilt and waste and failure. Among them is this one, addressed perhaps to his daughter. The context suggested by the companion poems is a painful and rancorous divorce. The poet is answering the child's question: "What have you done?" and the poet, father now, not child in search of the father, speaks with a tenderness that's wholly new, as if the question had thrown him off himself and allowed that feeling to come rushing in:

Pigeon, who are to me
Language and light,
And the long flight home,
Your question comes with coils
Which I am crawling from,
Be patient with my wound:
Too long I lay
In the folds of my preparation,
Sinuous in the sun,
A golden skin,
All pride, sores, excretion,
Blazing with death. O child,
From my angry side
Tumbles this agate heart,
Your prize, veined with the root
Of guilty life,
From which flow love and art.

What moves me most about this poem is simply the tone of voice. It isn't through with the old intensity but something has been accepted, taken in. What might have appealed to critics forty years ago is its substructure—the way those sinuous folds make the poet Lucifer while the wound makes him Christ, that the man who would have been the child's savior and protector is also the one who introduces her to the painful knowledge of good and evil, that from that double wound and double identity love flows, that the dove and the serpent are, as the old archetypes had insisted, one.

And there is another, more complex thing that moves me. It is that the father in this poem, for all his tenderness to the child, is thinking mainly about himself, pleading his own case. That is what the dramatic lyric has to dramatize: *I* in trouble, *I* suffering, *I* transformed. It is a form particularly susceptible to what Robert Pinsky has called, eloquently, "our hard-ons of self-concern." It doesn't say: imagine this. It says: imagine me. It is not the palm at the end of the mind, but the knot or wound of the lopping-off from which that palm might have grown, bleeding into our world. Reading "The Reckoning," I feel some of the same emotion I have felt whenever I read or hear that famous speech of Lear's to Cordelia: "Come, let's away to prison, we two alone will sing like birds i' the cage. . . ." Sometimes I weep at the pathos of it, sometimes I want to weep with rage that that crazy old man has learned nothing, that he *still* wants his daughter to himself. That is the "root of guilty life" in "The Reckoning," and Kunitz has got at it by dramatizing in a way that no discursive or meditative poem could. It gives an odd tartness to the release of the verb "flow" in the last line of the poem. In the back of my mind I hear "and flow and flow and flow . . ." like the pumping of the heart.

After *Passport to the War*, the poems don't strain to leap out of this world into another one. The crystal they look for is in our lives and the occasions of it are more various. Look, for example, at how the wound is delivered in "A Spark of Laurel." The poem registers an occasion described in *A Kind of Order, A Kind of Folly*. Kunitz was living—the poem suggests—in a desperate solitude on a farm in the Delaware Valley and a stranger showed up at his door, Theodore Roethke, and quoted some of Kunitz's lines to him:

This man, this poet, said,
"I've carried in my head
For twenty years and more
Some lines you wrote before
I knew the meaning of
Euripides or love"—
And gravely then intoned,
Lured from the underground
The greekness of my song
Still melancholy-young;
While she, long since forgotten,
For whom the song was written,
Burned wanton once again
Through centuries of rain,
Smiling as she must do,
To keep her legend true,
And struck the mortal blow,
But not that blood could flow.
Ha! Once again I heard
The transubstantial word
That is not mine to speak
Unless I break, I break;
The spiral verb that weaves
Through the crystal of our lives,
Of myth and water made
And incoherent blood;
What sirens on the coast
Trilled to Ulysses lost,
And Agamemnon's thigh
Opened at length to cry:
This laurel-sparking rhyme
That we repeat in time
Until the fathers rest
On the inhuman breast

That is both fire and stone,
Mother and mistress, one.

It is funny, and exultant, the wound delivered back to him from his own early poems. The moment seems to enact his own prophecy that he should have not love, but the pity and the pride of it. And if he must break to make poems, it is this time a smile he breaks into. Notice also, in case you had begun to think that he had learned to curb his excesses, that the song is cried by a wound in Agamemnon's thigh.

The wound keeps wanting to be sexual, and in many of the poems gathered in 1958, it is. There are poems of sexual enchantment, of the sexual wars, and, particularly in "She Wept, She Railed," celebration of a woman (or women) for whom the sexual wound is defiance, who won't, because of it, accept "the postures of the underling."

She wept, she railed, she spurned the meat
Men toss into a muslin cage
To make their spineless doxy bleat
For pleasure and for patronage,
As if she had no choice but eat
The lewd bait of a squalid age.

That moment when the lights go out
The years shape to a sprawling thing,
A marmoset with bloodied clout,
A pampered flank that learns to sing,
Without the grace, she cried, to doubt
The postures of the underling.

I thought of Judith in her tent,
Of Helen by the crackling wall,
Of Cressida, her bone-lust spent,
Of Catherine on the holy wheel:
I heard their woman-dust lament
The golden wound that does not heal.

What a wild air her small joints beat!
I only poured the raging wine
Until our bodies filled with light,
Mine with hers and hers with mine,
And we went out into the night
Where all the constellations shine.

"Beautiful," a friend said when I read her this poem. And then, "Not true, not true." What is true is that the Byzantium here is the ecstatic possibility when, wounded, proud, defiant—"touchy," we say—we turn to each other in this world. I think the poem is as much about art, about a turning away from the search for ice, crystal, and the father, as it is about love. The music feels like Roethke, or Roethke at this period feels like Kunitz. Many of the poems read as if they could be collaborations.

What about a poem without a wound in it? That brings us to "The Waltzer in the House," the eeriest, funniest, weirdest of Kunitz's poems. It even sounds, to my ear, slightly sinister. The mouse in this poem is the happy lover, I think, and the phallus, and the poet without a wound:

A sweet, a delicate white mouse,
A little blossom of a beast,
Is waltzing in the house
Among the crackers and the yeast.

O the swaying of his legs!
O the bobbing of his head!
The lady, beautiful and kind,
The blue-eyed mistress, lately wed,
Has almost laughed away her wits
To see the pretty mouse that sits
On his tiny pink behind
And swaying, bobbing, begs.

She feeds him tarts and curds,
Seed packaged for the birds,
And figs, and nuts, and cheese;
Polite as Pompadour to please
The dainty waltzer of her house,
The sweet, the delicate, the innocent white mouse.

As in a dream, as in a trance,
She loves his rhythmic elegance,
She laughs to see his bobbing dance.

The music of many of these poems is courtly, rich, formal, the imagery generalized. "Goose Pond" and "The Thief" move toward autobiography. "The Thief" is a poem I have liked a long time. The traumatic event in it is that the poet gets his pocket picked in Rome and it contains a brisk, clear statement of his theme: "All's motion here / And motion, like emotion, is impure." In "The Unwithered Garland" there is a female figure, loved for "her sacred flaw," "her wounding by the infinite," who teaches him that

Things are not only what they are:
They pass beyond themselves to learn
The tears of the particular.

It is the next book, *The Testing Tree*, that tests this proposition. The style has been radically stripped to support a series of experiments in harrowing simplicity, the tragic lyric in its plainest possible form. "The Portrait" is the clearest example, a poem so naked it made me uncomfortable when I first read it, still makes me uncomfortable, but which I've never forgotten:

My mother never forgave my father
for killing himself,
especially at such an awkward time
and in a public park,
that spring

when I was waiting to be born.
She locked his name
in her deepest cabinet
and would not let him out,
though I could hear him thumping.
When I came down from the attic
with the pastel portrait in my hand
of a long-lipped stranger
with a brave moustache
and deep brown level eyes,
she ripped it into shreds
without a single word
and slapped me hard.
In my sixty-fourth year
I can feel my cheek
still burning.

The risk of this poem is that it seems to allow us to do nothing but feel stunned with the speaker. In that way, it seems shockingly singular, as if all the work of the great artists of childhood—Dickens or Chaplin—were reduced to a single image of cruelty to a child, stinging down through time. In fact, in a dramatic lyric, something else happens. We come to realize that the portrait of the title, which seems to refer to the father, refers to the mother. It is a portrait of her, of a knot or wound locked so deep in the heart, it becomes the heart, and can't bleed through into the world we share. The burning on that cheek, then, becomes not the boy's, but the mother's, the burning of a refusal cold and deep and furious, and it makes the plainness of those first two lines—"My mother never forgave my father / for killing himself"—quite terrible. And what we are left with is not just the grown man's sense of the wrong done to the child, but his sense of the wrong the mother had done to herself, which was savage, and is over, and can't be helped.

One reading of the knot or wound, then, is simply this: we

hurt each other. And that is what lies behind another of these very bare poems, "The Catch":

It darted across the pond
toward our sunset perch,
weaving in, up, and around
a spindle of air,
this delicate engine
fired by impulse and glitter,
swift darning-needle,
gossamer dragon,
less image than thought,
and the thought come alive.
Swoosh went the net
with a practiced hand.
"Da-da, may I look too?"
You may look, child,
all you want.
This prize belongs to no one.
But you will pay all
your life for the privilege,
all your life.

This survey of the work should make it clear why Kunitz wrote "The Knot" and not "Of Mere Being." He isn't a poet of the palm at the end of the mind, however much we Americans hunger for that Adamic country. His subject is the long wound of becoming. "I know what I know," he says, "I shall never escape from strangeness or complete my journey." I think he is the least non-attached poet I know of. Past seventy, he is still answering the knock on the door:

What wakes me now
like the country doctor
startled in his sleep?
Why does my racing heart

shuffle down the hall
for the hundredth time
to answer the night-bell?
Whoever summons me has need of me.
How could I afford
to disobey that call?

There is, of course, no one there. Look at the fugue of transformations of feeling with which the poem ends:

. . . I know
I am not ready yet
and nobody stands on the stoop,
not even a stray cat
slouches under the sodium lamp.
Deceived! or self-deceived.
I can never atone for it.
Oh I should be the one
to swell the night with my alarm!
When the messenger comes again
I shall pretend
in a childish voice
my father is not home.

"What of the Night?" the poem is called. And asks. Death, which is the first and final wound? Guilt, which is how we take it inside us? Love, to which it gives birth? We are the only protectors, it says, and we are the thing that needs to be protected, and we are what it needs to be protected from. And so we "pretend" back to the first innocence where, pretending, we are authors of ourselves and where, as Blake says, the authors are in eternity because father isn't home. How rapidly and easily those last lines run us through that series of recognitions. And what faith that childish voice keeps with the young author of burning, prophetic poems.

Listening and Making

1/

I told a friend I was going to try to write something about prosody and he said, "Oh great." The two-beat phrase is a very American form of terminal irony. A guy in a bar in Charlottesville turned to me once and said, loudly but confidentially, "Ahmo find me a woman and fuck her twenty ways till Sunday." That's also a characteristic rhythm: ahmo FIND ME a WOman / and FUCK her TWENty WAYS till SUNday. Three beats and then a more emphatic four. A woman down the bar doubled the two-beat put-down. She said, "Good luck, asshole." Rhythms and rhythmic play make texture in our lives but they are hard to talk about and besides people don't like them to be talked about. Another friend wrote to me about an essay of mine in which I commented at some point on a "metrical inversion" in a line from a poem by Robert Lowell. He said he liked the piece well enough, but that one phrase—that finical tic of the educated mind—had filled him with rage. I think I understand why.

For a long time anthropological theory treated shamanism and spirit possession as separate phenomena. Shamanism was seen as a priestly tradition, a repertoire of techniques for acquiring vision. Spirit possession was a peripheral phenomenon, occurring mostly among women on some borderline between hysteria and Pentecostal religion. Or so it seemed until an English anthropologist, Ian Lewis, began to study the continuities between them. At which point it became clear that shamanism was usually a fully developed, male-dominated, politically central evolution of spirit possession; and that, in the harshly repressed lives of women in most primitive societies, new songs, chants, visions and psychic experiences keep welling up into cults which have their force because they are outside the entrenched means to vision. Because rhythm has direct access to the unconscious, because it can hypnotize us, enter our bodies and make us move, it is a power. And power is political.

That is why rhythm is always revolutionary ground. It is always the place where the organic rises to abolish the mechanical and where energy announces the abolition of tradition. New rhythms are new perceptions. In the nineteenth century, blank verse, the ode and ballad forms overthrew the heroic couplet. In the twentieth, vers libre overthrew the metrical dexterities of the Victorians. The latest of these revolutions occurred in the 1950s. It is variously dated from Charles Olson's essay "Projective Verse," from Allen Ginsberg's *Howl* and Jack Kerouac's spontaneous poetics or from Robert Lowell's conversion to William Carlos Williams in *Life Studies.* In the second generation of poets since 1950, the same slogans have been advanced and there is, in the magazines, an orthodoxy of relaxed free verse. Statements about rhythm emphasize its natural character. The rhythm of poetry is sometimes said to be based on the rhythm of work, but no one wonders then why we work rhythmically. The heartbeat—pa-thunk, pa-thunk, pa-thunk—is pointed to as a basis for rhythm, but if you think about it for a minute, it seems obvious that it is a little monotonous to account for much. Prosody is not much taught or talked about, since it was a form of institutional terrorism in the previous, metrical orthodoxy. And during this time, I think, there has been an observable falling off in the inventive force of poetry. A likely outcome would be an equally mindless metrical revival. And I think that would be too bad. The range of possibilities for the poem—from chant to prose—have been extended enormously in English in the past seventy years. Very few living poets—Robert Duncan comes to mind—work with that full range. What I want to try to do in this essay is talk about the part rhythm plays in the work of the imagination and suggest a way of thinking about the prosody of free verse. It is listening that I am interested in—in writers and readers—and the kind of making that can come from live, attentive listening.

Here is a poem by Gary Snyder, "August on Sourdough, A Visit from Dick Brewer":

> You hitched a thousand miles
> 　　　　　　　　north from San Francisco
> Hiked up the mountainside　a mile in the air
> The little cabin—one room—
> 　　　　　　　　walled in glass
> Meadows and snowfields,　　hundreds of peaks.
> We lay in our sleeping bags
> 　　　　　　　　　　talking half the night;
> Wind in the guy-cables　　summer mountain rain.
> Next morning I went with you
> 　　　　　　　　　　as far as the cliffs,
> Loaned you my poncho—　　the rain across the shale—
> You down the snowfield
> 　　　　　　　　flapping in the wind
> Waving a last goodbye　　half-hidden in the clouds
> To go on hitching
> 　　　　　　　　clear to New York;
> Me back to my mountain　　and far, far, west.

This poem is beautifully made, casual, tender, alive with space. It is worth remembering, since I want to argue that rhythm is at least partly a psychological matter, that twenty-five years ago the editors of most American literary magazines would have found it thin, eccentric, formless.

It belongs to a tradition of poems of leave-taking in China and Japan. Buson provides an instance:

You go,
I stay;
two autumns

And Basho another:

Seeing people off,
Being seen off,—
autumn in Kiso

Goodbyes are powerful, and Americans, who say them all the time, don't seem to write about them very much. In *A Zen Wave*, Robert Aitken's book about Basho, he observes that the Japanese, customarily, wave until a departing guest has disappeared from sight. We are more likely to turn away before that happens, not so much erasing the other person as turning inward, toward our own separateness, and getting on with it. Buson doesn't do that; he lets the moment define itself, lets the distance speak. And, in imagining his own separateness, he imagines his friend's. That last image—two autumns—speaks absolutely of the way in which each of us is alone, but it also tends to multiply, expand: two autumns, dozens of autumns, a million autumns, worlds and worlds, and whether that fact is happy or unhappy, he doesn't say; he says it is. Basho makes something different but similar of the fact that parting is like the process of individuation. The second line of his poem in Japanese reads *okuritsu hate wa*, literally *okuri* (seeing off) *tsu* (now) *hate* (goal, outcome, upshot) *wa* (particle indicating the subject). In the version I quote, R. H. Blyth has, nicely, rendered *hate wa* as a dash; comings and goings resolve into a time and a place, the ongoing world without subject or object. Basho's insight moves us a step further than Buson's. Many worlds, many subjectivities become one world which includes, among other things, all the individual worlds. How sharply you feel that world emerging, how sharply the self dissolving into it, he leaves up to you.

Robert Aitken has written a fine, brief commentary on this poem:

> Now being seen off; now seeing off—what is the upshot? Autumn in Kiso, rain in Manoa Valley, a gecko at the Maui zendo—*chi chi chichichi.*
>
> Paul Gauguin asked: "Where do we come from? What are we? Where are we going?" You will find these words inscribed in French in the corner of one of his greatest paintings, a wide prospect of Tahiti, children, young adults, old people, birds, animals, trees, and a strange idol. What is the upshot after all? Paul Gauguin painted it very beautifully.

Snyder's "August on Sourdough" seems to say something like what Buson says: you go, I go. And in its evocation of space and movement something of what Basho says; it creates a wide, windy world whose center is no particular person. One understanding of it might come from looking at the personal pronouns, at the way American speech distinguishes the self as subject from the self as object. But another way that Snyder tries to discover what he means is rhythmically. *Chi chi chichichi.* One two onetwothree. What does the sound have to say about wholeness or endings or movement or separation? What rhythm heals? To ask these questions, we have to ask what rhythm is and how it engages us.

2 /

Some ideas first. I want to suggest that our experience of rhythm has three distinct phases. Clear enough that it implies the apprehension of a pattern. We hear

one two

and we are hearing a sound. When we hear

one two
one two

we are beginning to hear a rhythm. If we listen to something like this,

one two
one
one two
one two three
one two
one two three
one two
one
one two

we attend to and can pick out three patterns of repetition:

one	one two	one two three
one	one two	one two three
one	one two	one two three
one	one two	one two three

Part of the explanation for this is that we are pattern-discerning animals, for whatever reason in our evolutionary history. We attend to a rhythm almost instinctively, listen to it for a while, and, if we decide it has no special significance for us, we can let it go; or put it away, not hearing it again unless it alters, signaling to us—as it would to a hunting or a grazing animal—that something in the environment is changed. This process is going on in us all the time, one way or another. It is the first stage, wakeful, animal, alert, of the experience of rhythm. And it is the place to which we are called by the first words of any poem or story. *Once upon a time; how many dawns chill from his rippling rest; it is a law universally acknowledged . . . ;*

fishbones walked the waves off Hatteras: it calls us to an intense, attentive consciousness. Probably that is what attracts some people to poetry, to writing generally, and it is probably what repels them, since the last thing many people want is to be conscious.

This threshold alertness is only the first phase of the experience of rhythm. The second includes the whole range of our experience of recurrent and varying sound. We enter, are made attentive, then something else begins to happen:

one two
one
one two three
one two
one two three

or this, from a musician-poet, Nils Petersen:

Whenas in silks
Whenas in silks
My Julia goes
My Julia goes
Then, then methinks (methinks)
How sweetly flows
Sweetly flows
The liquefaction (faction) (faction)
Of her clothes
  her clothes her clothes

We move from attention to pleasure, from necessity to a field of play. The principle is recurrence and variation. The effect is hard to describe. Interplay, weaving, dialogue, dance: every phrase that comes to mind is a metaphor. This need to speak metaphorically suggests that rhythm is an idiom of the unconscious, which is why it seems an echo of many other human activities.

When we listen to a rhythm, especially an insistent rhythm, there is often a moment or more of compelled attention in which the play and repetition of the sounds seem—I am pulled toward metaphor again—to draw us in or overwhelm us. That kind of listening can lead to something like trance. It is the feeling out of which comes another set of metaphors—magic, incantation—and practices. We know that rhythm has always been a mnemonic device, that metrical compositions are usually easier to remember than non-metrical ones, that in ancient times all laws were expressed in incantatory rhythms, that the oldest Greek and Latin words for poetry were also the oldest words for law. This is part of the basis for the connection between memory and inspiration: *O musa, memora mihi*, the Aeneid begins. Far back rhythm, memory, trance are connected to authority and magical power.

An instance from the Plains Sioux, in Frances Densmore's translation:

The whole world is coming
A nation is coming
A nation is coming

This song was made after the buffalo had been massacred by hide hunters. It is chant, magical invocation, designed to bring the herds down from Canada in the spring as they had always come.

Eagle has brought the message to the tribe
The father says so
The father says so

It is rhythmic repetition moving toward magic. *Enchantment*, we say, *incantation*, singing the song inward. Often it is accompanied by a slight rocking of the body.

From the north they are coming
The buffalo are coming
The buffalo are coming

At some point chant becomes hypnotic; it begins to induce the trance state, identified with possession.

Crow has brought the message to the tribe
The father says so
The father says so

Its effect can begin to be a feeling of terror and confinement. In medieval Europe you could ward off the devil by repeating a small prayer three hundred or five hundred times. The medical histories of hysteria describe instances when the chanter, once begun, was unable to stop.

The buffalo are coming
The buffalo are coming
The father says so
The father says so

Repetition makes us feel secure and variation makes us feel free. What these experiences must touch in us is the rhythm of our own individuation. It's easy enough to observe in small children the force of these pulls between the security of infancy and the freedom of their own separateness. When my oldest child was two or so, we used to take walks. He had a zen carpenter's feeling for distance, running ahead of me in an abandoned waddle, coming to an abrupt stop when he felt he had come to the very edge of some magical zone of protection which my presence generated, and then gazing back at me over his shoulder with a look of droll glee. He knew he was right out there on the edge—the distance seemed to be about eleven or twelve squares of sidewalk. Sometimes he would take one more step, then another, looking back each time, and if I uttered a warning sound he would collapse in hilarity which seemed to be a celebration of his own daring. I was listening at the same time to Miles Davis, to how far he was willing to move away from the melody, to the way the feeling intensified the further away from it he got, as if he were trying to describe what it is like to get out there so far into the wandering hunger for the next note that it seemed at the same time exultant and explosively lonely and probably impossible to come back ever. I was also reading Theodore Roethke, the long poems with their manic inward-driven nursery-rhyme rhythms:

The shape of a rat?
It's bigger than that.
It's sleek as an otter
With wide webby toes.
Just under the water
It usually goes.

And it made me feel that there was not, in this, much difference between child and grown-up, between my son's impulses and the tidal pulls of adult life, the desire for merger, union, loss of self and the desire for freedom, surprise, singularity. I think it is probably the coming together of our pattern-discerning alertness with this pull between polarities in our psychic life that determines our feelings about rhythm.

It is important that we both want a rapt symbiotic state and don't want it; that we want solitariness and self-sufficiency and don't want it. Rhythmic repetition initiates a sense of order. The feeling of magic comes from the way it puts us in touch with the promise of a deep sympathetic power in things: heartbeat, sunrise, summer solstice. This can be hypnotically peaceful; it can also be terrifying, to come so near self-abandonment and loss of autonomy, to whatever in ourselves wants to stay there in that sound, rocking and weeping, comforted. In the same way, freedom from pattern offers us at first an openness, a field of identity, room to move; and it contains the threat of chaos, rudderlessness, vacuity. Safety and magic on one side, freedom and movement on the other; their reverse faces are claustrophobia and obsession or agoraphobia and vertigo. They are the powers we move among, listening to a rhythm, as the soul in the bardo state moves among the heavens and the hells, and they are what makes the relation between repetition and variation in art dialectical and generative.

An example, from a metrical poem:

A slumber did my spirit seal,
I had no human fears;
She seemed a thing who could not feel
The touch of earthly years.

No motion has she now, no force.
She neither hears nor sees,
Rolled round in earth's diurnal course
With rocks and stones and trees.

In this poem of grief at the death of a young girl, Wordsworth brings us in the last lines to a small, majestic, orderly music in which we feel reconciled to the way the child has entered the natural universe. Like a cradle rocking, bringing us to rest. At least that is how I read the poem for a long time, until someone pointed out to me the randomness of the last sequence: rocks, stones, trees. What is the difference between a rock and a stone? Who knows? What difference could it make? Rocks and stones. She has passed into brute matter, into the huge, mute spaces that terrified Pascal. For a while, with all the bad habits of education, I wondered which was the correct interpretation. I've come to see that the poem is so memorable and haunting because the two readings and feelings are equally present, married there, and it is the expressive power of rhythm that makes this possible.

First we hear: an order is insisted upon by the meter; then

we listen, for that order is questioned immediately by the arrangement of the stanzas. Four beats in the first line, an insistent order; three beats in the second line, the same order but lighter, easier to live with. Four beats in the third line: the heavier order enters again, intensified slightly by the almost audible extra stress of "not feel." Three beats again in the fourth line, a lightening. The fifth line is interesting because the pause seems to promise an alteration in the pattern, to give us three beats, the lighter order, but no, after the pause we get two heavy stresses, "no force"; it almost says: were you wondering if "not feel" was two stresses? "Not feel" is two stresses. It is like a musical theme; we have begun to hear not just a play between three- and four-stress phrases, but a secondary drama of the four stresses tending toward a heavier and menacing five. In the sixth line we return to the three-stress pattern. In the seventh line the five stresses appear in full force, made large and dizzy by the long vowel sounds. They say, in effect, that from a human point of view an insistent order is equivalent to a chaos, and they are at the same time wondering, wonderful. In the last line we return to three stresses, the bearable rhythm, but we have already been made to hear the menace in the idea of order, so that last phrase, deliberate and random at once, leaves us with a deep and lingering uneasiness.

To speak of a sense of closure brings us to the third phase of rhythmic experience. Many things in the world have rhythms and many kinds of creatures seem to be moved by them but only human beings complete them. This last phase, the bringing of rhythmic interplay to a resolution, is the particular provenance of man as a maker. A rhythm is not a rhythmic form; in theory, at least, a rhythmic sequence, like some poetry readings, can go on forever, the only limits being the attention of the auditor and the endurance of the performer. Meter is that kind of sequence. The flow of blank verse suggests no natural stopping place of itself and most of the other metrical shapes, sonnets and the various stanzaic forms, are defined by their rhyme schemes. Daydream and hypnotic rhythm have it in common that their natural form is exhaustion. The resolution of rhythmic play, not just the coming down on one side or the other but the articulation of what ending feels like, is active making.

Think of the words you might want to use. *End*: to die. *Finish*: to be done with. *Conclude*: obligation over. *Complete*: to fulfill. *Consummate: really* to fulfill. *Close, terminate, arrive, leave off, release.* There are many senses of ending and they are drawn from our different experiences of it. There are rhythmic forms in nature—the day, a season, the life of a blossom. In human life, orgasm, the sentences in which we speak, falling asleep, the completion of tasks, the deaths we all see and the one death each of us must imagine. Many of our senses of ending are conventional—imagine the sound of a door opening: anticipation; of a door closing: finality. There are many possibilities of ending. In that way, each work of art is a three-line haiku. You go, I go—and the artist must provide the third line.

What hovers behind all this, I would guess, is a wish. Formally, the completion of a pattern imitates the satisfaction of a desire, a consummation, which is why orgasm is a preferred metaphor of conclusion. And because the material of poetry is language, it seems inevitable that an ending would also imitate the experience of insight. And because it is an ending, it will be death-obsessed. Sexual pleasure is a merging, a voluntary abandonment of the self; insight is a freeing, the central experience of our own originality. We don't know what death is. The wish behind the human play of artistic form is to know how these three are related: probably it is the hope that they are, or can be, the same thing. And there is another element to be added here, which belongs to the riddles of completion. When poet or reader listens through to the moment of resolution, it is over. The poet has not created until the thing is gone from his hands.

It's possible that what humans want from works of art are shapes of time in which the sense of coming to an end is also, as it very seldom is in the rest of life, a resolution. Hence the art formula common to television comedy and Wagner and the Shakespearean sonnet: tension, release; tension, release; tension, more tension, release. There is a large and familiar repertoire of formal techniques which produce this effect. It is probably a definition of a rigidifying art-practice that it has more answers than it has questions. In the early twentieth century, painting got rid of perspective, music of tonality, poetry of meter and rhyme so that they could tell what ending felt like again, and give it again the feel of making. It is this feeling of the made thing, of craft and of an event in time, that gives the poem—and the world—the feeling of historicity, of having been made by men, and therefore in movement, alive to our touch and to the possibility of change which the familiarity of convention is always deadening. The task is to listen to ourselves and make endings true enough to experience that they eliminate the ground for the old senses of completion or renew them.

So, there are three phases of the experience of rhythm: hearing it, developing it, bringing it to form. And real listening, like deep play, engages us in the issues of our lives. I want to look now at prosody, at ways of talking about how a rhythm is developed and brought to closure.

3 /

Some definitions. Metrical verse is a fixed pattern of stressed and unstressed syllables. In accentual verse, the number of strong stresses in a line is fixed, but the position of the stressed syllables is not and neither is the number or position of unstressed syllables. In free verse, neither the number nor the position of stressed and unstressed syllables is fixed. I have already remarked that meter is not the basis of rhythmic form. It is a way to determine the length of the line, but it is not, by itself, a way to shape a poem. For example, these lines by Yeats:

When you are old and grey and full of sleep
And nodding by the fire, take down this book,
And slowly read, and dream of the soft look
Your eyes had once, and of their shadows deep.

There is a metrical pattern. But what gives the passage the articulation of form is the pattern of pauses and stresses. It looks very different if we just indicate those:

When you are OLD and GREY/ and FULL of SLEEP
And NODding by the FIRE,/ TAKE DOWN this BOOK
And SLOWly READ,/ and DREAM of the SOFT LOOK
Your EYES HAD ONCE,/ and of their SHAdows DEEP.

It seems clear that the main function of the meter is to secure the lulling sound of the first line and a half. The sense of pattern is created by two- and three-stress phrases which tend to have thematic associations. The three-stress phrases, "take down this book," "dream of the soft look," "your eyes had once," carry the energy and urgency; the two-stress groups convey balance or resignation or fatality, "old and grey," "shadows deep." The three-stress phrase appears when it disrupts the balance of the first line and a half. The pattern looks like this:

2/2
2/3
2/3
3/2

The third line replays the theme; in the last line the pattern is reversed. Life and death, odd and even are the terms of play.

Even, says the first line. Odd, say the second and third lines. Even, says the fourth line, rhyming with the idea that the shadows of desire in young eyes are the shadows of mortality.

In many modernist poems, technically metrical, the use of the effects of metrical rhythm is extraordinarily powerful—they feel hacked out, freshly made—but the metrical pattern as a whole counts for very little: the rhythmic articulation exists almost entirely in the pattern of stresses and pauses:

> Túrning and túrning in the wídening gýre
> The fálcon cánnot heár the fálconer;
> Thińgs fáll apárt; the céntre cánnot hóld;
> Meŕe ánarchy is loośed upon the woŕld,
> The bloód-dimḿed tíde is loośed, and éverywhere
> The ceŕemony of ińnocence is drówned;
> The bést laćk áll convićtion, while the wórst
> Are fúll of paśsionate inténsity.

It doesn't take a very refined analysis to see that this varies three- and four-stress phrases. If Yeats had written:

> The bloód-dimḿed tíde is loósed;
> And éverywhere the ceŕemony of ińnocence is drówned;
> The bést laćk áll convićtion,
> While the woŕst are fúll of paśsionate inténsity

the passage would not be less regular, but the sound has gone dead. The extra unstressed syllables in the second and fourth lines make them seem to sprawl out, and the pattern of stresses feels leaden, fatal: 4, 4, 4, 4. As it is, Yeats gets the fatality but also a sense of something broken, unbalanced: 4/1, 3; 4/1, 3. The inference to be drawn from this pattern is that at the level of form the difference between the strategies of free and metrical verse is not very great.

The difference lies, rather, in the stages of announcing and developing a rhythm. Every metrical poem announces a relationship to the idea of order at the outset, though the range of relationships to that idea it can suggest is immense. Free-verse poems do not commit themselves so soon to a particular order, but they are poems, so they commit themselves to the idea of its possibility, and, as soon as recurrences begin to develop, an order begins to emerge. The difference is, in some ways, huge; the metrical poem begins with an assumption of human life which takes place in a pattern of orderly recurrence with which the poet must come to terms, the free-verse poem with an assumption of openness or chaos in which an order must be discovered. Another way to say this is to observe that most metrical poems, by establishing an order so quickly, move almost immediately from the stage of listening for an order to the stage of hearing it in dialogue with itself. They suppress animal attention in the rush to psychic magic and they do so by laying claim to art and the traditions of art at the beginning. The free-verse poem insists on the first stage of sensual attention, of possibility and emergence—which is one of the reasons why it has seemed fresher and more individual to the twentieth century. The prophetic poems of Yeats and the loose blank verse of the younger Eliot, by staying near to traditional prosodies, say in effect that there has been this order and it's falling apart, while Williams and the Pound of the *Cantos* say—to paraphrase Robert Pinget—listen, there is no lost feast at the bottom of memory, invent.

The free-verse poem, by stripping away familiar patterns of recurrence and keeping options open, is able to address the forms of closure with the sense that there are multiple possibilities and that the poem has to find its way to the right one. Here is a simple example of how this might work. We can begin with a small poem of Whitman, "Farm Picture":

Through the ample open door of the peaceful country barn,
A sunlit pasture field with cattle and horses feeding.
And haze and vista, and the far horizon fading away.

As I hear it, there are six stresses in the first line, and a brief pause after "door"; in the second, six with a pause after "field"; in the third, six again with a pause marked by the comma. You could call this accentual verse. You could even argue that it's metrical, a relaxed mix of iambs and anapests. But that won't tell us why it feels complete. Notice the pattern:

3/3
3/3
2/4

The principle is that for a thing to be complete, it has to change. And the kind of change indicates how you feel about that fact. Suppose the poem ended "and haze and vista." It would be an ending and it would radically change the meaning of the poem. That is the possibility open to the poet who has not decided how many stresses each line should have. Let's look at the possible endings. They make four or five different poems:

Through the ample open door of the peaceful country barn,
A sunlit pasture field with cattle and horses feeding.
And haze, and vista.

*

Through the ample open door of the peaceful country barn,
A sunlit pasture field with cattle and horses feeding.
And haze and vista, and the far horizon.

*

Through the ample open door of the peaceful country barn,
A sunlit pasture field with cattle and horses feeding.
And haze and vista, and the far horizon fading.

*

Through the ample open door of the peaceful country barn,
A sunlit pasture field with cattle and horses feeding.
And haze and vista, and the far horizon fading away.

All of these poems seem to me plausible. Three of them, at least, are interesting. The first poem is balanced: 3/3, 3/3, 1/1. To my ear, the last line is not excessively abrupt, but it throws a terrific weight of disappointment or longing onto what is not present, so that the balance of the last line, thunk/thunk, seems an ironic echo of the amplitude of the first two lines. (Though this hovers at the edge of something else because of that dialectical play in rhythm. A little punctuation could make the poem feel like a gasp of surprise such as Dr. Williams might feel:

> Through the ample open door of the peaceful country barn,
> A sunlit pasture field with cattle and horses feeding.
> And haze, and vista!)

The second poem is also balanced: 3/3, 3/3, 2/2. It feels to me too much so. If there is such a thing as sentimental form, this is sentimental form. It invokes the idea of horizon, but prettily, so that there is no tension between the solidity of the barnyard and the hazy vista. It is like bad genre painting, nothing is problematic; distance is pretty, closeness is pretty. The third poem is unbalanced: 3/3, 3/3, 2/3. The extra stress seems to evoke the asymmetry of what fades away and is lost. Three-stress phrases usually feel more open than two-stress phrases. (I think of Leonard Bernstein's remark: two is the rhythm of the body, three is the rhythm of the mind.) The first lines, two sets of three, reconcile those two rhythms, openness and the earth. The third line says unh-uh. We have to let go of the horizon in return for the presence and solidity of the earth. It is a melancholy poem. Whitman's poem is also balanced, but it contains the asymmetrical 2/4 line. Its feeling is most inclusive. The odd rhyme of "feeding" and "fading," which is an aspect of the theme of presence and absence, is muted and, though we take note of what is lost on the horizon, the rhythm is willing to include that loss in the solidity and presence of the scene.

The point of this should be obvious. All four, or five, poems say different things. A poet in a poem is searching for the one thing to be said, or the many things to be said one way. As soon as we start talking about alternative possibilities of form, we find ourselves talking about alternative contents. It is exactly here that the truism about the indissolubility of content and form acquires its meaning. The search for meaning in the content and shape in the rhythm are simultaneous, equivalent. That's why it doesn't matter too much which a writer attends to in composition, because the process attends to both. It is possible—the testimony on this seems pretty general—to pay attention consciously to one or the other exclusively; more often, writers experience a continual shifting back and forth between formal problems and problems of content, carrying the work forward at whichever level it wants to move. In the long run, though, no work can be alive, intelligent, imaginatively open, intense, at one level and not the other.

It should be clear by now that free-verse rhythm is not a movement between pattern and absence of pattern, but between phrases based on odd and even numbers of stresses:

> I loáf and invíte my sóul,
> I leán and loáf at my eáse, obsérving a spéar of súmmer gráss.

Three stresses in the first line, seven in the second with a strong pause after *ease*. The pattern is 3, 3/4. The first two clauses are almost equivalent. *I loaf and invite my soul.* Then, *I lean and loaf at my ease.* Had he written *observing a spear of grass*, all three phrases would be nearly equivalent and they would begin to build tension; instead he adds *summer*, the leaning and loafing season, and announces both at the level of sound and of content that this poem is going to be free and easy.

The line comes into this and so does the stanza. It is with them that we approach Pound's definition of rhythm, a form carved in time, and Williams' notion of the variable foot. Talking about the line as a "beat," as everyone who has struggled with the idea has been compelled to admit, doesn't make much sense if you are thinking of stress. But looked at from the point of view of rhythm as I've tried to describe it, I think it does. The metrical line proposes a relationship to order. So does a three- or four-line stanza. Imagine, it says, a movement through pattern. The stanza is a formal proposal, Apollonian and clear. In this, it says, I want to catch light or court a shaping spirit. Look at these lines from Louis Zukofsky's "4 Other Countries":

La Gloire in the black 2
    flags of the valley 2
of the -
    Loire 1

A lavender plough 2
    in Windermere 1
The French blue 2
    door 1

Of a gray 1
    stone 1
house in 1
    Angers 1

Walled farms, 2
    little lanes 2
of entry, orange- 1/1
    red roofs 2

The rhythm of this passage is based on the strong three-beat phrase: *lavender plough in Windermere, French blue door, gray stone house, little lanes of entry, orange-red roofs*; it doesn't appear in the notation of the rhythm because Zukofsky has broken it across the line, everywhere, into units of one or two stresses and passed the whole through the balanced proposal of the four-line stanza. Three here is the beat of the bodily world and it is resisted and shaped otherwise by the rhythm the poet cuts in time, in imitation, I think, of the perceptions of travel. At the level of content it is straightforward description but it is given the quality of insight because the aural and visual imaginations are so freshly and attentively at work. The line, when a poem is alive in its sound, measures: it is a proposal about listening.

4 /

It should be fairly easy to turn now to a poem like Gary Snyder's "August on Sourdough" and listen to what's going on. The first thing to notice about it is that it is made from paired lines or half-lines which imitate and underscore its theme. *You hitched a thousand miles,* then *north from San Francisco*; *hiked up the mountainside,* then *a mile in the air*. Sets of two. The one break in this pattern comes in the next pair of lines: *the little cabin—one room—walled in glass.* A set of three with the poem's place of communion at its center. Two and three. You go, I go, what is the upshot? It is, when we look at the pattern of stresses, a transformation of the two-stress rhythms into three-stress rhythms:

YOU HITCHED a THOUsand MILES
NORTH from SAN FranCISco
HIKED up the MOUNtainside   a MILE in the AIR
The LITtle CABin—ONE ROOM—
WALLED in GLASS
MEAdows and SNOWfields   HUNdreds of PEAKS.

Stress is relative and I have marked what I hear as the main stresses. The pattern looks like this:

4
3
2/2
2/2
2
2/2

The base rhythm is the paired two-stress phrases. The variation comes in the one three-stress phrase and in the set of three two-stress phrases. The paired phrases with a pause in between insist on twoness, on the separateness of the two friends. There is just enough variety to convey a sense of movement, and the overall effect is balanced, relaxed. It is very deft work.

We LAY in our SLEEPing BAGS
                    TALKing HALF the NIGHT;
WIND in the GUY CABLES   SUMmer MOUNtain RAIN.

This is the interlude in which the images and rhythm speak of the communion of friends. It is a quiet expansion from two- to three-stress phrases, and a different balance:

3
3
3/3

And then the parting:

NEXT MORNing I WENT WITH you
                    as FAR as the CLIFFS
LOANED you my PONCHo   the RAIN aCROSS the
    SHALE
YOU DOWN the SNOWfield
                    FLAPping in the WIND

WAVing a LAST GoodBYE   HALF-HIDden in the CLOUDS
To GO ON HITCHing   CLEAR to NEW YORK;
ME BACK to my MOUNtain   and FAR, FAR, WEST.

This is a more intricate restatement of the play between two and three stresses, but it ends emphatically with a rhythm based on threes. Two is an exchange, three is a circle of energy, Lewis Hyde has said, talking about economics. I would mark the primary pattern like this:

4
2
2/3
3/2
3/3
3/3
3/3

and that last phrase is carefully punctuated to sing it out: 1/1/1. It insists, finally, on a rhythmic pairing of open three-stress elements. This is, formally, the solution it offers to the problem of identity and separation in partings and—as we've seen—in ending poems.

The articulation of rhythmic form, though, doesn't indicate what are for me the small miracles of feeling in the rhythm throughout. There are at least three musical phrases in the poem that are announced and then transmuted. One of them is *a mile in the air* which is echoed in *hundreds of peaks* and again in *as far as the cliffs*, and then changed to a three-stress cadence in *clear to New York*. (NEW YORK is a West Coast pronunciation of N'York—the emphatic *new* is a celebration of movement.) In the same way, *meadows and snowfields*, a playful pair of falling rhythms—MEAdows, SNOWfields—like the falling rhythms of nursery rhymes, Bobby Shaftoe, Humpty

Dumpty, is repeated in *loaned you my poncho* so that it has become a memory of playful reciprocity, and then it is transformed by the urgency of movement into *you down the snowfield*. Most brilliant and moving to me is the sudden iambic phrase, *the rain across the shale*. It is suggested in the first line, *you hitched a thousand miles*, echoed in *talking half the night* and *summer mountain rain*. And then, clearly, the old orderliness of iambic meter rises up to make us feel an order of nature older than us and steadier in which our comings and goings mean very little. "Hailstorm on the rocks at Stony Pass," Basho said. "The rain it raineth every day," Shakespeare said. "Rocks and stones and trees," said Wordsworth. The juxtaposition of rhythms and orders, *loaned you my poncho, the rain across the shale*, before the poem's open windy farewell is a lyrical hesitation, a moment of hearing really astonishing, I think, in its warmth, sharp pathos and clear intelligence:

> Loaned you my poncho   the rain across the shale
> You down the snowfield . . .

It recapitulates the two worlds the poem speaks of, the little one, one room, walled in glass, and the big one, half-hidden in the clouds.

The freshness and life of this poem is not uncommon in the work of the 1950s when the younger poets were writing in the teeth of an institutionalized and deadening metrical facility. It was in those years, somewhere, that William Carlos Williams delivered a lecture to Theodore Roethke's students at the University of Washington, "The Poem as a Field of Action." "Imagism," he told them, "was not structural: that was the reason for its disappearance. . . . You can put it down as a general rule that when a poet, in the broadest sense, begins to devote himself to the *subject matter* of his poems, *genre*, he has come to the end of his poetic means." There is a wonderful sense of momentum in his talk and it is hard not to feel, though almost everyone writing now would claim him as a master, that that momentum has been lost. I think he identifies the symptom. Almost all the talk about poetry in the past few years has focused on issues of image and diction. There was a liveliness in the idea of hauling deep and surreal imagery into American poetry, but the deep image is no more structural than imagism: there was hardly any sense of what the rhythmic ground might be. Hence, stuff like this:

> He played banana drums and dreamed of felt.
> He discerned a tin angel in a caulking gun.
> His bounced checks and their imaginative *noms de plume*
> Glittered in the cash registers of abandoned motels.

etc. Five beats to the line. The imagery is unusual enough; the rhythm is absolutely conventional. The counterattack on this kind of writing has been that it should have a different content. So we have gotten an aggressive return to the conscious mind:

> Pets are a creation of the industrial revolution.
> And so is 'projective identification.'
> You feed the useless animal to remind you of animals
> While the terminology of relationship is elaborated.

One of these is writhing rebelliousness in the face of terminal ennui, the other is ironic intelligence in the face of same. The ennui is expressed by the simple, orderly, conformist, free-verse rhythms; that is the main message, and it can't be talked about if poetry is a matter of kinds of imagery and kinds of diction. Way below the content of a particular poem, the idea that rhythm is natural, bodily, spontaneous, has been transformed into the idea that it is simply a given, invisible or inevitable. What this expresses is a kind of spiritual death that follows from living in a world we feel we have no hope of changing.

I have it in mind that, during the Vietnam war, one of the

inventions of American technology was a small antipersonnel bomb that contained sharp fragments of plastic which, having torn through the flesh and lodged in the body, could not be found by an X-ray. Often I just think about the fact that some person created it. At other times I have thought about the fact that the bomb works on people just the way the rhythms of poetry do. And it seems to me then that there really are technes on the side of life and technes on the side of death. Durable and life-giving human inventions—tragedy, restaurants that stay open late at night, holding hands, the edible artichoke—were probably half discovered and half invented from the materials the world makes available, but I think that they were also the result of an active and attentive capacity for creation that humans have—that is, finally, the only freedom they have—and that a poetry that makes fresh and resilient forms extends the possibilities of being alive.

Four Reviews

Lost in Translation

A Part of Speech by Joseph Brodsky

The translation of Russian poetry has become the great border war of American letters. The friendship of Edmund Wilson and Vladimir Nabokov foundered on the rendering of Pushkin's *Eugene Onegin* and it was Nabokov who suggested that a suitable revenge for Robert Lowell's "imitations" of Russian poetry would be to translate him into Russian by turning his phrase "leathery love" into something like "the large football of passion." English translations of a brilliant and tragic generation of Russian poets—Nikolai Gumilev, shot down by a firing squad while he clutched a volume of Homer to his breast; Osip Mandelstam, starved to death in the labor camps; Marina Tsvetaeva, who hanged herself after twenty years of exile; Boris Pasternak and Anna Akhmatova, who survived to write the indelible poems of those years—have arrived in America, attended by an enormous amount of skirmishing at the barricades of the literary quarterlies.

Joseph Brodsky, spiritual heir to the tradition of Mandelstam and Akhmatova, has also inherited their difficult passage. He came to the attention of Americans in 1964 when, at the age of twenty-four, he was arrested by the Soviet government for "parasitism." Eight years later he was expelled from the Soviet Union and settled in the United States. A volume of his early work was published in 1973. *A Part of Speech* collects translations of some of his earlier work together with a large selection of poems written since his exile. The work was done by a group of translators under Brodsky's supervision and that, presumably, of his editors at Farrar, Straus & Giroux. It is a book to have looked forward to, not only because Americans have grown accustomed through writers like Nabokov and Czesław Miłosz to the haunting literature of exile being made in our midst, but also because Brodsky has lived in both faces of the mirror world of the cold war; and the rest of us, affected daily by its subliminal pressure, want his testimony. There are a handful of poems here to justify that hope, but for the most part reading *A Part of Speech* is like wandering through the ruins of what has been reported to be a noble building.

Just how bad the trouble is may be judged from these lines in "Lullaby of Cape Cod": "Therefore, sleep well. Sweet dreams. Knit up that sleeve. / Sleep as those only do who have gone pee-pee." Such fatal miscalculations of tone, candidates for any future *Stuffed Owl*, the famous anthology of great moments in the history of awful verse, are fairly common. For example:

> My blood is very cold—
> its cold is more withering
> than iced-to-the-bottom streams.
> People are not my thing.

And when the words are wrenched from the order of natural speech to meet the requirements of a poetic form, things get even worse:

> A thing can be battered, burned,
> gutted and broken up.
> Thrown out. And yet the thing
> never will yell, "Oh, fuck!"

The specific difficulties of getting Russian poetry into English are notorious. We are often reminded that Russian is an inflected, characteristically polysyllabic language, much more flexible in its word order than English. Moreover, English poetry is a much older art. Metrical poems in English have been written for over four hundred years, in Russian for something like two hundred. That is, in terms of exhausting the resources of meter and rhyme, Russian verse could be said to be as fresh as English poetry was at the end of the age of Pope. In America, a metrical poem is likely to conjure up the idea of the sort of poet who wears ties and lunches at the faculty club. In Russia, the metrical poem is ubiquitous. It can suggest, as it does in Akhmatova and Mandelstam, the moral force of an art practiced against great personal odds, but it was also used, often enough, to praise generals and the N.E.P. When Pablo Neruda won the Stalin Prize, he was known in Russia in versions of his poems that had been translated into rhymed iambic tetrameter quatrains, a spectacle on the order of watching a boa constrictor being fitted for a corset. The kind of poem Brodsky writes, difficult to render anyway, must, because of these differences in national tradition, be rendered with some attention to its form; and this makes for further difficulty when that form, translated into English, is in danger of being transposed at the same time into another key altogether.

This helps to account for the difficulty of the task, but not for the results, which sometimes read like first high school exercises in the composition of metrical poetry, or worse, like sophisticated parodies of those attempts, like Peter Quince himself:

The strength, the gallantry
are stolen away from my muscles cowardly.

or:

and a mulatto girl melts lovingly like chocolate
while in masculine embrace she purrs insensate . . .

or:

linked to weak gums, to heartburn brought about
by a diet unfamiliar and alien

or:

any erosion begins with willing,
the minimum of which is the heart, the basis
of stasis. Or so I was told in that oasis
of school. Remove, dear chums, your faces!

There are other lines which look like nothing so much as those typos from the *Des Moines Register* that *The New Yorker* likes to use as filler: "Thrushes chirp within the hairdo of the cypress."

The translators have clearly struggled with tone. Should Brodsky sound like Lowell? like Auden? Byron? Pope? A preferred solution, because Brodsky is an ironist, is that tediously bouncy rhythm produced by clever young Englishmen of indeterminate age down from the university and set to make a splash:

When you recall me in that land,
although this phrase isn't oracular—
a fact unthinkable for an
eye armed with tears as its binocular . . .

Another is to make him sound like an eighteenth-century hack rewriting Shakespeare:

to keep the mind from getting scorched
by horrid, all-consuming malice;

and if we both were saved from such
a fate and didn't drink this chalice . . .

And some of the writing is unclassifiable:

Something lipsticked stuffs
the ear with lacerating lengthy words,
like running fingers through a hairdo stiff
with lice . . .

Then there are the clichés of iambic rhythm, like the excessive use of the possessive case: "retreating north before winter's assault," "closed to the clash of day's discord," "July's conclusion merges with the rains," "rubbed by the light on space's surface." It is like reading a book that keeps sneezing. And the absurd poetic diction: "the vast wet of ocean," "a strengthless breeze." There is padding for the sake of rhyme: "The bright corona, / the crimson petals abuzz, acrawl with wings / of dragonflies, of wasps and bees with stings," and "I said that the leaf may destroy the bud: / what's fertile falls in fallow soil—a dud"; and the padding to which translators are tempted because there are so often fewer words in a line of Russian verse than in an English equivalent. This leads fairly often to massive redundancy:

Eyes can be bruised and hurt
by people as well as things.

In general, of all our organs the eye
alone retains its elasticity.

Poetry, Ford Madox Ford told Ezra Pound in 1912, must be at least as well written as prose. There is, in fact, a kind of contempt for poetry in letting language like this stand. What editor would have let that last sentence go, with its "alone" contradicting its "in general" and rendering the whole thing ludicrous, if he were working on a prose manuscript? Who, indeed, would print stuff like this?

Age is growth of a new but a very fine
hearing that only to silence hearkens.

Still, change for the best, since fright, horror, shudders
are alien to objects. So little puddles
won't be found under objects like under others
even when your small object is to expire

and trees stand queuing up for the narrow
sturgeon-like waves; that's the only type
of fish the Thames ever is fit to offer . . .

Brodsky, of course, cannot be held entirely responsible for this carnage. Readers who want to get a sense of his strength should turn immediately to the powerful title poem, "A Part of Speech," which is translated by Brodsky himself and is free from the grotesquerie that characterizes the book as a whole. There is other work that is equally fine. Richard Wilbur's "The Funeral of Bobo" is a brilliant poem in any language. George L. Kline's "Nunc Dimittis" is beautiful and very plain. Derek Walcott's version of the first of two "Letters from the Ming Dynasty" is flawless work, and so is the rich sequence of poems, "In England," translated by Alan Meyers. His version of "To Evgeny" is also very good. David McDuff's "Strophes" is uneven, but some sections of it are among the strongest work in the book.

Readers will also want to look at "Lullaby of Cape Cod." It is full of tasteless and hackneyed writing, but in passages seems as if it must be a poem of extraordinary interest. In an atmosphere of insomnia and stifling heat, the poet regards his situation:

Having sampled two
oceans as well as continents, I feel I know
what the globe itself must feel: there's nowhere to go.

Elsewhere is nothing more than a far-flung strew
of stars, burning away.

This is the clear, disenchanted vision which, in "To Evgeny," sees the pyramids of Mexico and takes their measure:

Bas-reliefs with sundry scenes, complete with writhing bits
of serpent bodies and the mysterious alphabet
of a tongue which never needed a word for "or."
What would they say if they could speak once more?
Nothing at all. At best, talk of triumph snatched
over some adjoining tribe of men, smashed
skulls. Or how pouring blood into bowls
sacrificed to the Sun God strengthened the latter's bowels;
how sacrifice of eight young and strong men before dark
guarantees a sunrise more surely than the lark.

The combination of sanity and cheerful disgust could be Pushkin's. He is paraphrased later in the poem: "everywhere dumbness and cruelty come up and say, 'Hello, / here we are!' " So the vision is partly moral and social, but it has been passed through romanticism; partly it derives from a sharp sense of the way the past unravels and is lost:

Old Nastasya is dead, I take it, and Pesterev, too, for sure
and if not, he's sitting drunk in the cellar or
is making something out of the headboard of our bed:
a wicket gate, say, or some kind of shed.

Nothing is Brodsky's theme, the struggle of consciousness against the horror and boredom of things. At his best, he sounds something like Robert Lowell when Lowell is sounding like Byron—jaded, nervous, quick-eyed, alert to any smallest hint that the world is something more than numbingly predictable; brutal and inert by turns. It is all the more ironic, then, that the nothingness this book most often calls up is the kind figured by Pope at the end of *The Dunciad* when the sheer accumulation of inept and unintelligent writing puts out all the lights: "Thy hand, great Anarch! lets the curtain fall, / And universal Darkness buries All."

What He Did

An Introduction to the Poetry of Yvor Winters by Elizabeth Isaacs

When Yvor Winters received the Bollingen Award for Poetry in 1955, the editor of one of the small magazines that had sprung up about that time remarked in print: "Winters is not a poet; he's a policeman." As a critic, brilliant, maddening, draconian, he terrorized American letters in the 1930s and 40s. His books, *Primitivism and Decadence* (1937), *Maule's Curse* (1938) and *The Anatomy of Nonsense* (1943), were a frontal assault on romanticism, American transcendentalism and modernism—in fact, on much of what had been written and admired in English in the nineteenth and twentieth centuries. The books are still readable. His prose style is clear, obdurate, scathing, completely self-assured. In a time when the criticism of poetry was a passionately serious matter, no one wrote about poems with more seriousness or passion.

This imposing figure makes the poetry hard to come to, and Elizabeth Isaacs, though her book begins with a pleasant account of a meeting with Winters, seems to have succumbed to the power of the criticism. She devotes two long, respectful chapters to it before considering a single poem. She makes a rather mechanical use of Winters' own critical apparatus. Aspects of the poetry are taken up singly: diction, imagery, verse forms, etc. It is not until the end of her book that we get, almost as an appendix, a somewhat laborious and dispirited analysis of ten poems. And she never looks askance at the critic who wrote and apparently believed, at one point, that "emotion in any situation must be as far as possible eliminated."

Yet the Winters we first meet in the poems is not the fierce old curmudgeon of Palo Alto, he is a tubercular boy, just beginning to read the moderns (neither Wallace Stevens nor Marianne Moore had published a book yet) in a New Mexico sanitarium. He had matriculated at the University of Chicago in 1917 at the age of sixteen and became ill after completing a year of school. He had also met Harriet Monroe, the editor of *Poetry*, and through her begun a correspondence with Marianne Moore. During the three years of his treatment and the following two, when he taught school in the parched, dusty mining towns of New Mexico, he read the magazines sent to him by Monroe and books from the New York Public Library that were loaned to him (illegally) by Moore.

The fascination of his early poems has very little to do with critical theory and much to do with watching what he read take root in the young man, his head full of Keats and Mallarmé, who looked out on the desert of the Southwest in 1919 and 1920 through the eyes of symbolist and imagist poetry. One of the earliest poems is a debate—a sort of verbal harlequinade in the symbolist manner—between a black puppet and a white puppet. You can already hear Stevens in it:

WHITE PUPPET

My life is green water seen
Through a white rose leaf.
It has a sheen.

BLACK PUPPET

A dry leaf on the ground
Is much like me.
It turns around
And then lies still.

The poem also borrows from native American mythology. Winters wrote the first pioneering essay on the early translators of American Indian songs in 1928. Here, Coyote, the trickster who will show up again in the poetry and fiction of the 1960s as a figure for the quick, untrappable impulse of life, first appears:

WHITE PUPPET

You have seen Coyote
Who flows like gold,
The runner in the night
With eartips like the air.

BLACK PUPPET

Coyote is green eyes
On dust whirl of yellow hair—
My passion is untold.

WHITE PUPPET

Coyote is an ether
That is shaken in the air.
He hovers about me
When the day is white.
He passes swifter
Than the runner in the night.

BLACK PUPPET

My passion is untold.

Imagist clarity and fastidiousness of diction have already begun to discipline this adolescent melancholy, and if "The Pines Are Shadows" is a wonderfully peculiar congeries of voices and modes, what follows is more wonderful still. In 1922 Winters published a book of one-line poems, got out of imagism, Japanese haiku and Ojibway song:

THE HUNTER

Run! In the magpie's shadow.

SPRING RAIN

My doorframe smells of leaves.

HIGH VALLEYS

In sleep I filled these lands.

THE ASPEN'S SONG

The summer holds me here.

He had, by this time, begun to publish reviews that would seem comic if they were not so startlingly prescient. The voice that solemnly declares Wallace Stevens' "Sunday Morning" to be one of the great poems written in English in the twentieth century belongs to a young man of twenty-two, and he is speaking of a poem that has not yet appeared in a book. In the work of his late twenties, however, when the desert landscape takes hold of him, William Carlos Williams has become Winters' model, and some of the poems in *The Bare Hills* (1927) are very good indeed. For instance, "Jose's Country":

A pale horse,
Mane of flowery dust,
Runs too far
For a sound
To cross the river.

Afternoon,
Swept by far hooves
That gleam
Like slow fruit

Falling
In the haze
Of pondered vision.

It is nothing.
Afternoon
Beyond a child's thought,
Where a falling stone
Would raise pale earth,
A fern ascending.

Poems like this are anything but what I expected when I first came to Winters' work, imagining that it would be a cross between Malvolio and John Foster Dulles. The poems are less supple than Williams', less playful than Stevens', but many of them are brilliantly hard and clear:

October
Comes and goes
And in the moonlight
I wait for winter.

The silence
Is like moonlight
In one thing:
That it hides nothing.

The appearance of *nothing* in this poem is perhaps a clue to the dramatic change in Winters' poetic style that occurred around 1930 and gave birth to the notorious critic. He had, following the dicta of the imagists, cleaned the windows of perception. There is, in many of these poems, nothing but a tense clear perception of the world and, in their music and movement, the feeling that emerges from that perception. He had, with admirable fidelity and discipline, taken the imagist poem to one of its limits: and, an American with Calvinist roots, he found the world that he rendered, the world that was not an idea of the world or an interpretation of the world or the world as a mysterious symbol of something other than itself, insupportable.

Alone is another word that shows up many times. Williams and Stevens, Eliot and Pound, H. D. had also come, each in his or her own way, to the imagist cul-de-sac, and each of them invented a way out. Williams decided (quite easily) that there were no ideas *but* in things. Stevens discoursed for another twenty-five years about the idea that there were no ideas. Winters, in the intense loneliness of provincial places—Cerillos, New Mexico; Boulder, Colorado; Moscow, Idaho—decided that imagism was a bad, dangerous method, that it could render experience but not judge experience, and that constantly calling up feelings that you couldn't understand made people crazy. "I stood unseen," he says, movingly, at the end of one of his poems of 1928. "The rough soil / is without depth, shadow, distance; and he / lies in harshcolored air, breathing, alone," he says at the end of another.

It is possible to imagine that, in different circumstances, he might have pushed through, that the loneliness, terror, even the hysteria that haunt some of his last free-verse poems might have found a different resolution. As it happens, he arrived at Stanford University to begin studies for a doctorate in English literature. In the desert he had discovered that the black puppet was right. There is the world, and there is man; and man should not confuse himself with the world, because he is going to die. He was drawn to the poets of the sixteenth and seventeenth century who held close to this fact: and, to the end of his own life, he always praised most highly those poems that look directly and without flinching at the loneliness of human death.

The poems that come after this conversion are the ones that most readers who know his poetry at all are apt to be familiar with. They are, in style and tone, amazingly unlike his early work:

Death. Nothing is simpler. One is dead.
The set face now will fade out; the bare fact,
Related movement, regular, intact,
Is reabsorbed, the clay is on the bed.
The soul is mortal, nothing: the dim head
On the dim pillow, less. . . .

He abandoned free verse and turned to meter and rhyme because he had decided that a poet could exercise more control over his materials when he composed in meter. Control was a crucial word for most of the New Critics, who tended to write about emotion the way the older Scott Fitzgerald wrote about alcohol. It is as if the inventions of modern American poetry, of Pound and Moore, Williams and H. D., had opened more psychic territory than the younger generation was prepared to explore. They wanted to go slow, to absorb the techniques and to understand what they implied. It is probably also the case that during a Depression and a world war they didn't want a medium so slippery, so full of inner agitations.

It was in this context that Winters became a figure. Where others were respectful, quizzical, imitating the excellent manners of T. S. Eliot's prose, Winters came out fighting, took the extreme positions that no one else was quite prepared to take. It was he who said that Emerson sold Hart Crane the Brooklyn Bridge, that Yeats with his Blavatsky and his gyres and Anglo-Irish country houses was an old bluff and a fascist, that Eliot's moral exhaustion was morally exhausting. This must have been very heady stuff to a younger generation who were writing in the shadow of elders who had not only done work of unprecedented brilliance but who also showed every sign of going on forever.

It was, nevertheless, a holding action. There was nothing wrong with Winters' return to metrical forms. He handles them with great power. Nor was there anything wrong with his choice of models. The poets he claimed or rediscovered—

Wyatt, Gascoigne, Raleigh, Greville, Jonson, Hardy, Robinson—were great poets. He has written about them stunningly in his last critical book, *Forms of Discovery*; and his classroom lectures—I had a chance to hear some of them in the years just before his death—were high drama. What is damaging about the later work is that, in addition to adopting the forms and themes of the English poets, he adopted their diction. He never solved for himself the problem of getting from image to discourse in the language of his time, and instead borrowed the solution of another age.

Just how damaging this is it is very hard to say and will probably have to be left to another generation to judge. Some of the writing is unbelievably bad. This, from a poem to his infant daughter:

Ah, could you now with thinking tongue
Discover what involvëd lies
In flesh and thought obscurely young,
What earth and age can worst devise!

But there are also poems, "Time and the Garden," "A Summer Commentary," "To the Holy Spirit," "At San Francisco Airport," of sustained power, that carry the weight of his terror and his deep sense that his own way of being in the world was limiting and took courage. Sometimes, in moments of calm, he was able to render—and to civilize—that sense of the steadiness of the earth he experienced early in New Mexico, as in "By the Road to the Airbase":

The calloused grass lies hard
Against the cracking plain:
Life is a grayish stain;
The salt marsh hems my yard.

Dry dikes rise hill on hill:
In sloughs of tidal slime

Shell fish deposit lime,
Wild sea-fowl creep at will.

The highway, like a beach,
Turns, whiter, shadowy, dry:
Loud, pale against the sky,
The bombing planes hold speech.

Yet fruit grows on the trees;
Here scholars pause to speak;
Through gardens bare and Greek,
I hear my neighbor's bees.

His generation of poets, which includes Kenneth Rexroth, George Oppen, Louis Zukofsky, Charles Reznikoff, Louise Bogan, Allen Tate, among others, wrote in an odd obscurity. The glamour of the first generation of modern poets seems to have passed directly from them to their explainers, and neither ordinary readers nor university English departments have really begun yet to absorb the work of the second generation. Winters is particularly a victim of this situation. He saw himself as a poet and wrote criticism to explain what had happened to him as a poet, but the more interesting explanation is in the poems themselves. His own final judgment of his work is disarmingly modest and accurate; it appears in the last poem he wrote before his death: "What I did was small but good." Of course, he thought a good poem was a very rare thing. Elizabeth Isaacs' book is one of the first studies of his poetry to appear. It is to be hoped that it will get him some readers and, perhaps, a critic as independent and combative as he was himself.

Creeley: His Metric

The Collected Poems of Robert Creeley, 1945–75

Someone tells the story that when Robert Creeley was at Harvard in the forties and began reading William Carlos Williams at a time when there was no professor to tell one how to read William Carlos Williams, he simply assumed that all of Williams' lines were end-stopped, so that when he began to write his own poems in the one genuinely original verbal music in the English language in the second half of the twentieth century, it was with a patient sense of apprenticeship. Which of course all writing is, so the story has a wonderful rightness, though I doubt it is true. Creeley is a very subtle and conscious artist; he saw something in that work that no one else had seen.

When Williams broke his lines in odd places, when he wrote

It's all in
the sound. A song.
Seldom a song. It should

be a song—made of
particulars, wasps,
a gentian—something
immediate, open

scissors, a lady's
eyes . . .

it is reasonably certain that those line breaks in awkward places where words are most riveted together were intended to speed up the movement. The break between *in* and *the* was so unnatural that it hurried you from one line to the next and, in doing so, imitated the swiftness of perception. At the same time, it roughened the poem visually, gave it the kind of ungainliness that Williams found beautiful. When he wanted a slow, grave line, he gave you the elements of the perception in neat, syntactical units with natural pauses at the line end:

Or the tree's leaves

that are not the tree
but mass to shape it

Creeley, the young man reading those poems in the time of the ascendancy of Eliot's prose, of a reawakened interest in the tetrameters of the old man Yeats, knew what everyone knows, that in a line of poetry the last position is emphatic, and whether by cunning or mistake, he read Williams accordingly, giving each line a full pause at the end. Try reading Williams that way, with a full stop at the end of the line. It syncopates the rhythm and throws an odd emphasis on the last word in the line:

It's all *in*
the sound. A *song.*
Seldom a song. It *should*

be a song—made *of*
particulars, *wasps,*
a gentian—*some*thing
immediate, *open*

scissors, a *lady's*
eyes . . .

What becomes visible is the strangeness of the struggle to articulate the fact of the sentence. Creeley was reading about how to make a song, all right, but with a completely new and equal attention to the operation the mind has to perform in order to do so.

It was a while before the rest of the world would be similarly struck. I remember when it happened to me, partly because I had just heard Creeley read at a poetry festival in England. I was lying on a beach in Cornwall in the early spring; it was unseasonably hot and, in the variability of that weather, one large dark cloud which seemed to be coming straight out of France passed over us and let fall two or three minutes of gentle snow. One of my friends, who was in London studying to be an analyst, had been reading to us from another new arrival to the Anglo-American shore, Jacques Lacan's *Ecrits.* Lacan seemed to be proposing that because the resolution of the Oedipus complex and the acquisition of language occurred around the same time, they were the same thing. The *non* of you-can't-have-your-mother and the *nom* of the father and his access to mastery of the world through symbols were identical, so that the laws of language were the very form of consciousness and they carried its freight of loss and guilt and symbolic power. The idea was fascinating—it made the simplest of language gestures explosive and puzzling—and very French—the bourgeois gentilhomme discovering this time that prose spoke him—but not really funny; all the spiritual loneliness of the twentieth century was in it.

It *should*

be a song, made of
particulars, *wasps*,
a gentian, *some*thing
immediate . . .

Should be, *of* particulars: the disjunctions make us feel, if not understand, the almost unformed, prehensile yearning that lurks inside every preposition. Inside, I found myself thinking, the prepositional disposition of the human mind and its fictions of location.

My wife was trying to learn to do group therapy from a Greek psychiatrist at a hospital near Cambridge. Her training thus far had consisted of listening to him trying to get the middle-class English trainees to say *I* instead of *one*. "*I* feel, *I* feel, *I* feel," he would scream in frustration. And an unruffled student replied, "But sometimes one means *one*, doesn't one?" It had seemed an amusing story about English reticence, but Lacan made you wonder if the American *I* was any more personal, any less a matter of pure acculturation. Creeley had written:

> As soon as
> I speak, I
> speaks. It
>
> wants to
> be free but
> impassive lies
>
> in the direction
> of its
>
> words . . .

It, Bruno Bettelheim has reminded us, is what Freud called the unconscious. Lacan seemed to be saying that all of language and all of the cultural assumptions that we inherit when we acquire language are the *I*, by virtue of which *it* had become inaccessible. I remember feeling disoriented by the idea. My friend, for reasons I still don't understand, seemed delighted. The weather passed over, heading west, and we were in sun again. "Freak snow," somebody said, "The guy is freak snow."

This explains something about Creeley's popularity in the sixties, which had puzzled me. How could a poet whom I found so austere and demanding attract such a wide and enthusiastic audience? I had sat with his poems so long before they yielded their meaning that it was dismaying to go into a college lounge jammed with people sitting on the floor, nodding their heads in profound sympathy and agreement with some poem they had only heard once. They weren't faking; the answer had to lie elsewhere, in the difference between what Susan Sontag has usefully called erotics and hermeneutics.

At the State University of New York at Buffalo, in the salad days of that amazing institution, I got a clue one day during a massive seminar on popular culture. The year must have been 1969; the room was packed with students and faculty dressed, as the style was, to their archetypes: Indians, buffalo hunters, yogin, metaphysical hoboes, rednecks, lumberjacks, Mandingo princes, lions, tigers, hawks, and bears. Everything the American middle class had repressed lounged in that room listening to speaker after speaker with beatific attention. Which took some doing. I remember in particular a graduate student from the Progressive Labor Party who read an exceedingly long essay on the parallels between Bob Dylan's career and the growth of political theory in the New Left. "John Wesley Harding," I think, corresponded to a reawakening of working-class consciousness among students and intellectuals. When he finished, Edgar Friedenburg, the sociologist, rose to speak. He is a dapper man and he wore a light gray suit with a striped broadcloth Brooks Brothers shirt. His glasses sat low on his nose, his hair was tousled, and he looked amused. He only managed one sentence: "I have been reflecting this afternoon that we are patient beings, and that, though popular culture deserves our most urgent attention, it requires from us a good deal less credence and more clearwater." Some of the audience laughed; and a student in front stood up, jabbed a finger forward, and said, "Friedenburg, it took twenty fucking years of repressive *fucking* education for you to learn to talk like that."

No wonder Creeley packed the halls. His audiences were extraordinarily sensitive to language and they did not distrust it, but they distrusted deeply the *assumption* of it. Beyond the issues in any particular poem, they heard that attitude shared and worked through when Creeley read:

One more day gone,
done, found in
the form of days.

It began, it
ended—was
forward, backward,

slow, fast, a
sun shone, clouds,
high in the air I was

for awhile with others,
then came down
on the ground again.

No moon. A room in
a hotel—to begin
again.

In the assumption of language, people get on airplanes at Kennedy, have good or bad flights, are reminded of various things such a passage might symbolize, land at Heathrow, take a black cab into London, and arrive at a little hotel just off Somethingorother Square, the whole experience thick with names and an inherence of literary and historical associations, all welded together by the grammatical assurance of the experiencing subject. That is not what this poem renders; it is just not that comforted or comforting. It renders, below these twentieth-century pleasures, what the mind must, slowly, in love and fear, perform to locate itself again, previous to any other discourse.

The erotics of language: the stunned, lovely, slow insistence on accuracy that the mind is, in language. I don't know what other rhythms could render this more movingly:

> It began, *it*
> ended—*was*
> forward, backward,
>
> slow, fast, *a*
> sun shone, clouds,
> high in the air I *was*
>
> for awhile with others . . .

"The organization of poetry," Creeley said in an interview in 1965, "has moved to a further articulation in which the rhythmic and sound structure now become not only evident but a primary coherence in the total organization of what's being experienced." And this: ". . . words are returned to an almost primal circumstance, by a technique that makes use of feedback, that is, a repetitive relocation of phrasing where words are returned to an almost objective state of presence so that they *speak* rather than someone speaking through them."

Poetics, for the last seventy years, has assumed the existence of a dialectical tension between conscious and unconscious thought. The system of analogies derived from Lévi-Strauss and Lacan and Derrida seems to assert that consciousness carries with it its own displaced and completely symbolic unconscious, that is, the structures of language by which consciousness is constituted; and this unconscious is to consciousness what language—"the collective, structural, unconscious system of differential relationships which constitute the possibility of any individual speech act"—is to particular acts of speech. This is what Creeley's mode and the attractiveness of his mode have to do with, at least much of the time; it is a poetics which addresses the tension between speaking and being spoken through language; and he makes a brilliant and unnerving music out of it.

It is a truism that the person who believes that consciousness is sufficient and in control is, by definition, out of control. Anyone who thinks of language merely as a tool used to perform a particular speech act is in the same condition. For the student in that audience, Professor Friedenburg's syntax was an illusion of mastery in a world manifestly and wildly out of control. I thought there was in it as well a good deal of resentment toward the forms of mastery that are possible. The confrontation was a stand-off. It interested me because the place where they stopped was precisely Robert Creeley's point of departure: the fact, as Lacan has innocently insisted, that there is in the nature of our use of language "something more meant than what we say."

A more familiar way to talk about this matter is to evoke the exposure scene in *The Wizard of Oz*, where the two visions of language are also two visions of mastery and power in general. I am thinking of the scene in which the wizard, a stern face on a huge screen, booms out his mighty definition of himself: I AM OZ; and Dorothy's little dog Toto, the only creature in the room not scared witless by the impressiveness of it all, trots up to the curtain and pulls it back, revealing a nervous man fiddling desperately at a control panel and speaking into a microphone. Language has such power that poets are always both the image on the screen and the figure at the controls who tries to act as a medium for that powerful projection. Creeley has dealt with this problem by always writing from the point of view of the man behind the curtain. In doing so, he arrived by instinct at terms very like those of the post-existentialist philosophers of consciousness. His own sources are native; he took his hints from the hipster sensibility of the late forties and fifties, from jazz improvisation with its departures from melody out of fascination with the possibilities of the instrument, and from action painting with its similar interest in its own media and its understanding of art and consciousness as acts.

If Lacan and hipster culture seem to have this meeting ground, it is no coincidence. What else is experience in the second half of the twentieth century about, but the sense of a world run by people with insane assurance who manipulate large and unmanageable forces over which they have almost no control? "The unsure egoist," Creeley wrote, "is not good for himself." But if he makes us conscious of the process by which ego comes into being, tries to make some purchase on the experience of its emergence, defines exactly what that purchase is and is not, he may be the writer above all worth listening to. It is also not a coincidence that Creeley wrote the poem of the decade about a world gone out of control and the crazy assumption of control that the ego makes:

drive, he sd, for
christ's sake, look
out where yr going.

To speak about only this issue in Creeley's work is, I know, to leave out almost everything. This beautifully produced book from the University of California Press contains almost seven hundred pages of verse. It is thirty years' work and is full of discoveries and rediscoveries. *For Love*, which must be one of the most widely admired books published since 1945, retains its intimacy and its sting. *Words*, which is central to the issue I've described, is work of painful, sometimes luminous austerity. *Pieces* is, among other things, a meditation on time, on temporality as the condition of consciousness and of art. It is imagistic in method, but its images are to the traditional image what an X-ray is to a photograph. It is also the book that began to irritate critics. It is full of small, wry musings like this:

> Thinking—and coincident
> experience of the situation.
>
> "I think he'll hit me."
> He does. Etc.

and

> People
> were walking
> by

He wants that *by* to suggest all of time even as it catches the comedy of the fact that people go for walks partly to walk *by* things, to do a leisurely imitation of mortality, to, as Creeley would say, etc. These small, quick dances of the mind do not always work, but for me at least they are never without interest. There is a lot here that is playful, verbal equivalents of those Jim Dine drawings which try to discover the difference between pencil scribbles and pubic hair. The exhilaration of them, of this body of work, is the sense of an artist for whom the rhythms of any articulation are a possible poetry. "Who comes," he says elsewhere, "comes on time." Also, "What do you want with the phone / if you won't answer it." What else have I left out? He is a love poet above all. And a poet of dark wit and irritability and friendship. Sometimes his poems can rip you open and then turn ironically aside. The worst reproach that can be made against his work is that some of it seems begun by Francis Bacon and finished by David Hockney. That can be dismaying, but the root of the impulse is also his great strength; it is a loathing for eloquence as a form of delusion and self-importance. If you go to Creeley as you go to some other poets, for love of the social power or the transforming grandeur of language, you are likely to find him either frightening or incomprehensible. His way has been to take the ordinary, threadbare phrases and sentences by which we locate ourselves and to put them under the immense pressure of the rhythms of poetry and to make out of that what dance or music there can be. In the end, his tradition is the New England one of Puritan self-examination which extends from Edward Taylor through Emily Dickinson to Robert Lowell. None of these writers is his own particular master, and he departs from them in making the impulses of his own speech the object of scrutiny. In any case, he is a master, one of the handful at work in America in any art.

McMichael's Pasadena

Four Good Things by James McMichael

It appears that, whether one likes the idea or not, it is going to be important to understand the culture of southern California, since it has had a hand in forming two presidents and provides what is apparently a congenial atmosphere for the retirement of a third. "Culture" may not be the word one would first choose to indicate the ambience of locker rooms at country club golf courses near Palm Springs and San Clemente; and you wonder if even Bertolt Brecht or Gabriel García Marquez—masters of the fact that the middle class hates to be reminded that its comfortable life is political—could make it interesting. Golf is a worrier's game, inward, concentrated, a matter of inches, invented by the same people who gave us Presbyterianism. The story of how water arrived in a desert place to grow the grass on which the game is played is the history of California politics. Afterward, men drink Jack Daniel's and play dominoes, or, newly arrived, couples sit around their pools, looking up the word for "Venetian blind" in a book called *Home Maid Spanish.* The helicopters overhead are the means the city of Pasadena has found to search for purse snatchers, who make their grabs on the main streets and then disappear into arroyos of almost impenetrable chaparral in the canyons. Odds are that the purse snatcher is descended from West Africans. The maid is most likely a mixture of Spanish and aboriginal, belonging to the race of peoples who made the Aleutian crossing five hundred years ago and are believed now to have originated in what we call Vietnam. It may not be a culture, but it is a complicated place, complicated and thin at the same time.

James McMichael's *Four Good Things* should ease the task of understanding. It is a new, remarkable long poem about—of all things—Pasadena. It is also about worry, death, taxes, planning, probability theory, insomnia, stamp collecting, cancer, domestic architecture, sex manuals, the Industrial Revolution, real estate, and—it is so un-Russian a book that one can actually say this—the American soul. It begins, tranquilly enough, with recollections of childhood. The narrator's father is a real estate developer; his mother, in an upstairs bedroom of their pleasant suburban house, is dying of cancer. So the poem announces its themes immediately: the idea of place and the dread and bewilderment of death. From there it moves out into its meditation on a quite amazing variety of related American subjects in which it has discovered this common pair of threads. Place, in the child's mind where the poem begins, is a masculine proposition, and a rather dubious one, the promise of the good life sketched out in survey maps, prospective buyers, and the cheerful desolation of lots. And the female propositions—death, repose—seem to flower from the middle of that promise. Place, which is everywhere present and palpable, is not quite real; and death, which is not present and everywhere palpable, is very real—and they are somehow married, though they seem not to talk to each other very much.

If this seems to be an accurate and scary definition of southern California, or at least one steadily suggested by the other writers of that place, Joan Didion and Raymond Chandler and Ross Macdonald, then it will also begin to suggest why I think James McMichael may have written a classic American book. It has the speculative range, the freedom of imagination and fierce, clear eye that make the work being produced by the post-Vietnam generation of American writers—Maxine Hong Kingston or Thomas Pynchon, for example—so interesting, but it also has the virtues of good, expository prose, of the essays of John McPhee or Edward Hoagland. The verse is quiet, lapidary; all the excitement is in watching McMichael take up one unpoetic subject after another and illuminate it by turning it back on the emotions of a child who is watching the city take shape around him and the people moving into their houses and who tries to find this activity a clue to what it is his father does all day and why his mother is dying.

It is not easy to demonstrate how he achieves this. It is a long, engrossing work and its effects are slow to develop, like a film full of languid dissolves. But the central technique is simply that he makes connections. What, for example, is the connection between Pasadena and the Industrial Revolution? One is that the characteristic style of California domestic architecture derives from the arts and crafts movement in Victorian England, which was a reaction against the machine production of domestic objects. The rich of Pasadena, whom a world market brought into being, made houses out of William Morris' criticism of the world market and its shabby production standards. Very beautiful houses, and McMichael describes the principle of their construction with a wonderfully quiet (and faintly nagging) accuracy:

The roof was
long and relatively flat. Beams above the frames of
doors and windows were much broader than the
frames themselves and paralleled the covered
entryways and porches. Even the stairs inside
were less than vertical, each section of the railing
carved from a single piece of teak and joined to
all the other teak—the notched and interlocking
kickplates, the splines and level boards that were
the facing of the well. Their stairs were furniture.
A bench along a landing had the same insistent
finish as the inglenook, the same square
ebony caps for screwheads as the chairs and tables.
Everything showed you how it went together.

This is the work of Greene and Greene, architects who, along with Bernard Maybeck in San Francisco, perfected the informal style of California houses. Architectural historians emphasize the use of natural materials, rough stone and redwood shingle, and the decision to expose rather than disguise workmanship. McMichael notices something else, not just the reassurance that seeing how things go together can give, but the fact that reassurance was needed. He notices the anxiety previous to the desire for place; and this leads him to think of his Irish-American neighbors in those ample and curiously uncomforting houses and of how their ancestors might have lived in Richard Arkwright's Manchester, when the world that made California possible was coming into being:

People were living in the seams,
in undercrofts of bridges and along the
rivers and canals where they could bathe, the water
warm from the boiler-tailings, dyes, and bleaches,
from the refuse that would lift through floors
of houserows slipping from the Irwell to the Irk.
Crosses on the Ordnance Maps of 1850 mark the streets

where five or more had died of typhus. Workers ate
only the tainted meats. Their foodstuffs were
adulterated: flour, with chalk or gypsum; pounded
nutshells in the pepper, sloe-leaves in the tea.
Mothers were back at work the same day they delivered,
milk dripping from their shirts. Each wet nurse
had a dozen babies. She'd give them Quietness—
a dose of treacle, sugar, and crude opium—
and they would look much older than they were.

The cottage industry skills that country people necessarily had in the eighteenth century and that William Morris and the Greenes hoped to revive were exactly what was not wanted in Manchester, as McMichael—taking Engels as his guide—observes:

Skills made a worker more
intractable and less dependent. As long as there were
'workers enough, and not all so insane as to prefer
dying to living,' their master had it as he wanted it.
He had the capital to shield himself against
uncertainties within the market. And when those came,
the workers were displaced and worked for less and were
"as much without volition as the rivers."

This seems to me another extraordinarily interesting perception. It is easy enough to see that capital was a shield against uncertainty; what is more interesting and subtle is McMichael's conception of its tendency to displace. The literature of the period is full of contrasts between wealth conceived as the repose of property and wealth conceived as the energy of capital. The repose of place was the old shield against the world; the new one is movement and the ability to act. The English poets have written many poems about the way that the old estates embody place; it is interesting that it took an American one to find the poetry of Manchester, and the system that displaced the very idea of place with the idea of a constant hunger for it:

> England had outgrown the continent of Europe.
> Free Trade was Jesus Christ. They formed their
> joint-stock companies and combines, and could count on
> triple rows of sheds, eight miles of granite docks,
> calm and deep water in all tides at Liverpool.
> They were still in that plain geography of
> "things in their places," of bales on
> hoisting-pulleys, and in ship-holds and, along the quays,
> the dry white scudding that they lost as waste.
> They were looking for those samenesses that make us feel we've
> broken through to something, through those
> unsure things that happen in a place in time to
> something like our safe, impalpable and self-sustaining
> plans that are always future.

Volition is, of course, what is wanted if one is going to combat uncertainties. Vigor and active will were the hallmarks of the Manchester entrepreneur and they are the ideas that every American presidential candidate tries to project about himself. And planning, McMichael reminds us, is the main human embodiment of will. Its purpose is to allay anxiety by showing us how we are going to get there. In fact, the poem insists, planning and anxiety are almost Siamese twins. It's when we are anxious that we start to plan; or, having experienced anxiety, we learn to plan before we begin to feel anxious, as a way of warding it off. Americans, in this account, with their city planning, economic planning, estate planning, family planning, with their game plans and savings plans and lay-away plans, would seem to be the most anxious people on earth.

And this fact is also made to connect to Pasadena where the planner's paradigm, probability theory, took root in the Jet Propulsion Laboratory of Aerojet International and at the California Institute of Technology and the Palomar Observatory, our own Stonehenge, where a large telescopic eye continually searches the heavens, trying to understand our place in the universe and to anticipate any unpleasant surprises:

The future was
successive and successful answers to those
questions it made sense to ask. How far from the
earth itself could we project? And what was light?
In the calculus of variations, what was the mean
process of behavior in a species, in a
social class? Could we computerize a place for
each of us within the equalizing
sameness of the plan? If we overlooked nothing,
no single difference of temperament or will,
if it were all accounted for and stored and if we
watched it periodically and found it yielded
more and newer orders, it would teach us how to
master what was probable and make it pure,
assign it a completeness like the past's.

It is in passages like these that McMichael comes close, it seems to me, to revealing something like the American soul, or one kind of American soul that has never been accommodated before to the language of poetry. It is not, perhaps, what we would like to see—it is certainly not the American soul of Whitman's *Leaves of Grass* or Hart Crane's *The Bridge*—but it is undeniably familiar, belongs undeniably to the materials of American life. McMichael, whether we like it or not, has taken the language of our technical resourcefulness, of our most prestigious professions and most admired accomplishments, and held it up for our inspection in a most surprising place—in the language of poetry. If it looks disturbed and impoverished, then we have learned something that it is important to think about.

Four Good Things drives this home, takes it all the way

inside, in a long tour-de-force passage describing insomnia and the way that worry keeps us awake. The whole of it which is brilliant and maddening—like certain stretches of Samuel Beckett or the *roman nouveau*—concludes with a funny (and somewhat creepy) revision of René Descartes, inventor for the West of algebra and of the idea that the only real place is what passes through our minds:

I work at breathing for awhile, listen to
Linda's and adopt it, a sleeper's breathing.
Mine would be slower. To breathe the way she breathes,
I'd have to be awake, and am, and have been awake
too long now and have given up on trying to know
exactly what I should be doing, how I could be
thinking about it all and changing. So I don't
care if I go back to sleep. Since it never works to
care about it, since my calmness when I care is
feigned and crazy, I don't care. I'll get up.
I'm too tired to get up . . . The certainty
sleep isn't there is me . . .

•

Feeling anxious and hungering to be in a place—sleep—where you can't be (because *you* is, by definition, conscious, not asleep) is a metaphor for American restlessness, for all our desires for place and roots. One sees it, as well, in McMichael's portrait of the Midwesterners who came to California (as if it were sleep or unconsciousness) for their piece of the American dream. It is a central irony of the poem—and another of its surprising perceptions—that in order to achieve the American —or any other kind of—dream, you have to be unconscious, which these displaced Iowans aren't exactly:

Living here was too much what they'd
thought it would be. The sequences of perfect days were
unavoidably what they'd come for. They should be making

more of what was there and possible at any
hour in that clear air. With all those possibilities
aligned for them along the tracks and poles and wires
they should be somewhere else since where they were was
old already with their being there.

Only a few brief passages in all the two thousand or so lines of this work seem to regard the world outside this uneasiness. One of them is written from the point of view of the dying mother, because she is the one figure in the poem who has had to accept what planning can only forestall, and so she is the one for whom death and pain have made the world more, not less, a place. It is a deeply affecting moment, and I can only quote a part of it:

It would be
pain alone that held its place, that couldn't be
planned away from that one body that was living it in
hope, not waiting, not afraid to know it wasn't
worth it, after all that pain. It was worth it. There were
people who made it worth it, and the world. A cat came
sleepily from a thick shrub and stopped and shook its head.
There was time between the bleatings of the horn to be
reminded and forget again the huckster and his fish
two streets away, then one, then out of hearing, gone,
the shadows of the fences less alert as the heat gave
way a little and the peas were shucked, all changes
watched for now as if one were confined and sitting up
in bed, alone, with nothing but the afternoon
outside along the ground toward the lilac and the
cactus in the foothills . . .

Against the possibility of looking out the window and seeing nothing but the afternoon, place the son's sense of what he learned, growing up in Pasadena:

With my conception, I was virtually
coincident with cancer in my mother's body.
To exist is to be *placed outside*, where there are
things to fear. My body. Me. The visible
pulse at my right ankle, thick blue vein, the skin,
sunlight on my ankle in a cold house, now.
When I'm afraid, I try to think of everything.
I try to change the possible by thinking some one
part of it and giving it a place—gratuitous
murder, accident, a flood, the separate and bizarre
pathologies that could be mine and final.
Worry is somewhat less possessive, less complete,
more frequent and deliberate, self-amused. It too
displaces where I am with something that I make
inside me. Each thing I worry is secure,
familiar, almost home. Its difference is
mine and not the world's. The house wren, when it sings, says
"Here I am." It looks around and says it.
My worrying and fear are notices that I don't
have a place outside and don't know how to
find or make one. They are as free of people as a
garden is, or as a plan.

Knowledge of our displacement, knowledge of death, these are consciousness for McMichael, and what consciousness does is worry and plan, though it hungers like the wren to say "Here I am," to make a place out of sleep or to make "Pasadena" or a house like a nest, to make love. Or to make poetry, which is the pure case of the human attempt to find in consciousness freedom from consciousness. That McMichael does not use the occasion of his long poem to celebrate poetry is the one un-American thing about it. It is also the most remarkable thing about it: this is a long American poem that stays in the world of ordinary consciousness, of history and fact and daily life. It does not wander into myth, nor does it surge into the dark of nature, into animals or plants or sexuality. The passage about lovemaking is about consciousness of lovemaking, about sex manuals and sexual technique, which is another symptom of anxiety and planning ahead. Our books on the subject are not about how to be with another person, they are about what to do, and so they too are "as free of people as a garden is, or as a plan."

•

In the first long American poem, Walt Whitman, with a great sense of how comic the idea was, made love to all of us, to the whole future. It is the central sense of possibility in his poem that we are beings who can, through imagination, make the future present. McMichael has exactly reversed this formulation and described a world that makes the present always future. And he also finds it comic—at least the writing about insomnia and the developers of Pasadena and Van Karman's wind tunnel at Cal Tech are funny—but very sad. Partly he seems to think that this is the human condition. We *are* displaced; we *do* have to plan. And partly he seems to want to understand it on economic and social grounds, to see capitalism—private or state—as an engine for continually displacing the present. Capital is itself a thrust toward the future, based on plans; and production is oriented to the future as well. The present, in economic thinking, exists as consumption only, as what is being used and passing out of our hands. It is what is being eaten up. And the clear sense of this in the poem is that it is both a disease and a great sadness.

There is another source for this vision, I think. McMichael belongs to the generation of writers, now about forty, who grew up in the social and economic expansion of the postwar years. It was probably most intense in California. And, as the others did, he watched the planning and the confidence and the technical inventiveness turn, with what seemed to the young unbelievable callousness and efficiency and fury, on Vietnam. That war was, perhaps, a paradigm of planning without people in the plan. The Vietnamese did not fit it and the American young who were supposed to fight the war did not fit it; and as the administration with a plan to win the war was replaced by an administration with a plan to end the war, the suffering seemed to go on forever. And a generation of American writers has come to look at the central mechanisms of American life with a deep, stunned, curious detachment, which, I think, the writing in this poem reflects beautifully.

At the present moment, when we have yet another California president with yet another set of plans—which would seem to include the intensification of a civil war in Central America, the suffering of the elderly and the marginally employed to provide a shield against uncertainties within the market, the shutting down of theaters and symphony orchestras and the selling of adulterated foodstuffs to the underdeveloped world —the detachment of *Four Good Things*, its precision and meditative quiet, seemed to me especially powerful—with the power art has of stinging us awake. In the last lines of the poem, as the narrator is falling asleep, his wife describes to him an afternoon spent skiing:

> The street was ice and hardly wide enough for
> two of them at a time, or for a cart.
> They felt showy in their bright nylon.
> A woman with a bowl looked at them from her door.
> Chickens. A covered water-trough. She told me
> more about the street and then remembered.
> What she was saying, she said, was that there were
> farmers out working in the snow.

After all the turnings, it seems radiant, this glimpse of the fact that there are people in the world.

Reading Miłosz

It might be useful to begin by invoking a time when one might turn to the work of Czesław Miłosz. The summer, let's say, of 1966. Picketing the napalm plant in Redwood City on a Thursday afternoon. Hazy autumnal light. You have seen the photographs of the faces of Vietnamese children. Imagine putting your hand on the stove. Imagine putting-your-hand-on-the-stove as a vaseline jelly. The children's faces, light brown skin in the beautiful technology of the American color photograph, look like deserts or moonscapes. Eyes the color of black olives, the inward look of the recently traumatized made more impassive by the frank agony of the adults who hold them. The phrase "licking their wounds" occurs to you. Now the wind off the bay buffets your large cardboard sign. It was handed to you by one of the Quaker organizers of the event. It says THIS MUST STOP NOW! Pathetic, really, and holding it among the other signs, LOVE NOT GUNS, HELL NO WE WON'T GO, BOMB DOW CHEMICAL, ANOTHER MOTHER FOR PEACE, you feel sheepish between gusts of affection for this ragtag army of an aroused middle class.

The man next to you, grey hair, grey beard, Yankee to the core—his look of rage and determination so intense he could be John Brown or Henry Clay—is wearing his infantryman's uniform from World War II. Ill-fitting. Absurd, in fact: next week he will shave his head to express solidarity with the Buddhists of Saigon; the week after, he starts to smear himself with red dye. In his uniform, shaved head, red dye, he takes to attending

Friends' meetings carrying the American flag. The war is driving people crazy. A professor whom you thought was an abject careerist—he advised graduate students always to browse in popular periodicals contemporary with the novels they were studying; you could almost always dig an article out that way—Dickens and the Public Hygiene Controversy; Melville and the Egyptian Vase Collection at the Brooklyn Museum—goes abroad for the summer, gets beat up by police at an antiwar demonstration in Brussels, and returns to wear jeans, T-shirt and a Mao cap to teach his course in Victorian bibliography. One of your friends, the son of an Air Force general, is arrested with dynamite in the trunk of his car; he was going to blow up Moffett Air Base. More wind. Speeches. When the sun starts to go down and it gets cold, you go home for dinner.

At a stop sign on the way, you glance at the car next to you, a big new station wagon pulling a motorboat on a trailer. Inside a man, a woman and two children. Evidently they are going on vacation. He is suntanned with a red and white polo shirt. She is wearing a peasant blouse and a golfer's visor, a thin anxious face. She smokes. Only the tops of the children's heads are visible in the back seat. They are probably bent to comics and coloring books. The husband jumps out of the car while the light is red, runs back to check his trailer hitch. Paunchy, wearing shorts. They seem like America to you, like a large, stupid pleasure boat. Banners as it comes into the harbor, a whistle like a tuba. They are going somewhere to foul a lake with gasoline. Their children will float in black inner tubes. Pester them to go to the concession stand. Suntan lotion. Drinks before dinner on a deck from which you can admire green pines, grey granite, blue sky. Huge steaks from cattle drugged for that purpose in feedlots in Manteca. More comics. Thousands of miles away, fear, violence, brothels, villages going up in an agony of flames.

Another time a senator shows up to give a speech to the

demonstrators at the napalm plant. He is the one senator who voted against the Tonkin Gulf resolution, which granted the White House its war powers. It is very windy that day. Trouble with the signs which seem to want to sail off into space and trouble with the amplifying system. The senator, however, can be heard clearly. Either it is a magic that attends power or he is a pro. The audience, standing in the parking lot of the chemical plant, the air full of seagulls, grows silent. They are tormented people, and deeply grateful to be listening to someone in authority. Morse begins: "I want to say at the outset that Lyndon Johnson and I are old friends. We have both served the Democratic Party for a long time, a very long time." You look at the faces trying to take that in. One woman's sign today says REAL PEOPLE ARE REALLY DYING THIS MINUTE. THINK! FEEL! *Think* and *feel* furiously underlined. She is straining forward to listen. "You know, we disagree about the war in Vietnam. I personally think it is a tragic mistake." A scattering of hopeful applause. "The president disagrees. That doesn't make us enemies. He called me just the other day about a transportation bill. And I said to him, 'Why, Mr. President, I'm pleased to hear from you. I was just thinking that we haven't seen much of each other lately.' And he said to me, 'Senator, you are a goddamn nuisance, but you're also a Democrat and you're also my friend and there's nobody else who can get this bill through and we both know our job is to bring home the bacon.'" The audience, people who dream at night of throwing their bodies in front of troop trains, is utterly silent now and all that delicate sense of strain has gone out of their attention. It might have been the day when the death of God was officially announced. "Senator." "Mr. President." They call each other by their lodge names, as if it were a grand joke. There was a memorable phrase from the debates among American intellectuals about the Eichmann trial—the banality of evil—and it sinks into you now with a light, feathery aptness that sickens. This is how the war is conducted. You think you can read internal debate in the curiously calm faces around you. There had been a lot of discussion of the causes of the war among people who had been living very well and wanted to find a name for the monstrous thing that their country had unleashed: capitalism, imperialism. But now in the mildness of the senator's self-regard and the mildness of the afternoon sky, it is as if you had fallen through a trapdoor to another set of questions. Beyond the chemical plant, there are clouds of white gulls over the garbage dump.

Thinking about myth, having an eye out always for any idea you think your professors won't want to hear, you remember someone saying that—Freud, Jung, Eliade aside—myth is about eating each other. It was man's first tool for sanctifying the food chain. And this pleased you because it seemed Marxist. Listening to lectures on literature and literary theory by a generation of professors in love with Henry James and Virginia Woolf, one of your friends had said he wanted to write a book called *Crude Materialism Reconsidered.* Neolithic hunters had looked around and figured it out: we kill each other and eat each other. You stuffed chickens so full of hormones you invented a new sex—that was capitalism. Peasants in Silesia who worked all day for someone else sat around huts at night listening to stories: but, Grandmother, what big teeth you have!—that was feudalism. And Christ had said: eat me, so people did, solemnly, for two thousand years. The world was a pig-out; or the matter-universe was a pig-out. As if there were some other universe to distinguish this one from.

The disease that was on me has various names; one of them is philosophy, theology and eschatology are others, and the only thing I knew about them for sure was that they were the enemies of poetry. My real teachers had been, for the most part, the American poets I was reading and studying, and I began to get a sense of just how radical the proposal of modernist poetics had been. No ideas, William Carlos Williams had insisted—but in things. And Ezra Pound had said that the natural object was *always* the adequate symbol. Pound's Fenellosa was the most extreme version of this because he called for a poetry built entirely from pictographs, as if no one had ever thought before and nothing needed to be thought that was not shot through with the energy of immediate observation. In practice, this meant that if one were to write about the antiwar demonstrations, the poem would likely end with an image: beyond the chemical plant, clouds of white gulls above the garbage dump. But those images had a way of always throwing the weight of meaning back on the innocence and discovery of the observer, and something in the dramatic ambivalence of that gesture rhymed with the permanent unconsciousness of the man with the boat and Senator Morse. It made me feel vaguely ashamed when I saw it in the poems I was reading. I could not formulate the problem for myself very exactly, but I wanted to read a poetry by people who did not assume that the great drama in their work was that everything in the world was happening to them for the first time. So, during those years, like many other young Americans who were writing poetry or contemplating writing poetry, I began to read hungrily in translations of European and Latin American poets, and the same impulse sent me to *The Captive Mind.*

1 /

By the time Czesław Miłosz's poetry became available in 1973, I had already described to myself a notion of it. In this essay I want to try to trace the development of Miłosz's work and say something about what I think its value is, but in order to do that want to begin by looking at my first confused conception of it. I think it is shared by many readers, interested in Miłosz and unsure what to make of him. I knew that he had begun in Lithuania as a "catastrophist," that catastrophism was one of those schools of European poetry, incomprehensible to

Americans, that defines itself by its reaction to a previous school. The dominant force in Polish poetry had been a group called Skamander. They had grown out of the optimism of a Poland finally free from foreign domination after the treaty of Versailles, and their work, formally traditional, was a celebration—Nietzschean or Bergsonian, as the fashions were—of the life-force: lyric, facile, optimistic. Skamander was opposed by another movement, the Vanguard, more severe, experimental, strongly interested in clarity and formal invention, rather like the imagists in England or the acmeists in Russia. The catastrophists—really a handful of Wilno undergraduates and recent graduates writing in Polish—were the second wave of the Vanguard, but they were the generation of poets to watch the onset of the world depression and Hitler's seizure of power in Germany. Skamander was out of the question, and so was the formal purity of the First Vanguard. "Form in poetry," Miłosz would write years later, "has many uses; one of them is, like refrigeration, to preserve bad meat."

Catastrophist poetry was surreal, apocalyptic. Unlike the First Vanguard, it was socially concerned, and unlike Skamander, it went in fear of poets who went in fear of general ideas. It wanted intellectual force in poetry. I don't know that this characterization is accurate, but it was very striking because catastrophism or something like it seemed a stage in the development of twentieth-century art that never happened in English-language poetry. There was a sort of Skamander in the Georgian poets, the Little Englanders. And a first vanguard with a cubist concern for definiteness and formal hardness, but no real second vanguard appeared, perhaps because of the brilliance of the first, perhaps because of the poverty of the Anglo-American philosophical tradition. Surrealism, in any case, never took root, in either England or America, the two countries in which the dominance of middle-class pragmatism in political life was most clearly established. Hart Crane's *The Bridge*, with its social concerns, its appropriation of the baroque, its surreal and visionary imagery, and its futurist fascination with machines, appeared to be a sort of splendid entryway to a building that was never built. Inside it were only Auden and Spender and the New Critics who, if they were interesting poets, seemed less than what might have happened.

The catastrophists got what they predicted and more. Miłosz, migrating from Wilno to Warsaw, lived through the Nazi occupation, the holocaust, and the Warsaw uprising, and emerged a very different poet. Here, there were a handful of poems one knew or had seen quoted in discussions of European literature. I think the ones I had seen were "Dedication" and "A Poor Christian Looks at the Ghetto." Dry poems, understated, harrowed by survival guilt. Poems that one wanted to describe as ironic, though, when you looked at them, you found no trace of overt irony. Then came his break with the People's Government of Poland and the writing of *The Captive Mind.* I read it for the first time as a freshman in a kind of fit that included *The Stranger, Nausea, No Exit, Waiting for Godot, Malone Dies, The Voyeur, The Waste Land.* (Modern literature: the setting was bucolic, orchards, dairy cattle grazing the hills, olive trees whitening in what wind there was. I noticed the contrast, but did not know that it could form the basis for a life's work in poetry. Miłosz arrived in California at just about that time.) I was to hear, from someone who had taken a course from him at Berkeley, that he had said that the best literary model for the twentieth century might be the gospel of Luke, rough, plain, synoptic.

And that was the figure that I pictured, the moralist in exile, a man who had witnessed the operations of the great beast and told terrible truths, with detachment, skepticism, with that whisper of unlocatable irony, in the plainest of language and who, almost one sensed as an amused response to the role he had to play, the émigré university professor in blond California, gave lectures on the Albigensian heresy, Jules Verne, the visions of the Virgin Mary vouchsafed to Vladimir Solovyov. And one also heard, vaguely, that he was a Christian, though of a dark, heretical kind. Having tasted a little of thought-in-extremity, it was pleasant to think that the hawk-like Lithuanian poet in the Berkeley hills had distilled it.

None of this was completely wrong—which is why it is completely wrong. When one turns from that austere moralist to the poems which appeared in 1973, here is what one finds:

> White, white, white. White city where women carry bread
> and vegetables, women born under the signs of the
> slow spinning of the zodiac
> And the jaws of fountains spout water in the green sun
> as in the old days of nuptials, of strolls under a
> cold aurora from one side of the city to the other.
> Buckles from schoolboys' belts buried in the dense earth,
> bunkers and sarcophagi bound with ropes of blackberry.
> Revelations of touch, again and again new beginnings, no
> knowledge, no memory ever accepted . . .

And this:

> The scent of fresh mown clover redeemed the perished
> armies and, in the car headlights, meadows glittered
> forever.
> An immense July night filled my mouth with the taste of
> rain and near Puybrun, by the bridges, my childhood
> was given back to me.
> The warm encampments of crickets chirped under a low
> cloud just as they had in our lost homeland where
> a wooden cart goes creaking.
> Borne by an inscrutable power, one century gone, I heard,
> beating in darkness, the heart of the living and the dead.

Here is a portrait of a painter:

Year after year he circled a thick tree
Shading his eyes with his hand and muttering admiringly.

How much he envied those who draw a tree with one line!
But metaphor seemed to him indecent.

He would leave symbols to the proud, busy with their causes.
He wanted to draw the name from the very thing by looking.

When he was old, he tugged at his tobacco-stained beard:
"I'd rather lose this way than win the way they do."

Like Peter Breughel the elder, he fell suddenly.
Trying to see his ass from between his legs.

And the tree still stood there, unattainable.
Veritable, true to the very core.

And a pantheist Madonna:

Paulina, her room behind the servants' quarters, with one
 window on the orchard
where I gather the best apples near the pigsty
squishing the warm muck of the dunghill with my big toe,
and the other window on the well (I love to drop the bucket down
and scare its inhabitants, the green frogs).
Paulina, a geranium, the chill of a dirt floor,
a hard bed with three pillows,
an iron crucifix and images of the saints,
decorated with palms and paper roses.
Paulina died long ago, but she exists.
And, I am somehow convinced, not just in my consciousness.

Above her rough Lithuanian peasant face
hovers a spindle of hummingbirds, and her flat calloused feet
are sprinkled by sapphire water in which a frolic

of dolphins, backs arched,
leap.

And this:

A coelentera, animal-flower, all pulsing flesh,
All fire, made from fallen bodies joined together by the black pin
of sex.
It breathes in the center of a galaxy, drawing to itself star after
star . . .

And, finally, this:

From childhood till old age ecstasy at sunrise.

This poet, so little like what one expected—and so much fuller, more passionate and tormented and, occasionally, funny—requires a different accounting. He is not, clearly, the embittered sage of my fantasy, nor is he the patriot and freedom fighter of his current Polish popularity. Of course, what one decides he is depends on a perception of the strength of his work. It seems to me now that the crucial moment in Miłosz's development did not occur in Warsaw during the war or in Paris at the time of his break with the Stalinist government of Poland. It happened sometime around 1959 or 1960 in his last years in France just before his move to Berkeley. The key spiritual or intellectual figure for this moment seems to be Simone Weil, and what she gave him—no doubt it could have come some other way, or was already there—was the permission which issued in the late, long sequences which are, I think, the most remarkable and characteristic poems in the body of his work. These include "Album of Dreams," "Throughout Our Lands," "The Chronicles of Pornic," "Bobo's Metamorphosis," "City Without a Name," "With Trumpets and Zithers," "From the Rising of the Sun," and "The Separate Notebooks."

2 /

Miłosz was, from the beginning, enmeshed in contradiction. To be born into the Polish gentry in Lithuania was a little like being born Anglo-Irish in Ireland. Lithuanian national consciousness was beginning to stir in his childhood. Lithuanians are not Slavs, their language (the oldest living Indo-European tongue) was spoken by peasants and artisans, and the target of the new nationalism was the Polish gentry to which Miłosz, though his family name on his mother's side was Lithuanian, belonged. To complicate matters, he was born, in 1911, a subject of the Russian Empire. Not quite a Lithuanian, not quite a Pole, and the political subject of another nation altogether. What he was for sure was a Roman Catholic, though this was qualified by the persistence of custom, of the old, pre-Christian earth magic of the countryside. And his education was Polish, qualified again by evocations of the former glories of the Grand Duchy of Lithuania. That is to say, he was a Westerner, with a spiritual heritage oriented toward Rome and a cultural one toward Paris, rooted in the half-magical geography of a particular river valley about which hung the legends of a perished (and therefore perishable) past. None of this (as he says in his autobiography) could have meant too much to a boy in short pants throwing stones in a river, but it was the seedbed of the imagination of a poet who would, later, write: "He would like to know who he was, but he does not know. He would like to be one, but he is a self-contradictory multitude, which gives him some joy, but more shame."

Poem on Frozen Time, 1933
Anthology of Social Poetry, ed. Miłosz & Folejewski, 1933
Three Winters, 1936

This complexity is already expressed in his earliest work. Only three poems from this period have appeared in book form in English—the "How Once He Was" section of *Selected Poems*—and they do not seem either very well translated or very strong. The best of the ones I have seen elsewhere* are "The Song," "Slow Rivers," and "The Gates of the Arsenal." "The Song" was the first of his poems to achieve wide circulation. I believe it was translated into French by his cousin Oscar Miłosz. It seems to be beautifully made—critics would speak of a reckless freedom of imagination in his early work, combined with a surprisingly classical strength in the phrasing—it rehearses lifelong themes and preoccupations, and more crucially it is choral. The poet does not speak in one voice but in many, none of them quite his own. And it has an intensity, an emotional nakedness which will leave his work and come back to it only slowly, long after the catastrophe that the young catastrophists prophesied had actually occurred.

The easiest voice to identify in "The Song" is that of the chorus. It says what time and nature say:

> Children throw balls, they dance on the meadow in threesomes,
> And women wash linen at streamside, fishing for the moon.
> All joy comes from the earth, there is no delight without her.
> Man is given to the earth only, let him desire no other.

Another voice in the poem, "She," seems to be human consciousness with its ambivalent love of the earth and its knowledge of sorrow and death:

> Oh, if there were one seed without rust inside me,
> One grain that could outlast it,
> Then I would sleep in the cradle . . .
> But there is nothing in me but fear,

* *For some sight translations and dating of poems discussed here as well as other information, I am indebted to Renata Gorcyzinski.*

Nothing but the running of dark waves . . .
I am the wind going out and not coming back,
Milkweed pollen on the black meadows of the world.

But any interpretation seems hopelessly reductive of her voice. Say she is the female soul, and that the seed inside her is gnostic, or, as Miłosz would say, Manichean: the impulse to reject nature, the matter-universe, entirely since time and change have nothing but death and loss to offer to the human soul. And she has not that one tone, but many—love of the world, a lover's rejection of the world, the desire for transcendence, anguish, despair—which also intensifies the polyphonic quality of the poem. Finally, there are the last voices. Whatever they are, they are calmer, less mesmeric and insistent than the voice of the chorus, and their name implies an eschatological vision: a way of seeing the world from the point of view of the end, when Time and Being are reconciled.

This poem was written in Wilno in 1934. The following year Miłosz went to Paris to study and his poems reflected more directly the influence of surrealism. But these poems—"Slow Rivers," "The Gates of the Arsenal"—with their strange imagery, their odd mixture of formal and experimental elements, and their intensified sense of historical disaster, are extensions of the themes of "The Song." In fact, the imagination of doom, colored by the conditions of Polish workers in a vermin-infested district of Paris, the Depression, the gathering cloud of the Spanish Civil War, Hitler's seizure of power in Germany, represents itself in the poems not so much as an evil perpetrated by men against men, but a sudden intensification of the natural process of decay and death. This is important, I think, for Miłosz's later experience of the Nazi occupation and of Marxist ideology. His imagination prepared him to see the events of those years as a speeded-up version of the destructive power of time, of what nature had in store for us anyway. This was an evil which was not just a defect of human political systems or even of human nature, but of nature itself. He writes about the year in Paris rather prophetically: "I was sharply attuned to a universal catastrophe, which was not just a fear of war. At night I used to dream a fatal ray was pursuing me and that when I reached a safe shore it finally pierced me through."

Invincible Song, ed. Miłosz, 1942 (clandestine anthology)
Jacques Maritain, *Through the Disaster*, tr. Miłosz, 1942 (clandestine publication)
Rescue, 1945 (poems)

But the war years—it is hard to speak of them as something that had the effect of altering a poet's style—submerged these issues which, whatever range they had, got their force from a young man's shocked recognition that he and everything he cared about had to perish. Perishing was suddenly a cheap commodity. Miłosz edited an anthology of anti-Nazi poetry, translated Maritain's book on the obligation to resist collaboration with the Nazis, and worked on the poems which, after the war, were published in *Rescue*. Eight of the thirty-nine poems have been translated into English. They appear in the section of the *Selected Poems* called "What He Learned," and several belong to a sequence entitled "Voices of Poor People." The masterpiece and oddity of *Rescue* is "The World." It is the "Songs of Innocence"—an emphatic celebration of being—set against "Songs of Experience" in the meditations on death, time, historical helplessness in "Voices of Poor People." "The World" seems to be a hymn, in the midst of destruction, to a small, imaginable, human cosmos, but a close reading will suggest how many other tones it glints with. Characteristically, the poems are most powerful when they are many-voiced, though Miłosz, throughout this period, made an enormous effort to strip down his style in order to say the few true and necessary things.

For American readers, "Dedication" is instructive in this way, especially because it bears comparison with a very famous poem on a similar subject, Yeats' "Easter 1916." "Dedication" was written in 1945. It begins:

> You whom I could not save
> Listen to me.
> Try to understand this simple speech as I would be ashamed of
> another.

It is addressed to the dead of the Warsaw uprising, which came in August 1944. At the order of the Polish government-in-exile, the clandestine Home Army in Warsaw rose against the Germans. "For two months," Miłosz writes in *The Captive Mind*, "a kilometer-high column of smoke and flames stood over Warsaw. Two hundred thousand people died in the street fighting. Those neighborhoods which were not levelled by bombs or by the fire of heavy artillery were burned down by SS squads. After the uprising, the city which once numbered over a million inhabitants was a wilderness of ruins, its population deported and its demolished streets literally cemeteries." When I first read this poem, it confused me; I was expecting a paean, appropriately understated and tightlipped, to political commitment. It is, of course, just the reverse of that, and to understand it completely one needs to know a little of the politics of the Warsaw underground and the situation of its writers.

Poland had been *the* liberal cause in Europe in the nineteenth century when radical chic consisted in attending programs of Chopin. Russian domination had done to Poland what English domination had done to Ireland. It forged a literature that was nationalistic, patriotic and romantic. Years later, in *Man Among Scorpions*, his study of the novelist and philosopher Stanisław Brzozowski, Miłosz paraphrased Brzozowski's analysis of what this had done to the intellectual life of Poland:

> According to him the anti-Russian complex sterilized the Poles intellectually and artistically, since it veiled from them the truth about the human condition. As a result, all the evil and suffering with which the human species had to contend was projected by them into a single, limited geographical frame of reference—in other words, blamed upon Russia. The more Russia assumed the shape of a monster, of an emanation of Hell responsible for all evil, the more accentuated was the illusory idea of the angelic nature of man. . . . This Polish reluctance to face the tragic element in life was loathsome to Brzozowski, who built his entire philosophy on the self-reliance of man in the face of the ahuman, in the face of chaos. Man was only that which he wins in the struggle . . . and this struggle *is* tragic, for in it values are not guaranteed, but must be continually created, through an existential act which postulates itself. It is for this reason that Brzozowski utters judgments so unflattering to the Polish sensibility. "The Polish sacrifice, which takes the place of all accepted forms, is but a desperate attempt to create instantly what must be created incessantly."

The problem this impulse to martyrdom created for writers in the underground was practical. In *The Captive Mind*, Miłosz looks at the case of his friend Jerzy Andrzejewski, author of *Ashes and Diamonds*. Andrzejewski had begun his career as an admirer of Bernanos and Conrad, and fashioned his first novel from their themes. In his stories of the occupied city, the earlier, Catholic sense of fidelity to moral principle in a tragic universe fell away, but the themes of courage and loyalty persisted. "When his dying heroes turned their eyes toward a mute heaven, they could find nothing there; they could only hope that their loyalty was not completely meaningless and that, in spite of everything, something in the universe responded to it."

A political crisis developed in the underground about 1943. Every day more young people were dying in the resistance, more Jews being deported. But it was also becoming clear that the German army had overextended itself. This made the question of what one died for more acute. The resistance, which had looked mainly to the moment, began to debate more earnestly the political shape of the future. One alternative was represented by the government-in-exile. For most intellectuals, that meant the Poland of the past, parliamentarianism, capitalism, nationalism, Catholicism, anti-Semitism. The Nazis had already demonstrated the final logic of nationalist politics. The other alternative was communism, not because the communists were strong among the various radical groups in Poland, but because it seemed most likely that the Red Army would liberate the country. In any case, the question of what one died for became practical. Or so it seemed when, suddenly, the signal for the uprising was given. The insurgents were armed with pistols, grenades, benzine bottles. The Soviet Army, just across the river, did not intervene on behalf of the Poles. Whether they could have done so is now a matter of historical debate, except in Poland where it is believed that the Russians gave false signals and then held back. They had nothing to lose by letting the resistance army of a country on which they had designs destroy itself. After sixty-three days and two hundred thousand deaths, the city was razed.

Miłosz gives this portrait of the aftermath. Andrzejewski is identified here as Alpha:

> Alpha, walking with me over the ruins of Warsaw, felt, as did all those who survived, one dominant emotion: anger. Many of his close friends lay in the shallow graves which abounded in that lunar landscape. The twenty-year-old poet Christopher, a thin asthmatic, physically no stronger than Marcel Proust, had died at his post sniping at SS tanks. With him the greatest hope of Polish poetry perished. His wife Barbara was wounded and died in a hospital, grasping a manuscript of her husband's verses in her hand. The poet Karol, son of the workers' quarter and author of a play about Homer, together with his inseparable comrade Marek, were blown up on a barricade the Germans dynamited. Alpha

knew, also, that the person he loved most in life had been deported to the concentration camp at Ravensbruck after the suppression of the uprising. He waited for her long after the end of the war until he finally had to accept the idea that she was no longer alive. His anger was directed against (those who had brought on the disaster), that terrible example of what happens when blind loyalty encounters the necessities of History. Just as his Catholic words had once rung false to him, so now his ethic of loyalty seemed a pretty but hollow concept.

Actually, Alpha was one of those who were responsible for what had happened. Could he not see the eyes of the young people gazing at him as he read his stories in clandestine authors' evenings? These were the young people who had died in the uprising: Lieutenant Zbyszek, Christopher, Barbara, Karol, Marek, and thousands like them. They had known there was no hope of victory and that their death was no more than a gesture in the face of an indifferent world. They had died without even asking whether there was some scale in which their deeds would be weighed. . . .

This is the context of "Dedication" and these are the people whom the poet addresses:

You whom I could not save
Listen to me
Try to understand this simple speech . . .

It is shocking, perhaps, that this judgment of the dead is harsh:

You mixed up farewell to an epoch with the beginning of a new
one.
Inspiration of hatred with lyrical beauty.
Blind force with accomplished shape.

Here is a valley of shallow Polish rivers. And an immense bridge
Going into white fog. Here is a broken city,

And the wind throws screams of gulls on your grave
As I am speaking with you.

Compare this to Yeats' elegy for the dead of the Easter Rebellion. The cases are different but similar enough to warrant the comparison, especially since Yeats believed—on very poor evidence—that England might grant independence to Ireland without being compelled to do so, and that the deaths on Easter Sunday in 1916 were unnecessary:

Hearts with one purpose alone
Through summer and winter seem
Enchanted to a stone
To trouble the living stream.

For Yeats, with his love of transformation, of the monumental, the martyrs, right or wrong, have become a monument. For Miłosz, it is the river that has survived and the white gulls and the fog. And it is clear that his judgment is not simply political. The young insurgents had made, for him, the mistake of confusing the historic and the lyrical, what belongs to time and what belongs to transcendence. And if Yeats' poem is deeply committed to the transformation of life, Miłosz's is committed to life itself, to the river and not to the gesture.

This is the burden of what he tells himself about poetry in the following stanza:

They used to pour on graves millet or poppy seeds
To feed the dead who would come disguised as birds.
I put this book here for you, who once lived
So that you should visit us no more.

It is not hard to see how the moralist of my mythologizing might have emerged from "Dedication," but the commitment that poem implies is, it seems to me, exactly contrary to

Miłosz's gifts as a poet. He had also written: "What strengthened me for you was lethal." And it is true. In "The World," in "Voices of Poor People," he had found himself as a poet, but a complicated and many-sided one. In the next few years, he was not allowed leisure to contemplate this problem, because his life then came to a crisis. It seems odd to say that the years of the occupation were not a crisis, but one can imagine the ways in which they weren't. The problem was survival. He was in the capital city, he had met his future wife, there was work to be done, and the face of the enemy was reasonably clear. Since all publication was forbidden, all writing was clandestine. There were no censors and so, for writers, no compromises to be made at the heart of their work. As to the People's Government of Poland, one could give oneself to it, with whatever reservations, if one was a progressive. Poland, after all, had to be rebuilt. It was when the political pressure of the new government on writers began to be felt that the moral crisis for Miłosz came.

3 /

The Captive Mind, 1953 (essays)
Seizure of Power, 1953 (novel)
Daylight, 1955 (poems)
The Issa Valley, 1955 (novel)
A Treatise on Poetry, 1957 (poem)
Native Realm, 1958 (autobiography)
Continents, 1958 (essays & translations)
Simone Weil, *Selected Works*, ed. & trans. Miłosz, 1958
plus four other volumes of translations

The work of this period is extraordinary in its variety and intensity of experience. The poems of the immediate postwar period, or what we have of them in English, "Mid-Twentieth Century Portrait," "Child of Europe," "The Spirit of the Laws," (only seven of the forty poems in *Daylight* have been translated), are the work of an ironist and moralist. "Mid-Twentieth Century Portrait" casts a cold eye on the scramble of intellectuals to appear politically correct for the new social order:

> Keeping one hand on Marx's writings, he reads the Bible in
>   private.
> His mocking eye on processions leaving burnt-out churches.
> His backdrop: a horseflesh-colored city in ruins.
> In his hand: a memento of a boy "Fascist" killed in the Uprising.

"Child of Europe" observes with bitter irony how conveniently the doctrine of historical necessity assuages survivor guilt:

> He who invokes history is always secure.
> The dead will not rise to witness against him.
>
> You can accuse them of any deed you like.
> Their reply will always be silence.

But, as admirable as this work may be, or, to use the poet's phrase, as "salutary," it is not where the sources of his poetry lay. It is hard even to make an intelligent guess about the poems of this period, since so few are available in English, but if "Greek Portrait" is any example, Miłosz had already, by 1948, when it was written, begun to feel the sting of censorship. It is the only poem of his I have seen that sounds like it was written by a Russian who had the habit of keeping one eye on his readers and one eye on the censor. The poem was written in Washington, D.C., where he was serving as a cultural attaché to the Polish government:

> My beard is thick, my eyelids half cover
> My eyes, as with those who know the value

Of visible things. I keep quiet as is proper
For a man who has learned that the human heart
Holds more than speech does. I have left behind
My native land, home and public office.
Not that I looked for profit or adventure.
I am no foreigner on board a ship.
My plain face, the face of a tax-collector,
Merchant, or soldier, makes me one of the crowd.
Nor do I refuse to pay due homage
To local gods. And I eat what others eat.
This much will suffice about myself.

He broke with the government in 1951 in Paris. The account of those years is in the prose that he wrote just afterward. But a great deal about it is implied by the steely bitterness of these poems. What seems clear about his decision is not only that he refused to be censored, or that he had watched his friends become the careerists and cynics that "Mid-Twentieth Century Portrait" had envisioned, but that philosophical Marxism which he was being asked to swallow whole touched his own deepest obsessions and that the Marxism-in-practice to which he was lending his support as a minor bureaucrat was in the process of erasing Lithuania from the map. For him, the two issues were intimately related. "The problem of the Baltics," he wrote in 1953 to underscore this point, "is much more important for every contemporary poet than are questions of style, metrics, and metaphor."

The first sentence of *The Captive Mind*—with its innocent chronicler's tone—reads: "It was only toward the middle of the twentieth century that the inhabitants of many European countries came, in general unpleasantly, to the realization that their fate could be influenced directly by intricate and abstruse books of philosophy." The philosophy he had in mind was not that of Marx and Engels, but the dialectical materialism of the mid-twentieth century which identified history, time, necessity and nature with the path of Eastern European socialism. Miłosz had had a Roman Catholic education. At the center of Christian thought in the West is the idea, or metaphor, of incarnation: through Christ, the divine had entered the world and created a bridge between matter and spirit, time and timelessness. The world was good and man could, therefore, approach the divine through the intermediary of the senses. It was possible for the mind of man to discern moral laws that underlie the universe, adapt itself to them and transcend time.

This training was to give him a particular view of dialectical materialism, for it seemed clear to him that its genius lay in taking the moral laws of earlier Western thought out of their heaven and locating them firmly in time. For him, the humanist thought of the Enlightenment which passed through Hegel and Engels and Marx in the nineteenth century and invented, in the twentieth, a history, time and nature bent only to the liberation of man was not a break with this species of Christian theology but its natural extension. And this view had an obvious appeal in a world that had been razed to the ground and for a people so long powerless to act on their own fate. It meant that you could rebuild, in time, in nature, on the tip of the wave of historical necessity, the world toward which history was tending. Hadn't he written in 1934: "Man is given to the earth only, let him desire no other." The truth was that a large part of Miłosz's nature would have made a very good materialist poet, a Pablo Neruda praising socks, cats and lemons, dying and being born.

But there was, as we have seen, that antinomy in his sense of the world between time and the lived, individual moment, absolute and perishable. How do you celebrate time, even if it is moving toward human liberation, when so much is lost along the way? What do you say about this or that moment of being if the future looks to you not like a wide road but a ravenous maw? An excellent example was still vivid in his memory. The official attitude taken toward the two hundred thousand dead of the Home Army was that they were nationalists and reactionaries, not much different from the fascists they fought against. Hadn't Miłosz himself written: "You mixed up farewell to an epoch with the beginning of a new one." He had, but he had also experienced, with that sense of amazement that became one of the permanent themes of his poetry, moments of being, of his own being, in the middle of the carnage, that made all time, nature, history a grotesque and inexplicable joke:

With disbelief I touch the cold marble,
with disbelief I touch my own hand.
It—is, and I—am, in living changeableness
while they are locked forever and ever
in their last word, their last glance,
as remote as the Emperor Valentinian
or the chiefs of the Massagetes, about whom I know nothing,
though hardly one year has passed, or two or three.

I may still cut trees in the woods of the far North,
I may speak from a platform or shoot a film
using techniques they never heard of.
I may learn the taste of fruit from ocean islands
and be photographed in an attire from the second half of the
 century
But they are forever like busts in frock coats and jabots
in some monstrous encyclopedia.

And he had had, like the mourning girl in "The Song," intimations of something absolute in that perishable moment, of some being that was not merely the verb *to be* waving from the window of the train on the way to the crematoria:

And yet I was near it so often,
I reached into the heart of metal, the soul of earth, of fire, of water,
And the unknown unveiled its face
as a night reveals itself, serene, mirrored by the tide.

Lustrous copper-leaved gardens greeted me
that disappear as soon as you touch them.

And he had had the impulse, if there was no absolute meaning at the heart of things, to put one there:

And I, with my anchor of pine on the sandy plain,
With the silenced memory of dead friends,
And the silenced memory of towns and rivers,
I was ready to tear out the heart of the earth with a knife
And put there a glowing diamond of shouting and complaints,
I was ready to smear the roots of trees with blood,
To invoke the names on their leaves,
To cover malachite of monuments with the skin of night
And write down in phosphorus Mene Tekel Upharsin
Shining with the traces of melting eyelids.

Perhaps these powerful and conflicting impulses could have been put aside, discounted as fairly abstruse in comparison to a civilization that had to be rebuilt, but there was the matter of the Baltics. In 1949, while he was at the Polish embassy in Washington, Miłosz received a letter from a family deported to Siberia from one of the Baltic states, forwarded to him by their relatives in Poland. They were working on a kolkhoz, a mother and two daughters, and their brief account of their life there was a thinly disguised plea for help. In *The Captive Mind* he meditates on their fate:

Possibly neither the mother nor the daughters were possessed of any particularly fine qualities. The mother went to church on Sundays with a thick prayerbook, but at home she was a stingy shrew. The daughters had nothing on their minds but frippery and the Saturday night dances on the grasses that were so loved in their native province. They read no serious books; the names of Plato and Hegel, Marx and Darwin meant nothing to them. These three women were deported because they were kulaks; their farm had nearly thirty hectares of land. The benefit mankind got out of their quiet life in the country was, aside from a certain number of kilograms of butter and cheese, very little.

The question arises as to whether or not one is allowed to destroy three such creatures in the name of higher ends. The Stalinist will answer that it is allowed. Christians and pseudo-Christians will answer that it is not. Neither the former nor the latter are entirely consistent. Ninety percent of the arguments used by Stalinists in their propaganda are based on man's injury to man. The appeal to moral indignation is always present in their slogans. Christians, on the other hand, maintain that it is wrong to harm others because every man has an inherent value; but having voiced such a noble opinion, many of them would not move a finger to help another person. It is not merely the fate of the Baltic states that leaves them indifferent. They are equally unconcerned about forms of destruction other than slaughter and compulsory deportation. For example, they regard the spiritual death of people condemned to work all day and to swallow the poison of films and television at night as completely normal.

In *Native Realm*, the distinction between Marxist and Catholic attitudes is even more blurred. For the Catholic Church, he had been taught, while it believed that the laws governing the universe could be discerned by man, did not believe all men would discern them. Hence it placed a great deal of importance on obedience and ritual. Miłosz put it this way, describing the Jesuit dialectician of his preparatory school, Hamster:

By going to Mass and receiving the sacraments, we absorb, in spite of ourselves, a certain *style*, which, just as copper is a good conductor of electricity, serves to guide us to the supernatural. Since men are weak, it would be madness to give them free rein, counting on their ability to find union with God on their own regardless of the style of their environment. Rather, one should make that union possible, if only for a few, by mass conditioning. Hamster, while forcing us to take part in rituals, doubtless had

> few illusions. But neither did his predecessors, who converted heretics with the sword.

It takes no special leap of imagination—especially if one has been coached by Dostoevsky's Grand Inquisitor—to see the perpetrators of Stalin's policy in the Baltics as Hamster's heirs.

What is fascinating about this polemic is that Miłosz is so engaged by the historical argument that he is not tempted merely to write off the fate of Lithuania to Russian imperialism, a more Marxist account, in the end, of what really did happen. He is engaged, I think, not only because anyone who lived through the war years would want to make some final sense of that experience, but also because the hunger for something like historical or philosophical detachment was in him from the beginning. The female voice in "The Song" had not only yearned for an imperishable moment, but for a way to stand above it:

> Then they, who live in the lies,
> Like weeds pulled all ways by the bay's wash,
> Would be to me what pine needles are
> To someone who looks at the woods from above, through the
> clouds.

It would be tempting, even soothing, to see the woman and her daughters from a tragic height, laboring and suffering, or imagining they are suffering, on a work farm somewhere beyond the Urals, their complaints, griefs, dreams as vivid, commonplace and repetitive as the chirping of birds. Miłosz would, in fact, in the next of his incarnations, encounter a poet with just such a view of the world, the Californian Robinson Jeffers, and he would say to him, as if he were saying it to himself:

> Better to carve suns and moons on the joints of crosses
> as was done in my district. To give feminine names

to the birches and firs. To implore protection
against mute and treacherous power
than to proclaim, as you did, an inhuman thing.

So it would seem that, in confronting the idea of historical necessity, he was also forced to confront its prehistory in Western thought and to struggle with the temptation to free himself from the tormenting idea of human suffering by identifying with a detached and tragic perspective. He had discovered, in this struggle, a cruel streak of egotism in the human desire for transcendence.

Many layers, in short, of his own imagination were engaged in his argument with dialectical materialism in Poland. In electing for exile, he had not only rejected the government of his country, he had come to the verge of rejecting the central vision of reality in Western culture. And, in rejecting that vision, he had not really chosen one. Or if he had, it was the one that appeared in the least complicated, most simply lyric moments in his poems. Because the whole edifice of these ratiocinations was based on his intimations of the absolute value of being and his refusal to give them up to anything—a theology of relative good, a just state at the end of history, the tragic exaltation of poetry. The next irony must have greeted him here. Cut off from his language and his audience, having offended both the literary left in Europe and the orthodox Catholic crusaders against Communism spawned by the Cold War, he found himself buried in the polemics of philosophy, memoir, essay, poetic treatise, novels, and the sibilant ironies of a poetry written by a minor embassy official in the middle of the night by the glowing electric lights of a large, innocent, half-barbarous country, given over, heart and soul, to Packards, Frigidaires, and the seemingly eternal Saturday afternoons of *l'homme moyen sensuel.* He had isolated himself almost completely in order to defend the central impulse of his poetry, but he had no guarantee that that impulse would be available to him again. What there is in *Day-*

light, at the very end, is a sort of prayer for its return, written in a Switzerland peaceful enough to suggest that another kind of life were possible:

> Wine sleeps in casks of Rhine oak.
> I am wakened by the bell of a chapel in the vineyards
> Of Mittelbergheim. I hear a small spring
> Trickling into a well in the yard, a clatter
> Of sabots in the street. . . .
>
> Fire, power, might, you who hold me
> In the palm of your hand whose furrows
> Are like immense gorges combed
> By southern wind. You who grant certainty
> In the hour of fear, in the week of doubt,
> It is too early, let the wine mature,
> Let the travelers sleep in Mittelbergheim.

4 /

It is in the work that emerges from the last years in France and the first years in California, I think, that Miłosz's poetry comes to its full power. It can be traced in the poems available in English: "No More," 1957; "King Popiel" and "Magpiety," 1958; "What Once Was Great," "The Master," "Album of Dreams," 1959; "What Does It Mean," "Heraclitus," and "The Chronicles of Pornic," 1960; "Should, Should Not," "Throughout Our Lands," 1961; "Bobo's Metamorphosis," 1962. And the path leads through the edition of Simone Weil's writings that he prepared in Polish in 1958. In that year, in *Native Realm*, speaking of the philosopher whom he nicknames Tiger, he characterizes his state of mind in this way: "In America, the contradiction inclined me toward *movement*, while in Paris, through my conversations with Tiger, it drove me back to *being*, and I tried to diagnose my case. Whoever commits himself to movement alone will destroy himself. Whoever disregards movement will also destroy himself, but in a different way. This, I said to myself, is the very core of my destiny—never to be satisfied with one or the other, only at moments to seize the unity of these opposites." Which explains very well why he would also seize on Weil's lucid and tormented prose.

"There is a contradiction," he says in the essay which prefaces his edition,

> between our longing for the good, and the cold universe absolutely indifferent to any values, subject to the iron necessity of cause and effect. That contradiction has been solved by the rationalists and progressives of various kinds who placed the good in this world, in matter, and usually in the future. The philosophy of Hegel and of his followers crowned those attempts by inventing the idea of the good in movement, walking toward fuller and fuller accomplishment in history. Simone Weil, a staunch determinist (in this respect she was not unlike Spinoza), combated such solutions as illegitimate. *Her efforts were directed toward making the contradiction as acute as possible.* Whoever tries to escape an inevitable contradiction by patching it up, is, she affirms, a coward. That is why she has been accused of having been too rigid and of having lacked a dialectical touch. Yet one can ask whether she was not more dialectical than many who practice the dialectical art by changing it into an art of compromises and who buy the unity of opposites too cheaply.

King Popiel, 1962 (poems)
Man Among Scorpions, 1962 (literary criticism)
Bobo's Metamorphosis, 1964 (poems)
Post-War Polish Poetry, 1965 (English translations)
Poems, 1967
City Without a Name, 1969 (poems)
Visions from San Francisco Bay, 1969 (essays)
The History of Polish Literature, 1969 (textbook, in English)

Weil, who taught philosophy briefly, was a student of Marx and she counted him among the liberators. She had only one serious criticism of him, and that was his undialectical supposition that the struggle for justice would ever end. Her own analysis of class struggle is clearly appealing to Miłosz. She believed that primitive man was oppressed by the forces of nature and only freed himself by the introduction of technical inventions, the division of labor and the organization of production. A community was able to control its environment only by introducing social controls, the division of society into those who order and those who obey. Thus, technical civilization, in freeing itself from nature, created a second mirrored nature in society itself. In Miłosz's formulation: "Oppression of man by man grows proportionally to the increase of his realm of action; it seems to be its necessary price. Facing nature, the member of a technical civilization holds the position of a god, but he is a slave of society." The need to resist oppressive power is, for her, continuous. To introduce a vision of a kingdom free from necessity into this world, though its emotional appeal could be a weapon in the hands of a revolutionary struggle, in the long run placed a more terrible weapon in the hands of any ruling elite, because they could do anything in its name and they had the force to do it. For Weil, man had been given a vision of freedom, but he lived in the kingdom of necessity. "Contradiction," she wrote, "is a lever of transcendence."

In his essay on her work, Miłosz mentions the point at which he parts company with Weil. He calls himself a Caliban to her Ariel; but he might have said that, unlike the young philosopher with her passionate asceticism, the author of *The Issa Valley* had taken eros as one of his teachers. But what Weil gave him, I think, was crucial: the permission to dwell in contradiction. And once that happened, eros—in the form of dream, memory, landscape—comes flooding back into his work. There is already a discernible relaxation in the wonderfully visualized "No More" (just how ironic is that poem?) and in the calm amusement with which he discovers in "Magpiety" that the oldest and most schoolmasterly dispute in Western philosophy underlies his hunger to possess the world through language. But what Miłosz needed in order to lay aside the polemics of the nineteen-fifties and to explore the suggestions of Simone Weil was a more ample form than the individual lyric, and he seems to have found it first in "Album of Dreams."

The form is a dream-journal with dated entries. The setting of the first entry can be identified by a detail. During the war, Miłosz, like many writers in Warsaw, worried about the survival of his manuscripts. This concern has been condensed in the manner of dream imagery to a plastic tape; and that artifact suggests one of the themes of the poem: the redemption of time.

> Did I mistake the house or the street
> or perhaps the staircase, though, once, I had been there every
> day?
> I looked through the keyhole. A kitchen: the same and not the
> same.
> And I carried, wound on a reel,
> a plastic tape narrow as a shoelace,
> that was everything I had written over the long years.
> I rang, uncertain whether I would hear that name.
> She stood before me in her saffron dress,
> unchanged, greeting me with a smile and without one tear of time.
> And in the morning chickadees were singing in the cedar.

And against this vision, another:

> They ordered us to pack our things, as the house was to be
> burned down.
> There was time to write a letter, but that letter was already with
> me.
> We laid down our bundles and sat against the wall.

They looked when we placed a violin on the top.
My little sons did not cry. Gravity and curiosity.
One of the soldiers brought a can of gasoline. Others were tearing
down curtains.

And against both of these, this more ambivalent image:

The halls of the infernal station, drafty, cold.
A knock at the door, the door opens
and my dead father appears in the doorway
but he is young, handsome, beloved.
He offers me his hand. I run away from him
down a spiral staircase, never-ending.

To dwell in contradiction: there is a freedom in the movement of this poem, in its collage of clashing elements (in one dream he joins Walt Whitman, outside a manor house owned by Emanuel Swedenborg, in a "dance of happy Hassidim"), that recalls his poems of the thirties. This one ends with a Buñuel- or Magritte-like marriage of the Wasteland to eros and time:

Our expedition rode into a land of dry lava.
Under us, perhaps, armor and crowns
but here there was not a tree,
not even lichen growing on the rocks,
and in the birdless sky, racing through filmy clouds,
the sun went down among masses of solid black.

Then slowly, in that complete stillness
not even the rustle of a lizard disturbed,
we heard gravel crunch under the truck wheels
and saw, suddenly, standing on a hill
a pink corset with fluttering ribbons.
Further on, a second and a third. So, baring our heads,
we walked toward them, temples in ruins.

By 1961 Miłosz had arrived in California, duly unimpressed by that dry Western landscape, but the event—or the place itself—seems to have increased his wonder at the sheer strangeness of time and he found a form to explore it in the loose, numbered sequences of one of the native poets. "Throughout Our Lands" begins:

> When I pass'd through a populous city
> (As Walt Whitman says, in the Polish version)
> when I pass'd through a populous city,
> for instance near San Francisco harbor, counting gulls,
> I thought that between men, women, and children there is
> something, neither happiness nor unhappiness.

It contains this little summa:

> If I had to tell what the world is for me
> I would take a hamster or a hedgehog or a mole
> and place him in a theater seat one evening
> and, bringing my ear close to his humid snout,
> would listen to what he says about the spotlights,
> the sounds of the music and the movements of the dance.

And this haunting poem about time and being and language:

> And the word revealed out of the darkness was *pear.*
> I hovered around it, hopping or trying my wings.
> But whenever I was just about to drink its sweetness, it withdrew.
> So I tried *Anjou*—then a gardener's corner,
> white paint scaling on wooden shutters,
> a dogwood bush and the rustling of departed people.
> So I tried *Comice*—then right away fields
> beyond this (not any other) palisade, a brook, countryside.
> So I tried Jargonelle. Bosc. Bergamot.
> No good. Between me and pear, equipages, countries.
> And so I have to live, with this spell on me.

The poem ends, appropriately, with a meditation on a wanderer, Cabeza de Vaca, a bookkeeper from Castile who became a god to the Indians of the Southwest and, imprisoned by his role, marched with them on foot from the Mexican Gulf to California. Miłosz imagines his return to civilization:

But afterwards? Who am I, the lace of cuffs
not mine, the table carved with lions not mine, Doña Clara's
fan, the Slipper under her gown—hell, no.
On all fours! On all fours!
Smear our thighs with war paint.
Lick the ground. Wha wha, hu hu.

In an essay in 1971 Miłosz expresses his admiration for Pasternak and his reservations about the Russian poet's carefully cultivated irrationalism. "He did not pluck fruits from the tree of reason, the tree of life was enough for him. Confronted by argument, he replied with a sacred dance." In many of these poems Miłosz seems tempted by the dance himself. But then, in the poems, he seems tempted by everything. The intoxications of Pasternak consort with the sobriety of Weil and coupled to them are surreal shifts of imagination and a sense of historical irony entirely Miłosz's own. In poem after poem—there is an immense formal variety, verse and prose, free verse and metrical verse, dithyramb, rondel, quotation, documentation—he tries to fashion out of his many interior voices Weil's lever of transcendence. The poems, "The Chronicles of the Town of Pornic" (four of its sections have been translated), "Bobo's Metamorphosis," "City Without a Name" (not translated), "With Trumpets and Zithers," "From the Rising of the Sun" (one long section of which has been—unfortunately—omitted from the English version), and the recent "Separate Notebooks," for all their range, comedy, torment, are surprisingly faithful to his central preoccupation: whether one should try to rescue being from the river of time by contemplating or embracing it.

Private Obligations, 1972 (essays)
Selected Poems, 1973 (earlier poems in English translation)
Where the Sun Rises, 1974 (poems)
The Land of Ulro, 1977 (essays)
Emperor of the Earth, 1977 (a selection of essays in English)
Bells in Winter, 1978 (later poems in English translation)
Collected Poems, 1981

Shape-shifting is the formal characteristic of these poems and, very often, metamorphosis is their theme. Miłosz requires the open forms not just to express a collage of different attitudes toward experience, but for the rather startling shifts in scale and perspective. Desire, in writing, is very often a matter of scale, and the riddle is the old one, whether one possesses being in desire or cessation of desire. In "Bobo's Metamorphosis," there is the mute up-close of sexuality:

> I was entering the interior of the lily on a bridge of brocade.

And a Swiftian revision of that perspective:

> Bobo, a nasty boy, was changed into a fly.
> In accordance with the rites of flies he washed himself by a rock
> of sugar
> And ran vertically into caves of cheese.

There is the extreme distance of the prophet and the fatalist in "From the Rising of the Sun":

> If the wax in our ears could melt, a moth on pine needles,
> A beetle half-eaten by a bird, a wounded lizard,
> Would all lie at the center of the expanding circles
> Of their vibrating agony. That piercing sound
> Would drown out the loud shots of bursting seeds and buds

And our child who gathers wild strawberries in a basket
Would not hear the trilling, nice after all, of the thrush.

And the bewildered, slightly distanced tenderness of "With Trumpets and Zithers":

The gift was never named. We lived and overhead stood a hot
light, created.
Castles on rocky spurs, herbs in river valleys, descents into the
bays under ash trees.
All past wars in the flesh, all loves, conch shells of the Celts,
Norman boats by the cliffs.
Breathing in, breathing out, o Elysium, we would kneel and kiss
the earth.

This shape-shifting, the many voices, times, places that speak through him, the incessant questioning of where to stand, how to see, what to say, induce a kind of ontological vertigo, a deep feeling of dread and wonder at being alive, and there is very little comfort in it, and no resolution.

The reason why these poems refuse to resolve themselves we have already glimpsed: Miłosz is reluctant to grant that power to poetry. There are many places, as one reads through it, where one feels the work might have rested. In the second of "The Separate Notebooks," for example, he invokes this passage from Schopenhauer:

> . . . the quiet contemplation of the natural object actually present, whether a landscape, a tree, a mountain or a building, whatever it may be; in as much as he loses himself in this object, i.e., forgets even his individuality, his will, and only continues to exist as the pure subject, the clear mirror of the object, so that it is as if the object alone were there, without anyone to perceive it, and he can no longer separate the perceiver from the perception but both have become one, because the whole consciousness is filled and occupied with one single sensuous picture; if thus the object has

> to such an extent passed out of all relation to the will, then that which is known is no longer the particular thing as such; but it is the *Idea*, the eternal form, the objectivity of the will at this grade; and, therefore, he who is sunk in this perception is no longer individual, for in such perception the individual has lost himself; but he is pure, will-less, powerless, timeless subject of knowledge.

One can imagine, granted the heavy weather of German philosophy in translation, resting in this vision. It is rather like the vision of "The last voices" in "The Song" and seems akin, too, to the vision of certain American poems, passages in "Little Gidding" or "The Palm at the End of the Mind." But Miłosz no sooner invokes it than he answers it with a lyric, one of his purest and most moving, addressed to the writer by a woman, a former lover, who is long dead:

> You talked, but after your talking all the rest remains.
> After your talking—poets, philosophers, contrivers of romances—
> Everything else, all the rest deduced inside the flesh
> Which lives and knows, not just what is permitted.
>
> I am a woman held fast now in the great silence.
> Not all creatures have your need for words.
> Birds you killed, fish you tossed into your boat:
> In what words will they find rest and in what Heaven?
>
> You received gifts from me; they were accepted.
> But you don't understand how to think about the dead.
> The smell of winter apples, of hoarfrost, and of linen.
> There are nothing but gifts on this poor, poor Earth.

And the poem will not rest here either; it is pulled on, to the next subject, under the imperative of the need to suffer multiplicity of being, which is finally what is meant I think by dwelling in contradiction.

5 /

I had first been drawn to Miłosz because I thought of him as a poet afflicted by large and desperate questions, and that intuition had certainly been accurate. But what I came to love about his work is that he is an erotic poet, and a poet of great inclusiveness, that he includes a great deal without any loss of emotional intensity, of lyric poetry's steady attention to the circular dance of being and suffering; and that is the source of the painfulness of his poems. Erotic poetry, like erotic experience, is usually intense because it is narrow and specific, mute and focused. What seems to happen to Miłosz is that, as the focus widens through a terrible and uncompromising love of his own vanished experience, the poetry, refusing to sacrifice the least sharpness of individual detail to that wider vision, makes a visceral leap into dualism or gnosticism, which brings us back to his attraction to Simone Weil.

One way to come at this is through the philosophical traditions of the Gnostics themselves. They had devised elegant demonstrations that creation was evil. Like this: evil is the absence of a good; since everything in the material universe is relative—hot is the absence of cold, salt the absence of sweet, sour, bitter—then everything is evil. Limitation itself is the evil of existence. Very few Cathar texts survived the destruction of this great religion of medieval Europe; one of them is a fragment of a sermon: "If the world were not evil in itself, every choice would not constitute a loss." For everything that is, there is something that cannot be. Charles Darwin, at the end of the nineteenth century, had written a history of matter based on this insight which had made it seem a source of hope. For the Cathars, in the twelfth, it meant that time and matter were a prison. To dwell in them, to see the world through them, was evil; to claim them as reality and to claim to be a master of that reality was the devil's work.

But Miłosz's approach to this problem was not logical and he had other teachers besides old books. It is useful to look again at his resistance to Stalinism and to the orthodox Catholic psychology of his childhood. Both Catholics and Marxists admitted to a sorting out of being. This wheat is good, this bad. This man sinned, that one didn't. This tendency is progressive, that one is reactionary. Imagine a child, having been told—by men who seemed to get a certain magisterial pleasure from the telling—that the good will live in bliss forever and the bad will suffer torture beyond the end of time; and imagine him trying to work out a picture of the God who devised this scheme. Then skip a few years and superimpose on that image a government that held its army on the other side of the river in order to let the Nazis dispose of two hundred thousand men and women whose death was inevitable because they did not understand the dialectic of history, and that removed families which had farmed Lithuanian valleys for generations to relocation camps east of the Urals because they had a petit-bourgeois grasp of the land question. One begins to understand the connection between Miłosz's fascination with gnosticism and his loathing for Marxism as he saw it practiced in his own country. If you do not want one grain of sand lost, one moment lost, if you do not admit to the inexorable logic of the death or suffering of a single living creature, then you might, by a leap of intuition, say that it is *all* evil, because then nothing could be judged. Because it all dwelt in limitation or contradiction or, as Blake said, in Ulro. But the universe could be saved if you posited a totally independent but parallel universe of good in which each thing also had an existence. Thus, when the matter-universe fell away, the good universe survived. In the meantime, living in the contingent, limited world of creation, you were, in the Manichean phrase, "a soul torn asunder, divided into fragments, crucified in space."

The poet who, in his public life, refused to become an accomplice of dialectical materialism as it existed in Eastern Europe also refused in the privacy of his vocation as a poet to become an accomplice of time and matter. This is a difficult step for the American imagination to take. "No ideas," Williams said, "but in things." And yet things go, they survive only to the extent that they are not merely things but also somehow eternal beings, more than themselves and more than our idea of them. To praise things, for Miłosz, is to praise the history of suffering; it is to collude with torture and mutilation and decay. This he refuses to do—and finds himself doing in poem after poem in spite of himself. In the end, he is left with the task of those heretical Christians, the pure ones: to suffer time, to contemplate being, and to live in the hope of the redemption of the world.

This is the assertion that emerges at the end of "From the Rising of the Sun":

> Yet I belong to those who believe in *apokatastasis.*
> That word that promises reverse movement,
> Not the one that was set in *katastasis,*
> And appears in the Acts 3, 21.
>
> It means: restoration. So believed St. Gregory of Nyssa,
> Johannes Scotus Erigena, Ruysbroeck and William Blake.
>
> For me, therefore, everything has a double existence.
> Both in time and when time shall be no more . . .

This *is* an assertion, and we have been taught to distrust them in poetry. It is quite extraordinary to look at a poem that tells because it suspects it would be a profanation to try to show, asserts because it is impossible to embody:

> I wanted to describe this, not that, basket of vegetables
> with a redheaded doll of a leek laid across it.
> And a stocking on the arm of a chair, a dress crumpled
> as it was, this way, no other.

I wanted to describe her, no one else, asleep on her belly,
made secure by the warmth of his leg.
Also a cat in the unique tower as purring he composes his
memorable book.

Not ships but one ship with a blue patch in the corner
of its sail.
Not streets, for once there was a street with a shop sign:
Schuhmacher Pupke.
And I tried in vain because what remains is the ever-
recurring basket.
And not she whose skin perhaps I, of all men, loved
but a grammatical form . . .

This is a poet who, after a life unimaginable to many of us, will settle for nothing less than absolute reparation:

It shall come to completion in the sixth millennium, or next
Tuesday.
The demiurge's workshop will be stilled. Unimaginable silence.
And the form of every single grain will be restored in glory.

Some Notes on the San Francisco Bay Area As a Culture Region: A Memoir

One of the women who babysat for me when I was a child was Portuguese. She had lived most of her life in Marin County, but her English was halting. I don't know why she lived in town, whether she was widowed or unmarried. Her name was Marianna Sequieros and her brothers were dairy farmers. They lived a few miles away on their ranch in a old white clapboard house, choked with lilacs when I knew it, with a dilapidated palm tree in the front yard and a half dozen peacocks trailing their tails in the dust. The brothers were selling off their land parcel by parcel to real estate developers, and by the time I was in the eighth grade the newest tract abutted the house itself.

I had just entered an essay contest sponsored by the National Legion for Decency in Motion Pictures. We were supposed to read a book and say why it would make a good movie. My teacher, Sister Reginald, a tall woman who used to play Robert Burns songs for us in music appreciation on rainy days and then sit at her desk dreamily listening and weeping, was very keen on the project. She assigned us each a book to read and made us write an essay. I didn't like the book I read, and with the encouragement of my older brother—for I understood that it was an act of rebellion—I wrote an essay on why it was not a good book and wouldn't make a good movie. I thought it was a vigorous composition and Marianna—though she could not read English, she checked our work when she arrived in the morning to see that it had a look of orderly diligence—examined and approved its appearance. But Sister Reginald did not like it much. She had long beautiful hands which she waved in the air like doves when she conducted us at Mass in the singing of the *Tantum Ergo* and *Pange Lingua* (in the recently rebuilt chapel of the Mission San Rafael, very nearly the last to be founded and built as a hospital because by that time the native Californians were dying of European diseases in great numbers) and, in the silent period, she beckoned me to her desk with a brief movement of her exquisite, tapering fingers. Her face was not beautiful. She was nicknamed The Beak. Face and hands were all we saw of the bodies of the nuns, who were covered otherwise by a whirling mass of white cloth which the Dominican order had worn since it was founded in the twelfth century in Spain and Northern Italy as a kind of papal CIA to root out the gnostic heresy of the Cathars.

I became interested in the Cathars, years later, from reading Robert Duncan. He must have acquired the interest from reading Ezra Pound and he also studied medieval history at Berkeley across the bay under the great historian Kantorowicz. At that moment, I think, he was in New York hanging around the edge of a literary group which had Anaïs Nin at its center and working on the poems in *Caesar's Gate*. A poisonous portrait of the young man can be found in the first volume of Nin's spiderweb of a diary. Duncan's foster parents were theosophists, which also explains his interest in occult lore—it belonged to his world as naturally as singing *Eat, tongue, the body of the mystery* in Latin belonged to mine—and he used that knowledge in *Bending the Bow* to draw an analogy between the American war in Vietnam and the final massacre of the Cathars at Montségur.

One poem lists the names of men and women killed by the crusaders:

At Montségur
that the heart be tried,
Corba de Perella,
Ermengarde d'Ussat,
Guilleline, Bruna, Arssendis,

Guillame de l'Isle,
Raymond de Marciliano,
Raymond-Guillame de Tornabois,
Arnald Domerc,
Arnald Dominique . . .

these among the seventeen
receiving the *consolamentum* to join the two hundred and ten
perfecti
at the field of the fiery martyrs, *Champs de Cramatch*,
until the name of the Roman Church with its heaped honors
stinks with the smell of their meat burning

Also at about this time, a misfit young ad-copy writer, Allen Ginsberg himself, looked out of the window of his Nob Hill apartment at the glowering face of an office building and was given his own *gnosis*, a vision of the very god of money and power:

What sphinx of cement and aluminum bashed open their
skulls and ate up their brains and imagination?
Moloch! Solitude! Filth! Ugliness! Ashcans and unob-
tainable dollars! Children screaming under the
stairways! Boys sobbing in armies! Old men weeping
in the parks!
Moloch! Moloch! Nightmare of Moloch! Moloch the loveless!
Mental Moloch! Moloch the heavy judger of men!

Moloch the incomprehensible prison! Moloch the cross-
 bone soulless jailhouse and Congress of sorrows!
 Moloch whose buildings are judgment! Moloch the
 vast stone of war! Moloch the stunned governments!
Moloch whose mind is pure machinery! Moloch whose blood
 is running money . . .

Reading these passages later would give me one idea of what it was that writing could be faithful to, but just then, Sister Reginald—dressed, I suddenly see, in exactly the style, solidly middle class, sexually modest, of the Cathar women who had been burned alive seven hundred years before—was explaining to me why *Stranded on an Atoll* would make a very educational Walt Disney film—snapping turtles, whole colonies of exotic sea birds, an octopus. She had freckles, Sister Reginald. And, though she was not beautiful, up close I thought her skin was pretty. She must have been younger than I am now, Italian probably, gone straight from a San Francisco high school to the convent—and what a romantic name she had chosen for herself! I found her account of the Walt Disney film completely convincing. I could see it, in Technicolor, the boys running down the reef to get their fish that the turtle was dragging off for himself. She told me I could ignore the regular classwork and rewrite my essay through the afternoon, which I did, and I think I was as much pleased by my rhapsody about the book as I was by my attack on it. I remember that I was able at one point to use the word "sylphin" got from a historical novel by F. Van Wyck Mason, but I also had the feeling that my brother would think I had knuckled under, so at the end of the day I told her that I wanted to take it home and recopy it; in fact I covered it with scrawls and erasures so that I had to recopy it. I wanted to explain to my brother that I had realized what a great movie *Stranded on an Atoll* would make.

He was unconvinced. We had a long conference that night in our upstairs room before pretending to go to sleep and turning on the radio. It was a ritual in our house—which was too disorganized to have very many rituals—that we had to go to bed at 9:45, which was fifteen minutes before our favorite radio show came on. Every night we went downstairs, kissed our parents—or our father, if my mother who was ill a lot wasn't there—goodnight, went upstairs, turned off the light, waited ten minutes, turned on the radio to warm it up, and listened to *I Love a Mystery*. My father knew perfectly well what we were doing and I think he approved. Two of his favorite books were *Penrod* and *Penrod and Sam*, by Booth Tarkington. They are about freckled, charming, disobedient boys from Indiana. I think it amused him that we were upstairs secretly listening to the radio—a Norman Rockwell cover from *The Saturday Evening Post*, which arrived at our house every Tuesday and to whose humor page my brother and I had already submitted poems, neatly written out in pencil. My father could have let us stay up until 10:15—he was at his desk, lodged in the corner of the dining room, writing on long yellow legal pads a book on strategy in contract bridge which was never published—but he didn't, and it taught me an attitude toward the truth I am still trying to unlearn, so that, years later again, when I read the opening lines of Robert Duncan's "In Place of Passage 22" from *Bending the Bow*,

> That Freedom and the Law are identical
> and are the nature of man—

I knew instantly that I couldn't understand what he meant and felt sick to my stomach.

That morning, though, I felt sick to my stomach because I had to walk to school, up D Street to Fifth—San Rafael, a little valley under a hill, was laid out by developers, after the Mission had failed and the Indians scattered, in the grid pattern of American urban development dreamed onto the blank land by Thomas Jefferson's love of land surveying and by economic convenience; the expressions "square deal" and "square meal" emerged, I read somewhere, from those rare speculators who didn't squeeze a few feet off each lot to jam in an extra one at the end; and the arrangement suggested the possibility of infinite expansion, though here it had only got as far as E Street and Fifth Street. Anyway, up those I walked to tell Sister Reginald that I was sticking to my first essay.

The nuns arrived from the convent in a taxicab. That started the day, if one were not serving early Mass for Father O'Meara, who liked plenty of Dry Sémillon in the chalice at six-thirty in the morning. All of the kids I couldn't stand lined up at the curb to greet the sisters and carry their briefcases to the classroom. This day I hovered at their edges, followed Sister Reginald into the classroom, and told her that I wanted to submit my first essay because it was what I really thought, not the second essay which was what she thought. The speech was prepared by my brother and I am ashamed to say that I think it was exactly as real or unreal to me as each of the essays. She heard me out, with chalk in her hand, standing at the desk, and then asked me gently, rather impressively, or at least there was something impressive about her tone, if I understood that I had very little chance of winning a contest having to do with why a book would make a good movie by writing an essay on why a book would make a bad movie. I said that I did, trying to match her tone, but in fact I didn't; she asked me if I would consider adding a sentence to the end of my essay saying that there were many interesting animals in the book and that it might make a good Walt Disney movie. She said it would improve my chances of winning, and I said I would, and I did. It turned out to be two sentences and she made me rewrite them several times.

I won second place in the essay contest. A kid from E Street School won first place with an essay on *Catcher in the Rye*, and it made me resent the public school kids for being allowed to read daring books. My prize was a ten-dollar money order from the Cottage Bookshop. It was presented at a luncheon ceremony in the dining room of the Rancho Rafael Motel. I went to the bookstore—for the first time, I think; it was where, four years later, I would buy Ginsberg's *Howl* because I read in the newspaper that it was a sexual book. But this first time I was at a loss. Out of all the books, which one to buy? I browsed, dizzy. It seemed impossible to choose, to have a basis for choice. In the end, I grabbed a small red book, a Modern Library Classic, entitled *A Comprehensive Anthology of American Poetry*. I chose it, I think, because its title was so clear that I thought I knew exactly what I was getting.

To my disappointment almost everything in the book was incomprehensible to me. But there was one poem I liked. I liked it so much, if "like" is the word, that it made me swoon, and made me understand what the word "swoon" meant. The poem went like this:

At night, by the fire,
The colors of the bushes
And of the fallen leaves,
Repeating themselves,
Turned in the room,
Like the leaves themselves
Turning in the wind.
Yes: but the color of the heavy hemlocks
Came striding
And I remembered the cry of the peacocks.

The colors of their tails
Were like the leaves themselves
Turning in the wind,
In the twilight wind.
They swept over the room,
Just as they flew from the boughs of the hemlocks
Down to the ground.
I heard them cry—the peacocks.
Was it a cry against the twilight

Or against the leaves themselves
Turning in the wind,
Turning as the flames
Turned in the fire,
Turning as the tails of the peacocks
Turned in the loud fire,
Loud as the hemlocks
Full of the cry of the peacocks?
Or was it a cry against the hemlocks?

Out of the window,
I saw how the planets gathered
Like the leaves themselves
Turning in the wind.
I saw how the night came,
Came striding like the color of the heavy hemlocks.
I felt afraid.
And I remembered the cry of the peacocks.

I read it over and over. I read it exactly the way I lined up for a roller-coaster ride with a dime tight in my fist at Playland across the bay in San Francisco. I see certain things about it now. I was full of not very conscious fear for my mother and it filled my days with gusts of childish terror and, obscurely, with a small boy's desire to do good. I suppose it was the acknowledgment of terror, of terror and beauty, in the poem that seemed to so wake me up, or hypnotize me, that I wanted to hold it close. The sensation was physical. It was the first physical sensation of the truthfulness of a thing that I had ever felt. Then, of course, I didn't see anything, or need to. The poem was unambiguously thrilling. A year later, in high school, I went on my first date. To Playland, and rode the roller coaster with a girl from my ninth-grade class who I thought the most beautiful being I had ever come close to in my life, which may also account for something of the previous year's swooning. And, as it happened, when we grew up, I married that girl.

But in the year of the essay contest, I was more interested in baseball than girls. Little League had arrived in Marin County, a small puddle of that organizing energy which seems to characterize nations in their empire phase. I played for a team sponsored by a businessmen's club. My best friend played for a team sponsored by an insurance company. His colors were green and white, mine were purple and gold. We wore our uniforms constantly, OPTIMISTS emblazoned across my chest, CALIFORNIA CASUALTY across his. His father was a Basque who had run away to sea, worked in the galleys of ships, married an Australian woman, and become a chef at a restaurant on Fisherman's Wharf. He, my friend, studied Slavic languages at Berkeley and is now a translator of Miłosz and Gombrowicz, living in Toronto. Sometimes we played games against other towns. When we played against Fairfax, we played at White's Hill School. My position was center field and just in back of it—so that if you hit a home run, it went in their yard—was the ranch house of the Sequieros brothers, completely surrounded by the new school and the tract of suburban houses from which issued every morning the men who took buses to work in the banks and insurance companies of San Francisco.

Playing center field in the late innings that summer, I heard the irritated, prenocturnal cries of the peacocks in the Sequieros brothers' yard. The cry of a peacock sounds like some hardwood being scraped against slate. It is not a pleasant sound, but on those summer evenings in the twilight, the game would be coming to an end, we would be winning or losing, I liked to listen—with a hollow in my stomach and the body of the mystery still to be lived—to the cries of those birds.

I never once associated them with the Wallace Stevens poem. Art hardly ever does seem to come to us at first as something connected to our own world; it always seems, in fact, to announce the existence of another, different one, which is what it shares with gnostic insight. That is why, I suppose, the next thing that artists have to learn is that this world is the other world. A creek ran by the baseball diamond at White's Hill School, just by the third base line. It was called Papermill Creek and it winds through western Marin and empties into the Pacific at Tomales Bay. I read many poems that pleased and startled me after "Domination of Black" but the first one to teach me that there could be an active connection between poetry and my own world was in a book by Kenneth Rexroth. Flipping through it, I came across this:

> Under the second moon the
> Salmon come, up Tomales
> Bay, up Papermill Creek, up
> The narrow gorges to their spawning
> Beds in Devil's Gulch. Although
> I expect them, I walk by the
> Stream and hear them splashing and
> Discover them each year with
> A start. When they are frightened
> They charge the shallows, their immense
> Red and blue bodies thrashing
> Out of the water over
> The cobbles; undisturbed, they
> Lie in pools. The struggling
> Males poise and dart and recoil.
> The females lie quiet, pulsing
> With birth. Soon all of them will
> Be dead, their handsome bodies
> Ragged and putrid, half the flesh
> Battered away by their great
> Lust . . .

Rexroth died this past spring. He was, like Penrod, a bad boy from Indiana. He came to San Francisco in the late 1920s, and in 1941 he published the first readable book of poems ever produced by a resident of the city. There were less than four hundred English speakers in all of California in 1841, so it took about a hundred years for colonization to produce the city that produced the book of poems. There had been earlier writers born here. But all that remains of California in the poems of Robert Frost, though he spent his summers in the Nicasio Valley through which Papermill Creek flowed, was the fear of his father's violence, and that has been transformed into the dark interiors of New England farms. Gertrude Stein took only the genteel provincial culture, imported here like horses, chairs, the machine age, and the English language, which she reacted against. Jack London and Robinson Jeffers, of roughly the same generation as Frost, were the first California writers, with the important exception of John Muir. Rexroth and Steinbeck belong to the second generation.

But *In What Hour*, Rexroth's first book, seems—with its open line, its almost Chinese plainness of syntax, its eye to the wilderness, anarchist politics, its cosmopolitanism, experimentalism, interest in Buddhism as a way of life and Christianity as a system of thought and calendar of the seasons, with its interest in pleasure, its urban and back-country meditations—to have invented the culture of the West Coast. It is a phenomenally fresh and enlivening book to read still; not perfect, and flawed when it is flawed in ways that I find unattractive, but very much alive. None of which mattered to me then. I was stunned by the presence of the creek in a poem. It made it seem possible that the peacocks in Wallace Stevens and the scraggly birds under the palm tree could inhabit the same place and made me think of Kenneth Rexroth with gratitude when I heard that he died. His poem ends like this:

I sit for a long time
In the chilly sunlight by
The pool below my cabin
And think of my own life—so much
Wasted, so much lost, all the
Pain, all the deaths and dead ends,

So very little gained after
It all. Late in the night I
Come down for a drink. I hear
Them rushing at one another
In the dark. The surface of
The pool rocks. The half moon throbs
On the broken water. It is black,
Frosty. Frail blades of ice form
On the edges. In the cold
Night the stream flows away, out
Of the mountains, towards the bay,
Bound on its long recurrent
Cycle from the sky to the sea.

Looking for Rilke

Last fall, in Paris, a friend promised to take me to the café, not far from Rue Monsieur-le-Prince, where Rilke was said to have breakfasted in the early years of the century when he was working as Rodin's secretary. I was glad for the pilgrimage because, of all poets, Rilke is the hardest to locate in a place. He was born a year after Robert Frost, in 1875, a little too soon to be a young modernist, and the dissimilarity between his work and Frost's is so great that the fact does not help to anchor for me a sense of his life. The house where he had lived in Prague as a child cannot be seen; it was destroyed during the war. Besides, Prague—"that, God forgive me, miserable city of subordinate existences," he had written—seemed to explain very little. In his childhood, it was the capital of Bohemia. Rilke's family belonged to the German-speaking minority that formed the city's professional class in those years. He was insulted once to be called a German, and, when the speaker corrected himself, "I meant, Austrian," Rilke said, "Not at all. In 1866 when the Austrians entered Prague, my parents shut their windows." He had a lifelong sense of his own homelessness.

Anyway, Rilke came to hate his native city. His father was a failed army officer who became a petty clerk for the railroad. His mother, a complicated woman, cold and fervent, driven alternately by a hunger for good society and by pious Roman Catholicism, was an affliction to him. There was probably nothing more suffocating than the life of a genteel, aspiring European household of the late nineteenth century in which failure brooded like a boarder who had to be appeased, or like the giant cockroach which was to appear in another Prague apartment in 1915. All his life Rilke carried that suffocation inside him; and it was very much on my mind because I had just been reading Stephen Mitchell's fresh, startlingly Rilkean translations of the poems. Here, finally, was a Rilke in English that would last for many generations. Walking through European cities with Mitchell's Rilke in my ear, trying to see with Rilke's eyes, I could begin to feel in the new downtowns, in the old city squares like stage sets with their baroque churches by the rivers and restored fortresses on the hills, the geography of that suffocation; it flares in the brilliant anger of the *Duino Elegies*—in the Fourth, for example, where the images that the world presents to him seem so much like a bad play that he swears he'd prefer a real puppet theater and imagines himself as a kind of demented critic who refuses to leave the theater until *something* happens:

Who has not sat, afraid, before his heart's
curtain? It rose: the scenery of farewell.
Easy to recognize. The well-known garden,
which swayed a little. Then the dancer came.
Not *him*. Enough! However lightly he moves,
he's costumed, made up—an ordinary man
who hurries home and walks in through the kitchen.
  I won't endure these half-filled human masks;
better, the puppet. It at least is full.
I'll put up with the stuffed skin, the wire, the face
that is nothing but appearance. Here. I'm waiting.
Even if the lights go out; even if someone
tells me, "That's all"; even if emptiness
floats toward me in a gray draft from the stage;
even if not one of my silent ancestors
stays seated with me, not one woman, not
the boy with the immovable brown eye—
I'll sit here anyway. One can always watch.

Or the Tenth, which envisions adult life as an especially tawdry carnival:

> And the shooting-gallery's targets of prettified happiness,
> which jump and kick back with a tinny sound
> when hit by some better marksman. From cheers to chance
> he goes staggering on as booths, with all sorts of attractions
> are wooing, drumming, and bawling. For adults only
> there is something special to see: how money multiplies, naked,
> right there on stage, money's genitals, nothing concealed,
> the whole action—educational, and guaranteed
> to increase your potency . . .

This anger is probably part of the reason why the Elegies took ten years to complete. Rilke seems to have needed, desperately, the feeling of freedom which he found only in open, windy spaces—Duino, Muzot.

Wandering the empty Sunday-morning warren of streets off Boulevard St.-Michel, remembering how passionately Rilke had argued that the life we live every day is not life, I began to feel that looking for him in this way was actively stupid. There was another friend with us, a Dutch journalist named Fred, who was hungry and could not have cared less where Rilke ate breakfast. It was Fred who asked me if I knew the name of the woman who had loaned Rilke a room in Duino Castle. I did. She was Princess Marie von Thurn und Taxis-Hohenlohe. Trying to imagine what it would mean to have a name like that discouraged me from thinking I would ever understand Rilke's social milieu. It signified a whole class of people, seen at a distance like brilliantly colored birds, which had been wiped out by the First World War. Fred was in Paris to interview the Rumanian writer E. M. Cioran, who has been called "the last philosopher in Europe," about the new European peace movement. He pointed out to us the little garret, tucked like a pigeon coop under the roof of a building just off the Place de l'Odéon, where Cioran lives and works, as if he hoped that it would serve as a reasonable substitute, or would at least drag us back to the present. For it was clear that my friend Richard was also looking for something that the memory of his student days in Paris had stirred in him. He had lost some map in his head and felt personally anxious to retrieve it.

And it was clear that he wasn't going to find it. The transience of our most vivid experience is the burden of another of Rilke's complaints, the one in the Second Elegy where he compares humans with angels:

> But we, when moved by deep feeling, evaporate; we
> breathe ourselves out and away; from moment to moment
> our emotion grows fainter, like a perfume. Though someone
> may tell us:
> "Yes, you've entered my bloodstream, the room, the whole
> springtime
> is filled with you . . ."—what does it matter? he can't contain us,
> we vanish inside him and around him. And those who are
> beautiful,
> oh who can retain them? Appearance ceaselessly rises
> in their face, and is gone. Like dew from the morning grass,
> what is ours floats into the air, like steam from a dish
> of hot food. O smile, where are you going? O upturned glance:
> new warm receding wave on the sea of the heart . . .
> alas, but that is what we *are*. Does the infinite space
> we dissolve into, taste of us then?

We abandoned the search, standing in front of a bar called King Kong, where Richard may have had breakfast in a former life of the establishment twenty years before and Rilke fifty years before that. The morning had begun to warm up, and the streets filled with people. Like many other young artists at the turn of the century, Rilke was drawn to Paris, and there, under the tutelage of Rodin, he began to be a great writer in the poems of *Neue Gedichte*, but he didn't altogether like the city, either its poverty or its glamour, both of which shocked him at first and saddened him later. It was hard, watching the street come alive with shopkeepers, students in long scarves, professors in sleek jackets solemnly lecturing companions of the previous night who walked shivering beside them, shoppers already out and armed with that French look of fanatic skepticism, not to set beside the scene the annihilating glimpse of the city in the Fifth Elegy:

> Squares, oh square in Paris, infinite showplace
> where the milliner Madame Lamort
> twists and winds the restless paths of the earth,
> those endless ribbons, and, from them, designs
> new bows, frills, flowers, ruffles, artificial fruits—, all
> falsely colored, —for the cheap
> winter bonnets of Fate.

The *Duino Elegies* are an argument against our lived, ordinary lives. And it is not surprising that they are. Rilke's special gift as a poet is that he does not seem to speak from the middle of life, that he is always calling us away from it. His poems have the feeling of being written from a great depth in himself. What makes them so seductive is that they also speak to the reader so intimately. They seem whispered or crooned into our inmost ear, insinuating us toward the same depth in ourselves. The effect can be hypnotic. When Rilke was dying in 1926—of a rare and particularly agonizing blood disease—he received a letter from the young Russian poet Marina Tsvetaeva. "You are not the poet I love most," she wrote to him. " 'Most' already implies comparison. You are poetry itself." And one knows that this is not hyperbole. That voice of Rilke's poems, calling us out of ourselves, or calling us into the deepest places in ourselves, is very near to what people mean by poetry. It is also what makes him difficult to read thoughtfully. He induces a kind of trance, as soon as the whispering begins:

Yes—the springtimes needed you. Often a star
was waiting for you to notice it. A wave rolled toward you
out of the distant past, or as you walked
under an open window, a violin
yielded itself to your hearing. All this was mission.
But could you accomplish it? Weren't you always
distracted by expectation, as if every event
announced a beloved? (Where can you find a place
to keep her, with all the huge strange thoughts inside you
going and coming and often staying all night.)

Look at how he bores into us. That caressing voice seems to be speaking to the solitary walker in each of us who is moved by springtimes, stars, oceans, the sound of music. And then he reminds us that those things touch off in us a deeper longing. First, there is the surprising statement that the world is a mission, and the more surprising question about our fitness for it. Then, with another question, he brings us to his intimacy with our deeper hunger. And then he goes below that, to the still more solitary self with its huge strange thoughts. It is as if he were peeling off layers of the apparent richness of the self, arguing us back to the poverty of a great, raw, objectless longing.

This is why the argument of the Elegies is against ordinary life. Nor does it admit, as comfort, any easy idea of transcendence. "Who, if I cried out," the poems begin, "would hear me among the angels' hierarchies?" And the implicit answer is "No one." The great, stormy movements of those poems that seem to open out and open out really aim to close in, to narrow, to limit: to bring us up against the huge nakedness and poverty of human longing. He himself did not necessarily see this project of his art clearly. The Elegies were begun in 1912 and he did not complete them until 1922. The last of them, the Fifth, Seventh, Eighth, Ninth and Tenth, were not composed until after he was visited, suddenly, by the early *Sonnets to Orpheus*. In the first of them, he speaks of the mythic project of Orpheus:

And where there had been
just a makeshift hut to receive the music,

a shelter nailed up out of their darkest longing,
with an entryway that shuddered in the wind—
you built a temple deep inside their hearing.

It is that hut I want to call attention to. It is how Rilke saw our unformed inner lives—what he is always telling us about ourselves. He was not, in the end, interested in Paris. There is very little evidence that he was interested in breakfasts (except for one occasion when he first discovered in 1901 a California health food—Quaker Oats—and enthusiastically sent a packet to his future wife, with the recipe—Boil water, add oats). He is always arguing against the world of days and habits, our blurred and blurring desires, "a makeshift hut to receive the music, / a shelter nailed up out of their darkest longing, / with an entryway that shuddered in the wind." This hut is the place one means when one says that Rilke wrote from a great depth in himself, and it is, I believe, what Marina Tsvetaeva meant when she said that Rilke *was* poetry. His work begins and ends with this conviction of an inner emptiness. It is what he says at the very beginning of the Elegies:

Don't you know *yet*? Fling the emptiness out of your arms
into the spaces we breathe; perhaps the birds
will feel the expanded air with more passionate flying.

It even provides a clue to the odd fact that Rilke started writing in French just before his death. The only explanation for it he ever offered was to say that he found the language useful, since there was "in German no exact equivalent for the French word *absence*, in the great positive sense with which Paul Valéry used it." For what Orpheus has done is to turn the hut of our emptiness into something positive, into a temple, and that is also apparently what Rilke felt Valéry had done. The project of his poetry, then, was to find, in art, a way to transform the emptiness, the radical deficiency, of human longing into something else.

•

This project was, to some extent, an inheritance—it recapitulates many currents in European poetry in the nineteenth century. The romantic poets at the beginning of it opened up the territory. Hölderlin spoke of a new poetry, almost overwhelmed by the discovery of an infinite human inwardness. And Wordsworth had said that poets had to give that inwardness a local habitation and a name. It is important to remember that when he said this he was still a political radical, sympathetic to the French Revolution, who believed that the social and artistic projects were parallel, because after the failed European revolutions of 1848, those two projects were divorced. For Baudelaire, nature had become a temple where one only read symbolic meanings, and the poet, like an albatross, was understood to be hopelessly ungainly on the ground of social life and graceful only in the air. Poets trafficked with the infinite. In the work of Mallarmé, this led to a changed notion of poetry itself. As the poet pulled away from the social world the words in a poem pulled away from referential meaning. Poetry was an art near to music. It did not reach down to the mere world of objects. It made a music which lifted the traces of objects where they half survived in the referential meaning of words—street, apple, tree—toward a place where they lived a little in the eternal stillness of the poem. Something like this idea—it went by the name of symbolism—was inherited by the last, decadent or Parnassian, generation of nineteenth-century poets. The poem was to have as little commerce as possible with the middle class; the poet, in his isolation, served only his art, which was itself in the service of beauty.

If there is any doubt that this ambience was felt by the young Rilke, it is dispelled by a description of him in provincial

Prague at the age of twenty-one. "He went about," one of his contemporaries wrote, "wearing an old-world frock coat, black cravat, and broad-brimmed black hat, clasping a long-stemmed iris and smiling, oblivious of the passersby, a forlorn smile into ineffable horizons." His attachment to the role of decadent and aesthete was qualified, however, by his interest in Nietzsche, particularly Nietzsche's Zarathustra, who had given a name to the yearning place that the young poet had already hollowed out in himself: the death of God. And it was Nietzsche who had defined the task of art: God-making. This interest of Rilke's was intensified by one of the important events in his life; he met a remarkable older writer, Lou Andreas-Salomé. She was thirty-four at the time. When she was eighteen, Nietzsche had fallen in love with her and proposed marriage. It was already part of her legend that her refusal of him was responsible for the philosopher's derangement. Later, she would become an associate of Sigmund Freud's. In 1913 she brought Rilke, who was terrified by the idea of mental health, to a Psycho-analytic Congress and introduced him to Freud, an experience which issued in Rilke's own descent into what he called "the mother experience" in the Third Duino Elegy. But in 1899, she took the young poet for a lover and, in that year and the next, accompanied him on a pair of trips to Russia.

His first readable work, the prose *Tales of God* and *The Book of Hours*, comes out of his experience of Russia and Nietzsche and Lou. The poems are written, appropriately enough, in the persona of a young Russian monk. A young monk because that could stand for Rilke's sense of his own apprenticeship and for the God who he felt was only just coming into being. Russian because it was on this trip, in the immense open spaces of the Russian countryside and in the bell-ringing churches of old Moscow, that Rilke first discovered a landscape which he felt corresponded to the size and terror and hushed stillnesses of his own inner life. The poems themselves are a beginning—they already have the qualities of Rilke's mind and imagination, but formally they belong to the dreamy, musical mold of the symbolist lyric. This is a reason why, I think, they sometimes seem more interesting in English translation than they really are. Here is an example. To understand the point I'm trying to make, the reader without German has to attend to it anyway and try reading the poem out loud, noticing the tinkling regularity of the meter and the neat finality of the rhymes, *Abendbrot* and *tot, geht* and *steht*.

Manchmal steht einer auf beim Abendbrot
und geht hinaus und geht und geht und geht,—
weil eine Kirche wo im Osten steht.

Und seine Kinder segnen ihm wie tot.

Und einer, welcher stirbt in seinem Haus,
bleibt drinnen wohnen, bleibt in Tisch und Glas,
so dass die Kinder in die Welt hinaus
zu jener Kirche ziehn, die er vergass.

Here is the poem in the vigorous translation of Robert Bly:

Sometimes a man stands up during supper
and walks outdoors, and keeps on walking,
because of a church that stands somewhere in the East.

And his children say blessings on him as if he were dead.

And another man, who remains inside his own house,
stays there, inside the dishes and in the glasses,
so that his children have to go far out into the world
toward that same church, which he forgot.

Rilke's theme is already present, the abandonment of ordinary life for the sake of a spiritual quest. And so is his intensity.

Robert Bly has muted it, by having the father *stay* rather than *die* in the house, but in either case the poem insists that the spirit will have no rest until the quest is undertaken, which is probably Rilke's understanding of his relationship to his own father. But the poem has a feeling of being too neat, too pat, which disappears, I think, in the English translation, which is a marvelous poem, but one made from the unmetered, unrhymed cadences of a poetic revolution that hadn't occurred yet. A way to hear this might be to look at an English poem on a similar theme. Yeats' "Lake Isle of Innisfree" is a little more luxuriant, but it has the same end-of-the-century music and the same desire to escape:

> I will arise and go now, and go to Innisfree,
> And a small cabin build there, of clay and wattles made:
> Nine bean-rows will I have there, a hive for the honeybee,
> And live alone in the bee-loud glade.

Imagine if you can a translation of this stanza into twentieth-century free verse:

> I'm going to get up now, and go west to Innisfree.
> I'll build a small cabin there out of reeds and clay.
> I'll make nine rows of beans and a hive for honeybees
> and I'll live by myself in that bee-loud valley.

What goes are the wistfulness and the music. They are replaced by a sense of active will and specificity, which aren't really in the original poem.

There is something else to notice in this comparison. In both Yeats and Rilke, the spiritual search or the aim of art does not occur inside life, but somewhere else. For Yeats and his readers, Innisfree could stand for the wild naturalness of the west of Ireland and for Irish nationalism and for the elsewhere of symbolist art. In Rilke's poem, a comfortably symbolic "church in the East" does similar work. It is easy to see, biographically, how potent a symbol it was for him. It combined the experience of Russia, his Nietzschean spiritual strivings, his artistic vocation and his first serious love affair. Heady stuff. But a church in the East is a long way from that tattered hut in the first Sonnet to Orpheus. In order to get there, Rilke had to descend into the terrible and painful sense of his own emptiness, which lay behind the hunger for the ideal. That, finally, is why *The Book of Hours* seems like apprentice work and why it seems so limited by the dexterity and gracefulness of its writing.

Rilke needed to think less about art as visionary recital and more about it as a practice. The next phase of his development gave him a chance to do that. It took him, almost directly upon his return from Russia, to Worpswede, an artists' colony in the fen country near Bremen. The atmosphere combined fresh air, the sensibility of the English arts-and-crafts movement, and landscape painting—it was here that Rilke developed his enthusiasm for Quaker Oats. The place brought him into contact with the plastic arts and with two women who played a large part in his life, the sculptor Clara Westhoff, whom he married, and the painter Paula Modersohn-Becker. The prose that grew out of these associations—"On Landscape," *Worpswede, Auguste Rodin*—deals with the visual arts and lent him both the title and the spirit of his next volume of poems, *The Book of Pictures*. It contains the poems through which many readers of Rilke first discover him. The religious tonality of *The Book of Hours* is gone, replaced by solitude and majestic sadness. These are the poems of invitation, of seductive intimacy, calling us away from ordinary life. *Wer du auch seist*, whoever you are, one of them begins, *am Abend tritt hinaus*, in the evening go outside, *aus deiner Stube*, out of your room, *drin du alles weisst*, where you know everything. The language is clear, calm, only slightly poetic. (The room, for example, is *Stube*, whereas Gregor Samsa suffers his domestic embarrassment in a more modern and neutral *Zimmer*.) Many of the poems are gorgeous, especially "Autumn Day," with the sad, rich cadence of its final lines:

> Whoever has no house now, will never have one.
> Whoever is alone will stay alone,
> will sit, read, write long letters through the evening,
> and wander on the boulevards, up and down,
> restlessly, while the dry leaves are blowing.

But it is possible to make an argument against these poems, to say that they are the first pleasant face of everything that is terrible and painful about human loneliness. Later, in the First Elegy, Rilke will say it: "Beauty is nothing but the beginning of terror . . ." Here, though, the poems—just slightly—tend to congratulate the poet and his reader for having feelings and experiencing beauty. Partly this was a matter of Rilke's temperament, but it is also partly a matter of symbolist aesthetics.

Let us locate the moment. Rilke arrived in Paris in 1902. His wife had been a student of Rodin's and through her he came to know the sculptor, then at the height of his fame, and eventually became his secretary. During this time, from 1902 to 1906, he worked on *The Book of Pictures*, but as early as 1903, another project, inspired by Rodin, was forming in his mind. What impressed him about Rodin was how hard he worked. Rilke's ideas of art had been based on the symbolist myth of solitary inspiration, in which the artist was a passive receptor of intimations of large spiritual realities. But Rodin *made things*, working hard for long hours with a great concentration of energy. And Rilke, following his example, began to think about a different kind of poem. He wanted to write poems, he said, "not about feelings, but about things he had felt." *Ding-Gedichte*, thing-poems, he called them, poems about looking at animals, people, sculptures, paintings, in which the focus was thrown off the lyrical speaker of the poem and onto the thing seen. From this experiment came *New Poems*, work done between 1903 and 1908.

And it is poetry of a different order. Phenomenal changes were in the air in the decade before the First World War. Apollinaire was also in Paris, writing the poems of *Alcools*. "Zone," in fact, with its twentieth-century freshness, seemed to be inventing the new age:

> After all you are weary of this ancient world.
>
> Shepherdess O Eiffel Tower your flock of bridges is bleating this
> morning.
>
> You have had enough of living in a Greek and Roman antiquity.

In London, Ezra Pound was on the verge of writing the first imagist poem, a vision of the Paris Métro. Osip Mandelstam was also in Paris in 1906, an awkward high school boy with funny ears. He would return to Russia and write a manifesto in 1910, "The Morning of Acmeism," which declared that symbolism with its theurgy and its Gothic yearning had come to an end. Pablo Picasso had startled the world, though the world didn't know it yet, with his *Demoiselles d'Avignon*. *New Poems* marks Rilke's participation in this great shift in sensibility. But, in fact, he never made himself over into a modernist poet. His work came to have, through Rodin, a feeling of being actively made, but it does not have that modernist sense of the active and refreshing presence of the world. He was not deeply touched by the explosion of German expressionism in 1911. His Picasso is the painter of the pink and blue periods, as the Fifth of the Elegies shows, the painter of melancholy and isolated saltimbanques. It is possible to see him, for all these reasons, as the last symbolist. He takes a great deal from the eyes and the working methods of Rodin, but he takes it on his own terms. For all their objectivity, *Neue Gedichte* are profoundly inward poems.

Inward and almost savage. When Rilke began to look at things, the first thing he looked at was a caged animal. "The

Panther" is a much celebrated poem. It is also a terrifying one. In it Rilke says something to himself that he hasn't quite said before; he discovers, looking at the big cat pacing behind the bars in the Paris zoo, that the world is not for him a series of symbols of the infinite but a cage. The shock of that discovery initiates the poem, which is half a self-portrait, half the recognition of some profound otherness, difference, emptiness, power in the animal he might have liked, ideally and comfortably, to become:

> His vision, from the constantly passing bars,
> has grown so weary that it cannot hold
> anything else. It seems to him there are
> a thousand bars; and behind the bars, no world.
>
> As he paces in cramped circles, over and over,
> the movement of his powerful soft strides
> is like a ritual dance around a center
> in which a mighty will stands paralyzed.
>
> Only at times, the curtain of the pupils
> lifts, quietly—. An image enters in,
> rushes down through the tensed, arrested muscles,
> plunges into the heart and is gone.

There is a second shock for me in those last lines—after all the concentration and furious accuracy in the articulation of the poem: nothing. The question is, Where does that image go? Or, to put it another way, What is in that animal's heart? The answer seems to be "Nowhere, nothing." Is that good or bad? Does the image disappear because the animal is so magnificently self-contained that he doesn't need it? Or does it die because he is encaged and can't use it? The answer seems to be "Both and neither." The poem doesn't answer a philosophical question, it presents or enacts a moment at which a will pacing around a center sees at the center nothing, and renders in that recognition a sudden, not at all pleasant, sense of liberation. Analogous poems may be helpful. The ones that occur to me are Buddhist. Basho, walking in the mountains in a storm, wrote: "Hailstones / on the rocks / at Stony Pass." Hard things striking hard things in a hard place: it is a poem about nothingness. Again, famously, he wrote the poem that invented haiku: "An old pond; / frog jumps in, / plop." Where did the frog go? Where the image taken in by the panther went. Rilke, deciding to write poems about really seeing, wrote immediately a poem about the exhaustion of seeing. It took him to a much deeper place, and stripped away entirely the lyrical ego of his early poems.

That ego did not, of course, disappear. "Archaic Torso of Apollo" is an agonizingly personal poem. Like "The Panther," it begins from a sense of shock. In this case, the feeling occurs because, looking at a mutilated piece of old Greek sculpture, he suddenly realizes that it is more real than he is—not more pefect but more real. It is even, as he sees it, sexually more alive than he is:

We cannot know his legendary head
with eyes like ripening fruit. And yet his torso
is still suffused with brilliance from inside,
like a lamp, in which his gaze, now turned to low,

gleams in all its power. Otherwise
the curved breast could not dazzle you so, nor could
a smile run through the placid hips and thighs
to that dark center where procreation flared.

Otherwise this stone would seem defaced
beneath the translucent cascade of the shoulders
and would not glisten like a wild beast's fur:

would not, from all the borders of itself,
burst like a star: for here there is no place
that does not see you. You must change your life.

Stephen Mitchell's translation, here as elsewhere, renders exactly Rilke's own sculptural articulation, so that it becomes possible for English readers to sense his inner, stylistic development. Formally, the main difference between *New Poems* and Rilke's earlier work lies in the way he uses the poetic line. In the earlier poems, the line and the image or idea contained in the sentence tend to coincide, as they do in this English version:

> Whoever has no house now, will never have one.
> Whoever is alone will stay alone.

There is a pause at the line-end, and this pause is emphasized by the rhyme. In other words, the ideal paradigm of the poetic form is always emphasized. This physical fact about a poem can express many different things, but in Rilke it tends to say, beneath whatever is actually being said, Look at how the movement of my thought, this flow of tender and melancholy images, is attuned to an ideal shape. There is a sense that the poet, making the poem, is loyal to the ideal rather than the actual. But in "Archaic Torso," the thought tends to muscle past the line-end to complete itself in a restless pause at midline, and then plunge onward. Sculpture provides an analogy. The sculpture of a human body is made up of certain clearly separate parts—the head, the tapering mass of the torso, etc. The delight of looking at it, the presence in it of the energy of its making, comes from the way the parts are seen to be related to one another, which is the sculptor's particular energy of seeing and creating. In this poem, the rhymes are still present *(Bug/trug, Drehen/gehen)*, but they are de-emphasized by the sinuous movement of the lines. The poem, as a result, seems absolutely given over to the moment of its making. That is why the torso in the poem, luminous, animal, radiantly sexual, feels so present and alive. It is also why, throughout *New Poems*, one feels that Rilke has made himself over into a twentieth-century poet.

And yet this is what would seem to be a classic nineteenth-century poem: a sonnet about the ideal perfection of a statue. The mere description would have induced nausea in Apollinaire, or the impulse to hang a FOR RENT sign on the sculpture. What makes it more than its subject is partly the furious concentration with which the poem is made, but also the persistent strangeness of Rilke's imagination. Characteristically, he begins with what is absent. "We cannot know his legendary head . . ." Absence, more mysterious and hopeful to Rilke than any presence, introduces immediately the idea of growth. *"Darin die Augenäpfel reiften"*—in which the eye-apples ripened—is the rather startling phrase in German. The ripening that he has imagined passes like light into the body of the Apollo where it becomes both animal and star, animal because it is at home in the world in a way that human beings are not, star because it also belongs to what is distant from us and perfected. In this poem the speaker stands at a midpoint between them, neither one thing nor the other. That is when the eyes come back into the poem. "For here there is no place that does not see you." It is an odd thing to say. What is seeing him is not there, and yet has passed everywhere into the torso, so that it makes the speaker visible—in the absence of those qualities in himself. That is what, for me, has always made the shock of the poem's last, imperative sentence almost sickening in its impact. There is a pause in that last line: *"die dich nicht sieht. Du musst . . ."* It is as if the brief silence—the heart-pause, Rilke calls it elsewhere—between *sieht* and *Du* were a well that filled suddenly with a tormented sense of our human incompleteness, from which leaps the demand for transformation: "You must change your life." The difference between this and other similar poems is that Rilke does not praise the perfection of art, he suffers it.

But there is also a counteremotion in the poem, just because the poet is being seen. Rilke had already spoken of this in a little essay, "Concerning Landscape," that he wrote in 1902:

> To see landscape thus, as something distant and foreign, something remote and unloving, something entirely self-contained, was necessary, if it was ever to be a medium and an occasion for an autonomous art; for it had to be distant and very different from us, if it was to be capable of becoming a redemptive symbol for our fate. It had to be almost hostile in its sublime indifference, if it was to give a new meaning to our existence . . . For we began to understand Nature only when we no longer understood it; when we felt that it was the Other, indifferent toward men, which has no wish to let us enter, then for the first time we stepped outside of Nature, alone, out of the lonely world.

He takes up this theme again, more forcibly and strangely, in a wonderful essay about dolls (*Puppe*, in German—the noun is feminine) written in 1914:

> . . . in a world in which fate and even God himself have become famous above all because they answer us with silence . . . the doll was the first to inflict on us that tremendous silence (larger than life) which later kept breathing on us out of space, whenever we came to the limits of our existence. It was facing the doll, as it stared at us, that we experienced for the first time (or am I mistaken?) that emptiness of feeling, that heart-pause, in which we could have vanished . . .

"Archaic Torso" reflects the attitude of the essay on landscape, whereas the fury and dark comedy of "Some Reflections on Dolls" is the tone of the early Elegies. Taken together they suggest the underlying rhythm of the thing-poems.

Looking at things, he saw nothing—or, to paraphrase Wallace Stevens, "the nothing"—that arose from his hunger for a more vivid and permanent world. He had a wonderful eye for almost anything he really looked at, dogs, children, qualities of light, works of art; but in the end he looked at them in order to take them inside himself and transform them: to soak them in his homelessness and spiritual hunger so that when he returned them to the world, they were no more at home in it than he was, and gave off unearthly light. In this dialectic, everything out there only drives him deeper inside himself, into the huge raw wound of his longing and the emptiness that fueled it. It is true that the Apollo answers him. Art answers him, but only by intensifying his desire to pass over into the country it represents. This explains to me why I have always thought that Rilke's attitude toward art seemed slightly mortuary, Poe-esque. There is something vaguely necrophiliac about it. "Archaic Torso" is primarily, stunningly, a poem about the hunger for life, but its last, darkest echoes carry the suspicion that its true provenance is death.

I think I should report that when I first recognized this impulse in these poems, I had a very strong, divided response. It made me feel, on the one hand, that Rilke was a very great poet, that he had gone deeper than almost any poet of his age and stayed there longer, and I felt, on the other hand, a sudden restless revulsion from the whole tradition of nineteenth- and early-twentieth-century poetry, or maybe from lyric poetry as such, because it seemed, finally, to have only one subject, the self, and the self—which is not life; we know this because it is what in us humans stands outside natural processes and says, "That's life over there"—had one subject, the fact that it was not life and must, therefore, be death, or if not death, death's bride, or if not death's bride, its lover and secret. It is not only that this portrait of the self's true dialectic has terrifying implications for our age—implications which the reader can conjure by imagining my friend Fred in his battered journalist's trenchcoat patiently interviewing the last philosopher in Europe on the prospects for our imminent and total extermination while the young on Boulevard St.-Michel dye their hair turquoise, dress in black and wear buttons that say "No Future" (so much for finding the Rilke of 1908)—but that it also has the effect of making my own self seem like a disease to me. This is very much a case of blaming the messenger. Rilke has clearly not abandoned the symbolist quest for the absolute in *New Poems*, he has dragged it, like a sick animal, into the twentieth century and brought it alive before us.

What about human relationships? They are more or less what we mean by life, once nature and art have been disposed of. Rilke had marked views on the subject. The short version is that he thought they were distraction and evasion. The purest creatures of his imagination, the angels of the Elegies, don't need relationship because they are complete as they are. They are "*mirrors*, which scoop up the beauty that has streamed from their face / and gather it back, into themselves, entire." In a late poem about childhood, he pictures a child at home by himself, beginning to feel his strange solitariness in the world. Then his parents come home and ruin everything. And in his version of the story of the prodigal son, the young man leaves home because he couldn't stand the fact that people loved him there, because what that really meant was that they wanted him to be their mirrors. "In their eyes he could see observation and sympathy, expectation, concern; in their presence he couldn't do anything without giving pleasure or pain. But what he wanted in those days was that profound indifference of heart which sometimes, early in the morning, in the fields, seized him with such purity . . ." And there is his version of the story of Orpheus and Eurydice. As he tells it, Eurydice is lucky to be in the underworld, where she is finally complete. She is not full of that hungry emptiness that made her open to love. "Her sex had closed / like a young flower at nightfall." And, in Rilke's version, Orpheus wants to ruin that, out of his need for her, and bring her back into the transitory world. But she is "no longer that man's property," and when Orpheus turns around to look at her, she is saved. The poem is stranger and more beautiful than this summary conveys, and the translation is one of Stephen Mitchell's triumphs.

The most extraordinary poem Rilke ever wrote on this theme is the "Requiem" of 1908. Its occasion was the death of his friend, one of the great German painters of the early part of the century, Paula Modersohn-Becker. Rilke met her, as we have seen, with Clara Westhoff at Worpswede, and he seems to have fallen in love with them both. Shortly after Paula became engaged to the painter Otto Modersohn, Rilke proposed marriage to Clara. They lived together only for a year or so, long enough to have a child and for Rilke to discover his unsuitability for domestic life. After that, they decided to give themselves the freedom they felt they needed as artists. Paula's life with Otto Modersohn had a different outcome. He was the director of Worpswede, a much more famous painter than she, and her life in his shadow became filled with domestic tasks. Eventually, she took a year off and went to Paris to be by herself and paint. During that year she was importuned with letters from her husband and her parents, urging her to return to Germany and take up the duties of a wife. Almost as soon as she did so, she became pregnant, and in the winter of 1907 she gave birth to a child and died shortly afterward. She is a very moving and original painter. Rilke, though he loved her company in the year at Worpswede and talked to her long hours about the idea of art (he wrote letters to Clara, one biographer observed, and poems to Paula), seems not to have understood her work while she was alive. It was apparently in the summer after her death, when he attended the Cézanne retrospective in Paris, that he realized, looking at Cézanne's late work, what a great painter she had been. Her death was a profound shock to him. "It stood in front of me," he wrote to a friend, "so huge and close that I could not shut my eyes." "Requiem" was written in the fall of that year. It was begun, appropriately enough, on the eve of All Hallows.

Part of its appeal is that it is so raw and personal a poem. It is not Rilke onstage, not the great necromancer of the Elegies with the seductive voice and the breathtaking shifts of argument which leap from image to surprising image. This poem, written in blank-verse paragraphs, proceeds in bursts: it has the awkwardness of grief, which seems to exhaust itself and then breaks out again. It is also full of awkward ideas, contrary emotions. For all these reasons, it is a poem that is probably more revealing and less self-preoccupied than anything else Rilke ever wrote. The opening lines address Paula's ghost. The anxiety that they express is not feigned.

> I have my dead, and I have let them go,
> and was amazed to see them so contented,
> so soon at home in being dead, so cheerful,
> so unlike their reputation. Only you
> return; brush past me, loiter, try to knock
> against something, so that the sound reveals
> your presence. Oh don't take from me what I
> am slowly learning. I'm sure you have gone astray
> if you are moved to homesickness for anything
> in this dimension. We transform these Things;
> they aren't real, they are only the reflections
> upon the polished surface of our being.

The fascination of these opening lines is the depth of Rilke's identification of art with death. I should confess that it is what put me off reading the poem for many years. It seemed like the poet at his most morbid and talky. It was not until this brilliant translation by Stephen Mitchell taught me to hear the nakedness of the voice in which the poem is spoken that I could even get through it. And when I did, it stunned me. Still, it is very peculiar: this is an Orpheus talking Eurydice *back down* into the underworld, telling her how wonderful it is to be dead:

> . . . that you too were frightened, and even now
> pulse with your fear, where fear can have no meaning;
> that you have lost even the smallest fragment
> of your eternity, Paula, and have entered
> here, where nothing yet exists; that out there,

bewildered for the first time, inattentive,
you didn't grasp the splendor of the infinite
forces, as on earth you grasped each Thing . . .

The key to this is the idea of mirroring. He imagines the artist as a polished surface, disinterested (and, in that, unlike the face of a parent or a lover), which mirrors the world back to itself and, by wanting nothing of it, makes it real. This is how he sees Paula Becker's calm self-portraits:

And at last, you saw yourself as a fruit, you stepped
out of your clothes and brought your naked body
before the mirror, you let yourself inside
down to your gaze; which stayed in front, immense,
and didn't say: I am that; no: this is.
So free of curiosity your gaze
had become, so unpossessive, of such true
poverty, it had no desire even
for you yourself; it wanted nothing: holy.

I don't think Rilke ever made a plainer statement of what he wanted art to be: cessation of desire; a place where our inner emptiness stops generating that need for things which mutilates the world and turns it into badly handled objects, where it becomes instead a pure, active, becalmed absence:

And that is how I have cherished you—deep inside
the mirror, where you put yourself, far away
from all the world. Why have you come like this
and so denied yourself?

The stubbornness of Rilke's conviction—and the wholeness of his imagination—only dawns on us when we see, later in the poem, how he takes up the idea of Paula's pregnancy. Flawed, somehow, by her own desire or by her husband's possessiveness, she has, he imagines, broken the perfect circuit of mirroring energy in her painting:

> Let us lament together that someone pulled you
> out of your mirror's depths. Can you still cry?
> No: I see you can't. You turned your tears'
> strength and pressure into your ripe gaze,
> and were transforming every fluid inside you
> into a strong reality, which would rise
> and circulate, in equilibrium, blindly.
> Then, for the last time, chance came in and tore you
> back, from the last step forward on your path,
> into a world where bodies have their will.

This distrust of birth seems so strange in the twentieth century, so literal, that it is as if it were drawn from an ancient text, the Tibetan or Egyptian Book of the Dead; as if Paula were Pandora opening the box, initiating, through desire, the whole endless natural cycle of birth and death:

> Ah let us lament. Do you know how hesitantly,
> how reluctantly your blood, when you called it back,
> returned from its incomparable circuit?
> How confused it was to take up once again
> the body's narrow circulation; how,
> full of mistrust and astonishment, it came
> flowing into the placenta . . .

There is a personal subtext here, of course: Rilke's jealousy of Otto Modersohn. (How could you have married that man?) And a deeper and more troubling one than that. He has tried to imagine himself inside a woman's body because of his own identification with what is female.

This needs looking at. It is a famous fact of Rilke's childhood in that apartment in Prague that his mother, having lost a baby girl in the year before his birth, raised her baby son as a girl.

She gave him a first name, René, which was sexually ambiguous (he changed it to Rainer after meeting Lou Andreas-Salomé), dressed him in beautifully feminine clothes, and called him, in coy games they played, "Miss." These practices ended when he went to school—the latter part of his schooling occurred at a particularly brutal military academy of his father's choosing. Far back in Rilke's childhood—and farther back than that, in his mother's unconscious wishes—there is a perfect little girl, brought into this world to replace a dead one.

This fact requires a second detour. The occasion of *The Sonnets to Orpheus* was the death of a young girl, Vera Knoop. She was the daughter of an acquaintance of Rilke's. A gifted dancer as a young child, she developed a glandular disease, which caused her to grow fat. She abandoned dance and turned to the piano, which she also played beautifully, while becoming more and more deformed, until her death at the age of nineteen. Orpheus, as we have seen, is the figure in the First Sonnet. Vera is the figure in the Second:

> And it was almost a girl who, stepping from
> this single harmony of song and lyre,
> appeared to me through her diaphanous form
> and made herself a bed inside my ear.
>
> And slept in me. Her sleep was everything:
> the awesome trees, the distances I had felt
> so deeply that I could touch them, meadows in spring:
> all wonders that had ever seized my heart.
>
> She slept the world. Singing god, how was that first
> sleep so perfect that she had no desire
> ever to wake? See: she arose and slept.
>
> Where is her death now? Ah, will you discover
> this theme before your song consumes itself?—
> Where is she vanishing? . . . A girl, almost. . . .

The connection of this poem to "Requiem" seems clear enough. Rilke was moved by the idea of young women artists because they represented his own deepest psychic sources. And, as girls practicing an art, they are emblems of eros in a kind of undifferentiated contact with being, before it has become sexuality and located itself in the world. Paula, unlike Vera Knoop, lived to be a woman. Almost all of Rilke's close friends were women. He was deeply sympathetic to the conflict which the claims of art and family caused in a woman's life. When those social claims seemed to kill Paula Becker, it confirmed his belief that life was the enemy of art, that sexuality and the world were the enemies of eros and eternity. It is for this reason that, in one of the strongest passages in the poem, he lashes out against her marriage:

> For *this* is wrong, if anything is wrong:
> not to enlarge the freedom of a love
> with all the inner freedom one can summon.
> We need, in love, to practice only this:
> letting each other go. For holding on
> comes easily; we do not need to learn it.

This is very striking; and I don't think we deny its power by noticing that, as is so often the case in Rilke, he is teaching his readers something they probably need to know more than he does. All the evidence of his own life is that he fled relationships, that he was always attracted by the first flaring of eros and terrified of its taking root. What was hard for *him*, as Louise Glück has observed, was holding on; and she believes that there is a certain amount of bad faith in his pretending otherwise. It is certainly the case that he was not possessive, or tempted to be. He chose solitude, and took the grief of his own loneliness as his teacher.

This solitude sends him back, in the first Orpheus poem and

in the dialectic of the *New Poems*, always to the ragged hut of his own inner emptiness. He did not trust relationships, but the truth was that he did not have much capacity for them either. Psychoanalysis is not to the point here; we all know enough about choosing solitude and then suffering loneliness not to imagine that because the details of Rilke's life are different from ours, his situation is aberrant and local. He has seen to it in his art that he can't be regarded as a case history. What one of his lovers said about him is what any reader of his poems would have guessed:

> His outcries of astonishment and admiration interrupted his partner's words. At the same time, I could not fend off the impression that basically they resolved themselves into monologues, or dialogues with an absent one—was it perhaps the angel? . . . In truth, he fulfilled himself with his own. Did he ever take pains, even in love, to see the partner as she was? Did he not usurp both roles?

It would be wrong to conclude from this, as some readers have, that Rilke was simply narcissistic, if we mean by that a person who looks lovingly into the shallow pool of himself. He was, if anything, androgynous. The term has come to stand for our earliest bi- or pan-sexuality, and this is not quite what I mean. Androgyny is the pull inward, the erotic pull of the other we sense buried in the self. Psychoanalysis speaks of the primary narcissism of infants, but in the sense in which we usually use that term, only an adult can be narcissistic. Rilke—partly because of that girl his mother had located at the center of his psychic life—was always drawn, first of all and finally, to the mysterious fact of his own existence. His own being was otherness to him. It compelled him in the way that sexual otherness compels lovers.

I think this is why, in "Requiem" and in the Elegies, he has a (for me tiresome) reverence for unrequited love and writes about sexual love as if those given over to it were saints of a mistaken religion:

> Lovers, gratified in each other, I am asking *you*
> about us. You hold each other. Where is your proof?

When the Elegies were nearly complete in 1922, when the whole labor of bringing them into being was finally over, he added a passage at the end of the Fifth. It reads like a final, petulant and funny exclamation point:

> Angel!: If there were a place that we didn't know of, and there,
> on some unsayable carpet, lovers displayed
> what they never could bring to mastery here—the bold
> exploits of their high-flying hearts,
> their towers of pleasure, their ladders
> that have long since been standing where there was no ground, leaning
> just on each other, trembling,—and could *master* all this,
> before the surrounding spectators, the innumerable soundless dead:
> Would these, then, throw down their final, forever saved-up,
> forever hidden, unknown to us, eternally valid
> coins of happiness before the at last
> genuinely smiling pair on the gratified
> carpet?

I love the energy, the comic desperation of the writing. No one has ever composed a more eloquent indictment of fucking: if it is so great, why hasn't it catapulted all the dead directly into heaven, why is the world still haunted by the ghosts of so much unsatisfied desire? But I would guess that most people have known what it meant to be one of that "genuinely smiling pair." They have felt the dead go pouring into heaven. "Copulation," Baudelaire said, accurately but with a great deal of disdain, "is the lyric of the mob." Walt Whitman would have cheerfully agreed, would have added that it was, therefore, what made the lyric—and politics—possible. Mostly, people experience the possibility of union with the other in their bodies, with other people. But it would seem that for Rilke this was not so. He defined love once as two solitudes that protect and border and greet each other. And though it is a moving statement, it leaves out the fury of that greeting. It makes people sound as if they were soap bubbles bouncing off one another, whereas each of those two solitudes is a charged field of its own energy, and when they meet, they give off brilliant sparks.

In any case, this is the answer to the question of Rilke's attitude toward human relationships. It is not that he was not involved, intensely and intimately, with other people. He was, all his life. But he always drew back from those relationships because, for him, the final confrontation was always with himself, and it is partly because he was such a peculiarly solitary being that his poems have so much to teach us. There are pleasures, forms of nourishment perhaps, that most people know and that he did not. What he knew about was the place that the need for that nourishment came from. And he knew how immensely difficult it is for us to inhabit that place, to be anything other than strangers to our own existence. To learn not to be a stranger is the burden of the *Duino Elegies*. It is what causes him, at the end of "Requiem," to take Paula's death inside in the way that she took the world and a child inside herself. It is an incredibly strange and moving moment, because he is asking her, almost, to impregnate him with her absence. Here is the prayer with which that poem ends:

> Do not return. If you can bear to, stay
> dead with the dead. The dead have their own tasks.
> But help me, if you can without distraction,
> as what is farthest sometimes helps: in me.

•

All of this wandering through Rilke's life should help a reader to hear clearly the many resonances of the cry that opens the *Duino Elegies*:

> Who, if I cried out, would hear me among the angels'
> hierarchies? and even if one of them pressed me
> suddenly against his heart: I would be consumed
> in that overwhelming existence. For beauty is nothing
> but the beginning of terror, which we still are just able to endure,
> and we are so awed because it serenely disdains
> to annihilate us. Every angel is terrifying.
>   And so I hold myself back and swallow the call-note
> of my dark sobbing. . . .

Even when it has become familiar to us, this intensity of grief registers its shock. Not the world, the young man in Prague had vowed sixteen years before, an iris in his fist, but the infinite. Now he calls that vow back. In a stroke, he has leapt to the center of his imagination and cut out from under himself the ground of his own art. It is hard to know what is most breathtaking about the moment, the shock of self-understanding or the stifled cry.

The angels embody the sense of absence which had been at the center of Rilke's willed and difficult life. They are absolute fulfillment. Or rather, absolute fulfillment if it existed, without any diminishment of intensity, completely outside us. You feel a sunset open up an emptiness inside you which keeps growing and growing and you want to hold on to that feeling forever; only you want it to be a feeling of power, of completeness and repose: that is longing for the angel. You feel a passion for someone so intense that the memory of their smell makes you dizzy and you would gladly throw yourself down the well of that other person, if the long hurtle in the darkness would then be perfect inside you: that is the same longing. The angel is desire, if it were not desire, if it were pure being. Lived close to long enough, it turns every experience into desolation, because beauty is not what we want at those moments, death is what we want, an end to limit, an end to time. And—it is hard to think of Rilke as ironic, as anything but passionately earnest, but the Elegies glint with dark, comic irony—death doesn't even want us; it doesn't want us or not want us. All of this has come clear suddenly in Rilke's immensely supple syntax. He has defined and relinquished the source of a longing and regret so pure, it has sickened the roots of his life. It seems to me an act of great courage. And it enacts a spiritual loneliness so deep, so lacking in consolation, that there is nothing in modern writing that can touch it. The company it belongs to is the third act of *King Lear* and certain passages in Dostoevsky's novels.

Only the first two poems came to him at Duino in the winter of 1912. But the conception of them—that there would be ten, that they would arrive somewhere—came in a flash with these first few lines. He wrote down the beginning of the last Elegy, "Someday, emerging at last from the violent insight, / let me sing out jubilation and praise to assenting angels," and made a start on several others, then the impulse died away. It is not surprising that it did. He had committed himself to taking all of his yearning inside himself, its beauty and destructive contradictions, everything he had seen—thrust of tower and cathedral, the watercolor sadness of the city embankments of European rivers, night, spring, dogs, plaintiveness of violins, as if he were swallowing *Malte*—and to integrate it somehow so that he could emerge praising. The project needed to gestate and he needed to live with his desolation. The record of the last years before the war is restless traveling, inability to write, make-work, a little real work, discontent. Even his letters echo the decision of the First Elegy:

> I am sick to death of Paris, it is a city of the damned. I always knew that; but in the old days an angel interpreted their torments

to me. Now I have to explain them to myself and I can find no decent elucidation.

It was going to cost him a great deal, but the gains were already great. The main one is the incredible fluidity of the early Elegies. It is as if, not having a place to stand, the author of these poems is everywhere. Really, they are the nearest thing in the writing of the twentieth century to the flight of birds. They dive, soar, swoop, belly up, loop over. Look again at a passage that I quoted earlier:

But we, when moved by deep feeling, evaporate; we
breathe ourselves out and away; from moment to moment
our emotion grows fainter, like a perfume. Though someone may
    tell us:
"Yes, you've entered my bloodstream, the room, the whole
    springtime
is filled with you . . ."—what does it matter? he can't contain us,
we vanish inside and around him. And those who are beautiful,
oh who can retain them? Appearance ceaselessly rises
in their face, and is gone. Like dew from the morning grass,
what is ours floats into the air, like steam from a dish
of hot food. O smile, where are you going? O upturned glance:
new warm receding wave on the sea of the heart . . .
alas, but that is what we *are*. Does the infinite space
we dissolve into, taste of us then? . . .

The subject is the volatility of emotion; what is extraordinary is the volatility of the writing itself. Beginning with a communal *we*, it becomes a young woman addressed by her lover, the lover who addresses her, a man gazing at beautiful women, and then, moving from the expression of faces to dew on the grass to steam coming off food to waves receding from shore, leaps to a metaphor of space. This energy and freedom of movement become, in the long run, not just how the poem is written but what it is about. But it was ten years before that recognition was accomplished.

The narrative here becomes complicated. The facts are that Rilke moved from place to place before the war broke out. He was in Germany at the time and so was detained there, for the most part bored, passive and unhappy. Then he wandered for three more years, from 1919 to 1922, before he settled in Switzerland. The Third Elegy—the Freud Elegy, if you will, or the one in which he uses what he had seen of psychoanalysis to construct an argument against sexuality as a home for desire—had been finished in Paris in 1913. Most of the Sixth, which he called the Hero Elegy, was written in the same year in Spain. It is an attempt to pursue the questions that end the Third, I think, and sits rather uneasily in its position in the final text. The Fourth was written in Germany during the war. It came in a burst of creative energy which ended very quickly because Rilke was drafted, a grim enough event for a man whose only permanent hatred was for the military academy of his adolescence. The poem seems almost to anticipate the event. It is one of his darkest, full of the atmosphere of the war years, though it is about other things—the father he could not please, the women he could not live with, the self he had chosen to inhabit which seemed to have no meaning but its own death. It is full of disgust with the obsessive scenery and the repetitive melodrama of his own heart, but it is also stubborn:

> am I not right
> to feel as if I *must* stay seated, must
> wait before the puppet stage, or, rather,
> gaze at it so intensely that at last,
> to balance my gaze, an angel has to come and
> make the stuffed skins startle into life.
> Angel and puppet: a real play, finally.

He can't get rid of the wish for the angel, but the puppet, one remembers from the essay on dolls, is akin to those wooden, wide-eyed creatures that teach us the indifference of the angels by receiving impassively the pure ardor of our childish affections. There is a glimpse of reconciliation here. At the end of the poem, with a glance at the war, he redefines his task:

Murderers are easy
to understand. But this: that one can contain
death, the whole of death, even before
life has begun, can hold it to one's heart
gently, and not refuse to go on living,
is inexpressible.

This brings us to Muzot and the winter of 1922. Rilke was forty-seven years old, settled in a small house in the Valais region. Suddenly, in less than a month, he finished the Elegies and wrote the fifty-nine *Sonnets to Orpheus.* It is fairly astonishing, not just because of the quantity and quality of work produced in so short a time, but because it represents a transformation of the terms of his art. Simply—as simply as he himself announces it in the First Sonnet—Orpheus replaces the angel:

A tree ascended there. Oh pure transcendence!
Oh Orpheus sings! Oh tall tree in the ear!
And all things hushed. Yet even in that silence
a new beginning, beckoning, change appeared.

This is a shudder of hearing and seeing. It is also almost giddy with pleasure—how that tall tree in the ear has offended literal-minded critics! Rilke had not written a poem that mattered to him in four years, he had written very little for almost twice that long. And now the inner music has began again. What is happening in this poem is that he recognizes it and greets it.

It is possible to say something about what this means. If the angel is the personal demon of Rilke's inner life, it is also a figure for a very old habit of human spirituality, as old, at least, as the Vedic hymns. All dualisms spring from it, and all cult religions of death and resurrection. For Rilke, however, the angels were never hermetic knowledge. They were the ordinary idea, the one that belongs to children at home by themselves looking in the mirror, to lovers bewildered by the intensity of their feelings, to solitaries out walking after dinner: whenever our souls make us strangers to the world. Everyone knows that impulse—and the one that follows from it, the impulse to imagine that we were meant to be the citizens of some other place. It is from this sensation that the angels come into existence, creating in this world their ambience of pure loss. It is the ambience in which Rilke had moved and the one that Orpheus sweeps away.

He is, of course, a figure for poetry, as an energy that moves inside this world, not outside it. He is that emotion or imagination of estrangement as it returns to the world, moving among things, touching them with the knowledge of death which they acquire when they acquire their names in human language. Through Orpheus, Rilke has suddenly seen a way to hack at the taproot of yearning and projection that produced the angels. It is a phenomenal moment, for announcing, as Nietzsche did, that God is dead is one thing—this was, after all, a relief, no more patriarch, no more ultimate explanation, which never made any sense in the first place, of human suffering—but to take the sense of abandonment which follows from that announcement, and the whole European spiritual tradition on which it was based, inside oneself and transform it there, is another. For once the angel is gone, once it ceases to exist as a primary term of comparison by which all human life is found wanting, then life itself becomes the measure and source of value, and the task of poetry is not god-making, but the creation and affirmation of the world.

The death of a young girl prompted this discovery, but it was the experience of hearing the music rise in himself to greet

Vera Knoop's death and all of his own unassuageable grief, I think, that finally jarred Rilke loose. He *felt* the energy of life starting up out of death in this most profound and ordinary way. That is why Orpheus also represents more than poetry. He stands where human beings stand, in the middle of life and death, coming and going. And so Rilke is also able not only to greet his presence, but to accept his absence:

> Erect no gravestone to his memory; just
> let the rose blossom each year for his sake.
> For it *is* Orpheus. Wherever he has passed
> through this or that. We do not need to look
>
> for other names. When there is poetry,
> it is Orpheus singing. He lightly comes and goes.

From here, it is not far to the completed Elegies. The final breakthrough, I think, occurs in the Third Sonnet. Creature of habit, Rilke compares us with Orpheus and is again dismayed:

> A god can do it. But will you tell me how
> a man can penetrate through the lyre's strings?
> Our mind is split. And at the shadowed crossing
> of heart-roads, there is no temple for Apollo.

You can almost hear the music of the beauty of what we are not, cranking up again. But he resists, or leaps across. The last thing he had to give up was this seductive presentation in his poems of beautifully unsatisfied desire. And when that goes, as it does for a moment in the seventh line of this poem, we come to the untranslatable heart of Rilke's late poetry: *Gesang ist Dasein*, singing is being, or song is reality, the moment when the pure activity of being consciously alive is sufficient to itself:

Song, as you have taught it, is not desire,
not wooing any grace that can be achieved;
song is reality. Simple, for a god.
But when can *we* be real? When does he pour

the earth, the stars, into us? Young man,
it is not your loving, even if your mouth
was forced wide open by your own voice—learn

to forget that passionate music. It will end.
True singing is a different breath, about
nothing. A gust inside the god. A wind.

I love the way this moves. There is that second stutter after the discovery, "But when can *we* be real?" and then he lectures himself; and then he is simply taken up into the singing, an embrace altogether unlike the annihilating arms of the angel.

Rilke wrote the twenty-six poems of the first half of the Sonnets in less than four days. Then he turned to the Elegies and the change is immediately apparent. He began with the Seventh:

Not wooing, no longer shall wooing, voice that has outgrown it,
be the nature of your cry; but instead, you would cry out as
    purely as a bird
when the quickly ascending season lifts him up, nearly forgetting
that he is a suffering creature and not just a single heart
being flung into brightness, into the intimate skies. . . .

They culminate, for me, in the Ninth which, though it proceeds by self-questioning, is, like the First Sonnet, almost crazy with happiness. Listen:

. . . when the traveler returns from the mountain-slopes into the
    valley,

> he brings, not a handful of earth, unsayable to others, but instead
> some word he has gained, some pure word, the yellow and blue
> gentian. Perhaps we are *here* in order to say: house,
> bridge, fountain, gate, pitcher, fruit-tree, window . . .
>
> . . . .
>
> *Here* is the time for the *sayable*, *here* is its homeland.
> Speak and bear witness.
>
> . . . .
>
> Praise this world to the angel, not the unsayable one,
> you can't impress *him* with glorious emotion; in the universe
> where he feels more powerfully, you are a novice. So show him
> something simple which, formed over generations,
> lives as our own, near our hand and within our gaze.
> Tell him of Things. He will stand astonished; . . .
>
> . . . .
>
> Look, I am living. On what? Neither childhood nor future
> grows any smaller . . .

The transformation here is complete. It is wonderful just to be able to watch the world come flooding in on this poet, who had held it off for so long. Human feeling is not so problematical here. It does not just evaporate; it flows through things and constitutes them. And, in the deepest sense, it is not even to the point. Feeling, after all, belongs to the angels. They are the masters of intensity. The point is to show, to praise. Being human, the poem says, being in the world is to be constantly making one's place in language, in consciousness, in imagination. The work, "*steige zurück in den reinen Bezug*," is "to rise again into pure relation." Singing *is* being. It creates our presence. This echoes his description of Paula Becker painting, so absorbed that she was able to say *This is*, and it foreshadows the last of the *Sonnets to Orpheus*:

> whisper to the silent earth: I'm flowing.
> To the flashing water say: I am.

The second part of the Sonnets, twenty-nine of them, came on the heels of the Elegies. They are a sort of long suite of gratitude at having finished the larger, darker poem. And though there are a few really terrible poems among them—imprecations against the machine age in Kiplingesque meters—they are, for the most part, very strange and subtle work, full of calm, like light circulating in water. Orpheus has mostly disappeared from them, as the angel disappeared from the Elegies. Vera Knoop is the central figure. She is also Eurydice and, I would guess, that young girl who was Rilke's dream of his earliest self, pure art, perfect attention, death. The Thirteenth Sonnet is central. He begins it by reminding himself again that the way to be here is to have already let go:

> Be ahead of all parting, as though it already were
> behind you, like the winter that has just gone by.
> For among these winters there is one so endlessly winter
> that only by wintering through it will your heart survive.

The next line is the remarkable one. It echoes and revises the common Christian prayer for the dead: *Wohn im Gott*, dwell in God:

> Be forever dead in Eurydice—more gladly arise
> into the seamless life proclaimed in your song.
> Here, in the realm of decline, among momentary days,
> be the crystal cup that shattered even as it rang.

I think that readers, to have the full force of this, must also hold in mind the Second Sonnet, where that young girl first appeared, making a bed inside his ear:

> And slept in me. Her sleep was everything:
> the awesome trees, the distances I had felt

so deeply that I could touch them, meadows in spring:
all wonders that had ever seized my heart.

She slept the world. . . .

Earlier, I said that Rilke's project was the transformation of human longing into something else. Eurydice is that something else. She is Koré, Persephone, the ancient figure from vegetation myth, and she is also a figure for Rilke's own, peculiar psychology and the unfolding drama of his poems: mirror, dancer, flower, cup. She is the calm at the center of immense contradiction. Most of all, and most surprisingly, she is the Buddha of his "Buddha in Glory," the sweet kernel of the world, a positive emptiness from which death flows back into life. That is why the end of this poem so much resembles and contrasts with the stony moment at the end of "The Panther." Through Eurydice, it would seem (in the Thirteenth Sonnet), he is able to experience his own death, to add it to hers, and disappear with perfect equanimity:

Be—and yet know the great void where all things begin,
the infinite source of our inmost vibration,
so that, this once, you may give it your perfect assent.

To all that is used-up, and to all the muffled and dumb
creatures in the world's full reserve, the unsayable sums,
joyfully add your*self*, and cancel the count.

Sei—the German says—*und wisse zugleich des Nicht-Seins Bedingung*. It is difficult to render those meanings created by adding one noun to another. Be—and know at the same time Non-Being's condition. Or the Non-Being which is the condition of Being. The nearest translation, perhaps, comes from the *Tao Te Ching*:

The ten thousand things are born of being.
Being is born of non-being.

Eurydice has become the non-being from which being is born; he has planted her, quietly, at the center of himself. In the peace that follows, and the tenderness, the ending of the poem is almost flippant: cancel the count.

Rilke lived for another five years past this moment. He wrote many more poems, and the odd contradictions in his character persisted in his habits. He maintained a fairly strict personal privacy and then devoted most of it to voluminous social correspondence. One of the letters that he wrote during that time is addressed to a young man who had asked for advice. "When I think now of myself in my youth," Rilke writes, "I realize that it was for me absolutely a case of having to go away at the risk of annoying and hurting. I cannot describe to you our Austrian circumstances of that time . . . What I write as an artist will probably be marked, to the end, by traces of that opposition by means of which I set myself on my own course. And yet if you ask me, I would not want *this* to be what emanated above all from my works. It is not struggle and revolt, not the deserting of what surrounds and claims us that I would wish young people to deduce from my writings, but rather that they should bear in a new conciliatory spirit what is given, offered . . ." This is partly, of course, the perpetual advice of middle age, but what a contrast to the sometimes sanctimonious tone of *Letters to a Young Poet*. About his own work, he is exactly right. It is everywhere marked by furious opposition. And if it is the record of a man who wrestled with an angel, it is also the record of a very rare human victory.

All that really remained for him to do was to become his Eurydice. He set about the task scrupulously, specifying the churchyard at Raron near Muzot where he was to be buried, and even the gravestone, if it could be found, a very plain one, old and like his father's. He even wrote the small poem that became his epitaph:

> Rose, oh pure contradiction, joy
> of being No-one's sleep under so many
> lids.

Another shiver of pleasure. It is like the moment in "Song of Myself" when Walt Whitman says, ". . . look for me under your boot-soles." Rilke died on December 26, 1926, and was buried in the earth he had chosen.

Images

1/

Just down from the mountains, early August. Lugging my youngest child from the car, I noticed that his perfectly relaxed body was getting heavier every year. When I undressed his slack limbs, he woke up enough to mumble, "I like my own bed," then fell back down, all the way down, into sleep. The sensation of his weight was still in my arms as I shut the door.

In our bed, in a bundled, parti-colored mass of light grandmother's quilt, our eldest son. Aspirin on the dresser beside the bed, Kleenex, pencils, Nicolaides' *The Natural Way To Draw*, Kerouac's *The Dharma Bums*. Twenty years old, home from college, in love, working construction, he gets a summer cold and in our absence climbs into our bed to nurse himself.

The kitchen, with that mix of familiarity and strangeness that absence gives a room, is clean and smells strongly of bruised apples still simmering from the afternoon heat. On the table a note in the large open hand of my daughter. "Sweethearts, I've gone to work! Muffins in the drawer, coffee in the fridge. Pick me up at four." She graduated from high school in June. Evidently, she had friends over last night, got up earlier than they to go to her job at the merry-go-round in the park. In the cleanliness of the kitchen, the large freedom of her hand, even the choice of a red pen, are written a kind of independence and command, a new delicious pleasure in herself. High school seniors, a friend remarked, are older than college freshmen.

The moon is just rising at midnight. It is past half, a swollen egg, and floods the rooms with light. I walk around checking. Everything seems all right. Outside on the deck where they have been spread to dry, beach towels in the moonlight.

"*If the Spectator,*" Blake wrote, "*could enter into these Images in his Imagination, approaching them on the Fiery Chariot of his Contemplative Thought . . . or could make a Friend & Companion of one of these Images of wonder . . . then would he arise from his grave, then would he meet the Lord in the Air & then would he be happy*" And Eliot wrote:

> I am moved by fancies that are curled
> Around these images and cling

Last summer I had written about beach towels drying on a fence at the end of August in the early morning heat. I think it pleased me as much as anything I wrote last year, but I knew that it had seemed slight to everyone who saw it. I had somehow not gotten it right. If this were the seventeenth century, Japan, if I were Kikaku or Rensetsu, I would have gone to the master, Basho, and said, "How about this? 'Beach towels drying in the moonlight.' " And Basho would have said, "Hass, you have Edo-taste. You have the weakness of trying to say something unusual. 'Beach towels drying on a fence' is perhaps not good enough. 'Beach towels drying in the moonlight' is bad, even if it seems better at first, like one of those trees that flowers but bears no fruit." Ten years or more they spent together, trying to understand how to make an image.

In our room, our son having been dislodged tactfully from the bed, my wife in the lamplight is rubbing lotion into her skin and examining mosquito bites. That morning we had been lying on warm granite beside a lake the melting snow fed and her breasts are a little sunburned.

We had driven down late in an old car with a new transmission that made shifting difficult. Cool air, then the flat heat of the central valley, the traffic moving in fluid patterns like schooling fish. In bed the freedom and coolness of the sheets is one very good thing, and the pouring out of those images that night driving suppresses is another. Languorous, hallucinatory, they may be the best thing about summer.

Gradually, I pick one out. We are in camp in the morning. Cleaning up after breakfast, talking. I am fiddling with a Coleman lantern. One of our friends is remembering a time, at eighteen or nineteen, when she began to develop a repetition compulsion. Its rituals—handwashing, rechecking pilot lights, lying in bed at night in the grip of nameless anxiety because she could not remember if, bathing, she had washed her vagina and anus in the proper order, performing tasks and then obsessively performing them again—were invading her life and she was terrified. Her parents, so embarrassed by the idea of mental illness that they could not bring themselves to speak of it, finally arranged for her to see a psychiatrist contacted by her father through the health insurance officer of the company he worked for. A stone building downtown. Frosted glass, tile floors, walnut paneling.

Telling us this, she is rapt, alive to the memory. She has a skillet in one hand, a scouring pad in the other. Both hang limply at her sides for a moment while she considers. We are camped on a granite shelf in the saddle of a canyon. Silver Creek runs past our camp and one can see it glinting and leaping down the long valley to a meadow in the distance where it joins the south fork of the Carson River. High walls of granite on either side, ridges of cedar and pine, snowpatches, an immense blue sky. Just above her on a juniper limb a Stellar's jay is eyeing the grains of cooked millet she has scraped onto the ground.

"I asked him, I told him what was happening and said there was just one thing I wanted to know and that was, was I ever going to get over this? and he said, probably not." Suddenly she burst into tears. The occasion of the story was parents;

another friend, shaking out a sleeping bag, began to talk about her mother, how when she was about to leave a marriage of twenty years, her mother had called her to say that she was cold-hearted for not responding to the fact that her younger sister, the darling of the family, had lost a suitcase while traveling in Europe. She had not at first seen her friend's tears, and she trailed off now, her milder grievance suspended. The first woman was sitting on the ground, sobbing, her shoulders shaking. The man she was with came up and put a hand on her shoulder. My son, who had been assiduously practicing a card trick someone had taught him the night before and half-listening to the conversation, flicked me a quick look. Was this good sadness or bad sadness? And then went back to manipulating the cards.

The woman on the ground, forty years old now, long past that terror, stopped crying, took a couple of deep breaths, sighed, got up and began to clean the pan again. "The thing is, I guess, he was right in a way. I don't suppose we ever get over anything." The jay had alit on the ground at a safe distance, still eyeing the millet. Someone else said, "Yeah. A healed bone hurts in the winter." My son looked at his mother this time, to see, I think, if she regarded this proposition as true. Resumptions are a curious spectacle. The boyfriend now felt rather wooden with his hand protectively on his lover's shoulder. He gave her an awkward hug. The other friend, embarrassed at not having caught the woman's tone, made a connection that had not quite been there between the two stories. It was the social equivalent of parting one's hair at the ear to camouflage baldness. No one is deceived, it looks peculiar, but it is an acceptable convention.

In stories, in incidents that might be stories, I suppose there is always a moment, different for different memories, when the image, the set of relationships that seem actually to reveal something about life, forms. Lying in bed, what came to me all in one swiftness was the forty-year-old woman, lithe-bodied, with the beginnings of hard lines around the eyes and mouth, in the morning light, in dusty thermal underwear, with a pan and scouring pad hanging slackly in her hands and the startled, becalmed, remembering look on her face, just before the access of grief; and the jay in the tree above the white millet grains scattered among brown pine needles; and the oblivious friend telling her story; and the alert, small boy practicing a card trick; and the long moraine of glacier-smooth granite behind them that the river traversed and the green meadow in the far distance, with just a foam of white wildflowers flecking it; and me, I suppose, the watcher fiddling with his lantern.

Chekhov recorded this in his notebook: "They were mineral water bottles with preserved cherries in them." The context lost—is a mineral water bottle equivalent to a Coke bottle? what sort of diligence, refinement, husbandry do the preserved cherries imply?—it still gives a small, intense thrill of pleasure. Perhaps the very loss of context, like the lost context of the animals drawn on the walls of the Lascaux caves, intensifies it. What we see clearly is not perhaps the heart of reality toward which the image leaps, but the quiet attention that is the form of the impulse to leap. Here are some other entries from his notebook:

> A bedroom. The light of the moon shines so brightly through the window that even the buttons on his nightshirt are visible.
>
> They undressed the corpse but had no time to take off the gloves; a corpse in gloves.
>
> In July the red bird sings the whole morning.
>
> Prostitutes in Monte Carlo, the whole tone of the place. The palm trees, it seems, are prostitutes, and the chickens are prostitutes.
>
> An actress who spoiled all her parts by very bad acting,—and this continued all her life long until she died. Nobody liked her;

she ruined all the best parts; and yet she went on acting until she was seventy.

He got a bronze medal for the census of 1897.

A clever fresh sensible girl. When she bathed, he noticed her ribcage, her skinny behind. He got to hate her.

This is very close to the temperament of Japanese poets. Here is one by Issa:

> The man pulling radishes
> pointed my way
> with a radish.

And, from the opposite point of view, by Buson:

> Digging in the field—
> the man who asked the way
> has disappeared.

January 16 was a holiday in the Japan of the Tokugawa Shogunate. Apprentices who had been sent from home to learn a trade were given a day off to visit their families. The day also had associations with kite-flying. Buson gives us one kid on his way home:

> Apprentice's holiday:
> hops over kite string,
> keeps going.

That easy leap is like William Carlos Williams, but it is when you start thinking about the kite tugging in the wind that the poem opens up. Often enough, when a thing is seen clearly, there is a sense of absence about it—it is true of impressionist painting—as if, the more palpable it is, the more some immense subterranean displacement seems to be working in it; as if at the point of truest observation the visible and invisible exerted enormous counterpressure. Some of Buson's poems seem to comment on this directly:

> Mustard flowers,
> no whale in sight,
> the sea darkening.

Images haunt. There is a whole mythology built on this fact: Cézanne painting till his eyes bled, Wordsworth wandering the Lake Country hills in an impassioned daze. Blake describes it very well, and so did the colleague of Tu Fu who said to him, "It is like being alive twice." Images are not quite ideas, they are stiller than that, with less implication outside themselves. And they are not myth, they do not have that explanatory power; they are nearer to pure story. Nor are they always metaphors; they do not say this is that, they say this is. In the nineteenth century one would have said that what compelled us about them was a sense of the eternal. And it is something like that, some feeling in the arrest of the image that what perishes and what lasts forever have been brought into conjunction, and accompanying that sensation is a feeling of release from the self. Antonio Machado wrote, "*Hoy es siempre todavía.*" Yet today is always. And Czesław Miłosz, "*Tylko trwa wieczna chwila.*" Only the moment is eternal.

For me, at least, there is a delicate balance in this matter. Walking through the rooms of my house on a moonlit August night, with a sharp sense of my children each at a particular moment in their lives and changing, with three or four shed, curled leaves from a Benjamin fig on the floor of the dining room and a spider, in that moonlight, already set to work in one of them, and the dark outline of an old Monterey pine against the sky outside the window, the one thing about the house that seems not to have changed in the years of my living in it, it is possible to feel my life, in a quiet ecstatic helplessness, as a long slow hurtle through the forms of things. I think I resist that sensation because there is a kind of passivity in it; I suppose that I fear it would make me careless of those things that need concentration to attend to.

But I would equally doubt its absence, which is what we usually mean by fact. The terror of facts is the purity of their arbitrariness. I live in this place, rather than that. Have this life, rather than that. It is August not September for physical and historical reasons too boring to go into and I am a man approaching middle age in the American century, which means I've had it easy, and I have three children, somewhere near the average, and I've just come home from summer vacation in an unreliable car. This is the *selva oscura.* Not that it isn't true, but that it is not the particular truth. It is the average, which is different from the common; arbitrary, the enemy of form. The stillness of the instant exists by virtue of its velocity. It is eternal because it is gone in a second. This was the paradox Wallace Stevens had in mind when he wrote:

> Beauty is momentary in the mind,
>
> the fitful tracing of a portal,
> but in the flesh it is immortal.

It is this crossing of paths that the image seems to reconcile, and so it haunts us.

When Buson was dying in the winter of 1783, one of his friends reports, he spoke to his night nurse about the life of poetry. "Even being sick like this, my fondness for the way is beyond reason, and I try to make haiku. The high stage of *my dream hovers over the withered fields* is impossible for me to reach. Therefore, the old poet Basho's greatness is supremely moving to me now." The poem he refers to is Basho's last, written when he was taken ill on a visit to Osaka in the fall of

1694. *Tabi ni yamite yume wa kare-no wo kakeme guru,* it goes:

> Sick on a journey,
> my dream hovers
> over the withered fields.

Basho, late in his life, seems to have been torn between the way of religion and the way of art. He tried to stop writing poetry, he said, but was unable to do so, and he felt the choice as a kind of failure. He kept coming back to the search for the image. Some of his late poems have great serenity; all of them are solitary. This is one of the last, in R. H. Blyth's translation:

> Deep autumn,
> my neighbor, how
> does he live, I wonder?

Capable of enormous clarity, of an extraordinary emotional range, there is at the center of his work—as at the center of Rilke's or Baudelaire's—a sense of the sickness or incompleteness of existence. There is also a sense—rather like the sensation of driving when you lie in bed after a night of driving—of the unappeasable habit of the image. *Kare-no,* in Basho's last poem, means "withered fields." It is one of the conventional phrases of seasonal reference that almost all haiku contain. It identifies the time as late fall. Here it also means, I think, "the traditional phrase 'withered fields.' " His dream wanders in the world and in the poem indistinguishably.

It would seem wild with restlessness and grief if it were not for the firmness of the syntax—and for something else that is a little difficult to describe. The phrase *yume wa. Yume* is dream or dreams, *wa* a particle indicating what's being talked about. One often sees it translated "as for." It is such a common feature of Japanese that to translate it at all is to begin to translate the culture rather than the language—and I don't know very much about either Japanese culture or the Japanese language. I have studied these poems without learning to speak Japanese and I am afraid of a beginner's tendency to exaggerate differences. A literal translation might be *as for dream it hovers* or *wanders.* I asked a Japanese friend if it would be closer to translate the poem into English, "my dream wanders . . ." or French, "La rêve s'égare . . ." He shrugged hopelessly.

"There is no French word for dream, to me, that doesn't have the meaning of delusion. And all the words for wandering suggest error." He shook his head at the peculiarity of the French. "And everything in English has to be pinned down, your dream, my dream, and all the verbs are physical. *Yume wa,*" he made large circles with both hands, "means dream, the whole thing," more gestures, "*dream.*"

Whatever the translation it is that turn of phrase that gives the poem its deepest, most amazing effect. It is why the poem does not record sickness, yearning, unsatisfied hunger. Nor is it exactly objective or detached. It sits just in between, not detached but not attached either. Intense sadness and calm: nonattached, the Buddhists would say. It was this extraordinary act of consciousness that Buson was remembering in his dying master: *as for dream, it wanders the withered fields.*

2 /

Because it is summer, I have been in the mountains again and am now back at the typewriter. Basho's death poem running through my mind. We had been hiking in Desolation Wilderness. There had been a late thaw and the trails were still covered with snow. The sunlight was brilliant with it and the meadows were swampy and lush with blue lupine and fireweed and larkspur. Toward late afternoon we were descending from Susy Lake. We had eaten lunch, swum, skidded down snowbanks, and were headed home after dousing ourselves with mosquito repellant. The sky was clouding up and there were faint rolls of thunder over Echo Peak. I began to get a prickly sensation on the back of my neck and recognized the onset of an allergic reaction I sometimes get. I ignored it and kept walking, a hop-skip descent down a canyon, granite boulders on one side, a green, sharply rising hillside of pine, manzanita and flowering currant on the other. The inside of my mouth began to swell and that alarmed me. I knew it signaled a generalized allergic reaction, though I had never had one before—the danger is that the throat will swell up and close. I waited for my son to catch up, took a couple of antihistamines from his pack, swallowed them and kept going. My body was beginning to itch all over and we were a couple of hours from the trailhead. Probably I should have sat still.

I was sweating thickly and I could feel my balance going. I didn't know whether it was the effect of the medicine or of what my body was doing or some combination of the two. There was a bitter taste in my mouth, sweat laced with mosquito repellant. I wondered if what I was feeling was fear. I didn't think so; I expected the antihistamines to work. But I also knew that I am a terrific denier of all forms of anxiety. Very dizzy, I stopped to consider what I *was* feeling. The worst was that my son might have to punch a hole in my trachea with a Swiss Army knife while someone else ran down the trail for help. No, I thought, the worst was that I would die. I felt an odd kind of equanimity at the thought. Dying in the mountains seemed all right. The snow melt around me flowed down into the creek and passed through several lakes into the Truckee River and the Truckee flowed into the south fork of the Yuba and the Yuba into the Sacramento which flowed into San Francisco Bay and out through the Golden Gate. Among deaths, I didn't mind dying at a source in my native place. My two older children were almost grown and I thought about my youngest. My death would be hardest for him, and I thought it would change his life in the way that pain and loss change life, but it would not maim him. He was almost twelve. He had grandfathers, an older brother, many aunts and uncles, a sister and a mother he adored. I thought he would grow up carrying a grief. My wife and I had been through a very difficult passage in our life together during the last year, and I felt close to her. I had an intimate, painful sense of the way that I would survive in her memory; and I thought that it would be better in many ways to be a widow at forty than at fifty or sixty. The book of poems I had been working on felt like a mess to me, muddied, failed. I let it go in my mind. And was left feeling bothered that this essay would go unfinished, a promising start dwindled to a too-technical analysis of Basho's *yume wa kare-no wo kakeme guru.*

A rapid series of thoughts, more images than thoughts, in a very dizzy head. My skin burned, and I felt—one last popeyed prehistoric fish hauled up out of the depths—intense shame at being helpless before my family. A vague, half-articulated sense that much of my life had been based on a confusion between bodily confidence and will. And then, suddenly—I was looking up toward the forested hillside and the sky—everything green in the landscape turned white, and the whole scene flared and shuddered as if it were on fire. My legs gave way. I sat down, then lay down, then closed my eyes. The others had caught up and I picked out my wife's voice, felt her putting something soft under my head. I opened my eyes again and saw her face and the hillside opposite flickering and subsiding. I breathed easily and deeply and knew—what I thought I had known all along—that I was going to be all right. In fact, the antihistamines took hold and the rash on my skin cooled very quickly, leaving me slightly dizzy. I listened to the voices of my wife, my sister-in-law and my youngest son and kept my eyes closed. I felt a little chagrined, then suddenly and deeply tranquil.

During the rest of the walk down I was pleasantly light-headed, and my youngest son walked beside me, chattering all the way. I had been pretty consciously collecting and considering images all day—the spray from a waterfall shaking the petals of the delicate yellow mimulus at creekside; my son lifting his arms above his head in exultation when we first glimpsed through trees and snow the islands of Aloha Lake and the dark metamorphic canyon behind it; a group of teenagers we passed at Heather Lake: they were throwing snowballs at each other and each had a different corporate logo on his T-shirt. And my daughter had told us a story about something that happened to her the night before. She had gone from our cabin to the lake for a late swim. Across the way at Chambers Landing, a concert was in progress, the road to the beach was blocked, so she had to climb a fence. She could glimpse the rows of people in folding chairs, dressed for summer, and the San Francisco Chamber Orchestra in black. There was no one else in the icy water and the sun was going down, an immense tender rose out to the west. And she swam in it, and the intricate music of Vivaldi drifted to her across the water. An apotheosis of being eighteen; it reminded me of a poem of sheer joy by Issa:

> Naked
> on a naked horse
> in pouring rain!

I had also seen, that day, a dead marmot just off the trail and at least a thousand feet below what I thought was that animal's normal range. The long, auburn body looked slack, broken; it hadn't stiffened yet. The first thing I saw when I looked closer was a black ant scurrying out of the marmot's nostril.

That image lingered for a while. There were ants all over the animal's body, looking busy and happy and industrious. A foraging party, and very fast on their feet. They raced this way and that, signaling to each other, hurrying on, about as conscious of being on the tawny, dead creature as we were of being on a planet or as the earth was of wars in El Salvador and Lebanon and Chad. But the place in me to which the image sank did not have to do primarily with the shock of the food chain (which, Joseph Campbell says, is the basis of man's need for myth) or with human politics. The summer had been crowded with people, visitors, friends, children, their friends; even backpacking, I had gone with groups. This week had been a large gathering of grandparents, parents, brothers and sisters, in-laws, children. The communal rhythms of family life have their deep satisfactions—even the logistics of them. The true haiku of my days just then would have gone something like this: "Bill and Leif want to climb Mount Tallac and Karen and I are taking the Volkswagen to go fishing, so can you and Mom walk to the beach now and pick up Luke at Peter's later in Grandma's car?" A means to a means to a means, Randall Jarrell called it. It was beginning to be too much of a good thing, and trading away solitude for these other pleasures for so long had begun to eat me up. I suppose I was also feeling, paradoxically, the submerged melancholy of the end of summer. If I had written about what I had seen, if we had, as the Japanese did, a set of conventions that could carry all that weight, I think I would probably have gotten it wrong by identifying too closely with the animal:

> Mid-August:
> black ants, and the little dead marmot's
> half-closed eye.

This image, like the others, seemed partial to me walking down the mountain, glimpses of life, but not the heart of it. At Susy Lake, however, I felt as if I had been granted a death vision: white trees, white grass, white leaves; the snow patches and flowering currant suddenly dark beside them; and everything there, rock, tree, cloud, sky, shuddering and blazing. It was a sense, past speaking, past these words, that everything, all of the earth and time itself, was alive and burning.

3 /

Buson's last poem—he dictated it to his friend Gekkei, then fell asleep and died before morning—is difficult to get the quickness and condensation of in English. *Shiraume ni akuru yo bakari to nari ni keri.* "That one," he is said to have murmured, as if it were an afterthought, "should have a title, 'Early Spring.' " One rendering of it might be:

> In the white plum tree,
> night to next day just
> turning.

Edith Shiffert translates it:

> With white plum blossoms
> these nights to the faint light of dawn
> are turning.

It notices the way light in the early spring, just before dawn, comes first to the white blossoms, and it has Buson's characteristic freshness and precision. It locates a moment of origin, of the coming into being, endlessly, of the world and the world's images, and because it is about these things, it is about light.

Not surprising. Yosa Buson was a painter as well as a poet. Born in 1715, he lived during a relatively settled and prosperous time in Japanese history. He seems to have been rather poor most of his life, and fairly good-natured about it. In his later years, he taught poetry and did paintings on commission. He was a Buddhist of the Jodo or Pure Land sect—which is to say that there was nothing especially unconventional about his religious beliefs. He married, rather late and very happily, as far as one can tell, and he had a daughter he worried about. In his youth he participated in a revival of Chinese art and literature at a time when elders frowned upon the activity. He studied the painters of northern and southern Sung and the Tang dynasty poet-painter Wang Wei; in the histories of Japanese art, he is spoken of as one of the major figures in the group who painted in the Chinese or literary-man's style. The name suggests bookish painting, but, while there was in it a certain cultivation of Chinese sensibility—of *chinoiserie*, someone might have said of an early-twentieth-century artist—it was in fact a return to the deft, clear-spirited simplicity of Zen Buddhist and Taoist art.

Light, light and color and a painterly combination of intensity and detachment, are in Buson's work from the beginning; he has an amazingly alert and wakeful eye, and he requires the same in his reader. Here is a spring poem; it could be glossed by Pound's "*All things are a flowing, sage Heraclitus says,*" or Goethe's last words, "*More light! more light!*" but it takes the intensity of its sense of flux from pure seeing:

Green shoots,
white water,
the barley yellowing.

And there is this poem which resembles Li Po's "The Jeweled Staircase's Grievance":

Blossoms on the pear—
and a woman in moonlight
reading a letter.

Courtly women during the period powdered their faces; they were white; so are the pear blossoms, and the moon, and the moon's reflection on the paper. The woman has gone outside to read it, so the letter is probably very personal. But the poem is a study in those four shades of white. It throbs with them, and with desire, and with the spring night the blossoms imply; and the seeing of those colors gives it, for all its intensity, a painterly calm.

Buson's edge of detachment can be fierce:

  The mason's finger
bleeds
  near azaleas.

or touched by pathos:

  Spring rain—
soaking on the roof
  a rag doll.

Or miraculously transparent:

  Clear water,
the mason
  cools his chisel in it.

Matthew Arnold said that poetry is a criticism of life. Ezra Pound said that it is about as much a criticism of life as a hot poker is a criticism of the bucket of cold water it is plunged into. This poem is, among other things, a figure for art, for the moment when the hunger for the image comes to rest in the image. It is also about work, tools, heat exchange, transparency, and summer. It also registers the sensation of clarity and the sensation of perceiving it, and points to the difficulty of saying that an image is "about" anything.

In *The Empire of Signs*, Roland Barthes resolves this problem by saying that Japanese poems are about nothing, pure signifiers without the hawk's swoop of signification, because they signify only themselves. He quotes by way of evidence a poem of Basho:

> How admirable!
> to see lightning and not think
> life is fleeting.

But this poem does not seem to be itself an example. It makes a point, and the point is clear enough: to *see* lightning. But that idea does not make it a poem. What makes it a poem is the way that it renders the sensation of having an idea, the slightly comic feeling that the thought itself is the sudden vacuum and after-whiff of lightning; so that, while the poem seems to be about seeing lightning without preconception, it is much more about being lightning, or being struck by the lightning of thought. It is in this sense that the image stands for itself. It is a moment of insight that is a figure for a moment of insight, and this is why Buson's poem seems to keep expanding past its metaphorical targets, past art, past tools, past coolness and summer, until it seems to be not about but equal in status with being and the mysteriousness of being.

The first impulse toward any art is, no doubt, to make something, to act on the world. Other impulses—to make sense, to mirror, to transform—catch differences of emphasis, but end by being hard to tell apart. Discourse wants to make sense, metaphor to transform, metonymy to mirror. But Basho's little poem which seems to make a statement has a metaphor at its center—thought is lightning—and is ultimately an image. Always, in poetry, metaphor and discourse mirror their own moments. When Denise Levertov writes

> We are the humans, men who can make;
> whose language imagines *mercy*,
> *lovingkindness*; we have believed one another
> mirrored forms of a God we felt as good—

And when Yeats writes

> Love is like the lion's tooth

the lines have some of their force because they are moments of individual revelation, and they get that from the physical properties of the verse. In this sense, the formality of poetry makes all poems images. But Roland Barthes is also right to insist that this is more purely evident in the Japanese tradition.

There is a way of getting at these issues through Western poetry in which the pure image has been, until the twentieth century, relatively rare. Consider this poem by Walt Whitman:

> In some unused lagoon, some nameless bay,
> On sluggish, lonesome waters, anchored near the shore,
> An old, dismasted, gray and batter'd ship, disabled, done,
> After free voyages to all the seas on earth, haul'd up at last and
> hawser'd tight,
> Lies rusting, mouldering.

It was written in 1888 and belongs to *Sands at Seventy*. One sees, immediately, that it is about old age. It is an extended metaphor, a kind of equation. Metaphor, in general, lays one linguistic pattern against another. It can do so with a suddenness and force that rearrange categories of thought. But in the extended metaphor, the mind hesitates for a moment, sees the connection, and the orderliness of signification is resumed while the mind reads both sides of the code. It is something like walking railroad tracks. Many things can govern the manner in which we take that walk, bewilderment, amusement, grace, suspense, dread, but there is always an arrival at the signified, at the assurance of meaning. Now consider this:

> On a flat road runs the well-train'd runner,
> He is lean and sinewy with muscular legs,

He is thinly clothed, he leans forward as he runs,
With lightly closed fists and arms partially rais'd.

The poem dates from 1867 and it does not clearly signify anything but itself. Health? Energy? A program for poetry? It does not seem reducible in the way that the ship is reducible to old age. And what is remarkable about it seems to have gone unnoticed. It is—with the possible exception of a couple of poems by Jonathan Swift, "Description of the Morning" and "Description of a City Shower," one of the first poems of its kind in the English language. There are other, similar poems in Whitman, notably "Cavalry Crossing a Ford":

A line in long array where they wind betwixt green islands,
They take a serpentine course, their arms flash in the sun—hark
to the musical clank,
Behold the silvery river, in it the splashing horses loitering stop
to drink,
Behold the brown-faced men, each group, each person a picture,
the negligent rest on the saddles,
Some emerge on the opposite bank, others are just entering the
ford—while,
Scarlet and white and snowy blue,
The guidon flags flutter gayly in the wind.

This one, written in 1865, may have taken hints from the new art of photography, or from romantic genre painting, or even from Homer. It is, in any case, phenomenal—a poem that does not comment on itself, interpret itself, draw a moral from itself. It simply presents and by presenting asserts the adequacy and completeness of our experience of the physical world.

It can, of course, be read. Whitman seems to insist on that American flag which was, for him, a symbol of the struggle for emancipation, but he knew too much about what happened to the bodies of those young men for us to suppose that this is a patriotic tableau. One could speak of the vitality and tragedy of war. And the river invites symbolic interpretation. But one never for a moment feels that what Whitman saw is being fashioned to the shape of an idea. There is other evidence that he was experimenting with this kind of poem. "A Farm Picture" dates from the same year:

Through the ample open door of the peaceful country barn,
A sunlit pasture field with cattle and horses feeding,
And haze and vista, and the far horizon fading away.

This is in the spirit of Buson's

Night deepens—
sleep in the villages
and the sound of falling water.

or Issa's

Noon—
orioles singing,
the river flows in silence.

But Whitman's panoramic poems are remarkable partly because they are so rare. Repeated often enough, they would pall rather quickly. There are thousands of them in Japanese, mostly banal. Akira Kurosawa remarks ironically in his autobiography that during the war years the militarist censorship conducted a two-pronged attack on art by mutilating films and encouraging a haiku revival to keep people's minds on chrysanthemums and waterfalls. Not that an art based on natural objects could not be an adequate response to war—Monet's water-lily paintings, for example—but that it must be art of a fairly high order, like this by Buson:

A mustard field;
the moon in the east,
the sun in the west.

It is so good, I think, because it belongs to a particular moment of the day and year, that pallor of the moon and the reddish, liquid heaviness of the setting sun, and the way the acid yellow of mustard fields is muted in the late afternoon; it is really that quietening and darkening of the color of the mustard plants that is the subject of the poem, though it is set against the larger, breathtaking and precarious harmony of the sky. Smallness of detail gives power to images and this poem, immense in one way, has that smallness. Metonymy rather than metaphor is the characteristic form of the image, because all our seeing is metonymic. *Parts of a World*, Wallace Stevens called a book of poems. The world is glimpses, moment by moment, in our experience of it.

"A Glimpse" is the title of another of Walt Whitman's poems, a still earlier one, written in 1860, and a more complicated image:

> A glimpse through an interstice caught,
> Of a crowd of workmen and drivers in a bar-room around the
> stove late of a winter night, and I unremarked seated in a
> corner,
> Of a youth who loves me and whom I love, silently approaching
> and seating himself near, that he may hold me by the hand,
> A long while amid the noises coming and going, of drinking and
> oath and smutty jest,
> There we two, content, happy in being together, speaking little,
> perhaps not a word.

I am afraid to say too much about this poem. Perhaps the best way to get at it is simply to enumerate the possibilities implied by that "glimpse through an interstice caught." Either it is pure wish, sudden and vivid; or it is half wish, half out-of-the-body experience, a sudden seeing of himself inside as he passes a saloon; or he is actually there and imagining himself or someone else catching a quick look at the scene. In all of these possibilities, the poem is suffused with Whitman's loneliness—*sabi,* Basho would say—and with his odd, delicate, almost comic imagination of communion. "Interstice" is perfect because it is a perfectly sphinxlike word. One of the things it refers to is that moment of hesitation when the train of signification stops, when, suspended outside it and outside the world's law of one-thing-leads-to-another, seeing and the thing seen have stillness and weight for a brief while and are circumscribed by silence.

Metaphor, with its transforming urgency and energy, has been much more common as a mode in European literatures. The classic texts of imagism—which seems to have been an idea that Ezra Pound had for a few days in around 1910—are not much more than condensed, swiftly presented metaphors. Pound's

The apparition of these faces in the crowd;
Petals on a wet, black bough.

and H.D.'s

Whirl up, sea—
Whirl your pointed pines,
Splash your great pines
On our rocks,
Hurl your green over us,
Cover us with your pools of fir.

are usually discussed in exclusively technical terms so that it is hard to see anymore that they are about anything but how to be an imagist poem. H.D.'s "Oread" is not very good, in fact, a boiled-down symbolist lyric, too hortatory, too dramatic for its small space. Pound's poem is, of course, splendid, but what is it? Something that would matter, if this were a Japanese poem, and does not matter in this one is whether or not Pound is seeing the bough of that fruit tree. Which is not likely. Chestnuts or pollarded plane trees by the metro entrance. The reason it would matter to the Japanese poets has to do with the knife edge of subjectivity and objectivity in perception. Basho told a disciple that the trouble with most poems was that they were either subjective or objective, and when the disciple said, "You mean, too subjective or too objective?" Basho said, "No." If the plum blossoms were there in the rain, Pound would be mirroring that apparition. The sensation is, in fact, that he thinks, seeing the tired white faces emerging from the gloom, of petals on a wet, black bough. As a result, the poem makes us feel, mainly, not the perishableness of things or their transitory beauty, but the suddenness with which a man has a thought.

Many haiku have the same quickness. It is built into the poems by their odd grammar. There is a poem by Issa, for example, that goes like this:

In this world,
we walk on the roof of Hell,
gazing at flowers.

Yo no naka wa jigoku no ue no hanami kana. It is constructed out of a rapid series of genitives. *No* is a possessive which follows its subject. *Yo no naka* is an idiomatic expression. Literally, world's middle; it is usually translated "in this world" or "in this world of ours." *Hanami* is "flower-seeing"; it implies a holiday, the cherry blossom festival, getting dressed up, promenading, etc. The last word, *kana,* functions as an exclamation point, a grammatical intensification. So, the movement of the poem looks like this:

Yo	world
no	's
naka	middle
wa	as-for

jigoku	hell
no	's
ue	top
no	's
hanami	flower-seeing
kana	(!)

It is very fast. But the speed is part of the convention of the poem. Though it is striking, it is not especially striking. The poem is about how fast Issa sees what he sees; it is also, and equally, about the fact that in this world we walk on the roof of hell gazing at flowers.

Another, still more remarkable poem of this kind by Issa looks like this:

Dry creek
glimpsed
by lightning.

To get it, one needs to imagine the interstice in the universe that a near lightning bolt rips open. Issa is in the dark; lightning; a sudden glimpse of its fierce zigzag configuration and below it the zigzag configuration of the creek, all at once, in bright, brief, unnatural light; then darkness again. This poem does throw immense weight onto the observer, in the dark, having been given a vision of the raw energy of the world. It has occurred to me that one way to see European culture clearly is to hold this poem up to *Paradise Lost.* All of that monumental urgency and grandeur, the restless, sinuous metaphorical texture, the stories, men and women, subject and prince, God, pride, rebellion, the problem of evil, the problem of freedom; and *dry creek glimpsed by lightning.* They seem, without diminishing each other, two very different and very powerful figures for the life of art.

Pound comes much closer to the Japanese spirit of the image

in the poems that he wrote after "In the Station of the Metro," and through that work and the work of William Carlos Williams, that energy enters twentieth-century poetry. Interestingly, it died out in Japan at about the same time. In the year before Pound wrote his poem in London, Kataro Takamura, a young poet and sculptor, was traveling in Europe. Later he would become one of the writers who remade Japanese poetry, but on this occasion he kept a journal in which he jotted a few haiku. It is a very odd way for the story to end:

Donatello's horseman
is blue
in the spring wind.

and

Will I have
an Italian woman
this spring evening?

and

Spring rain—
Giotto's wall paintings
their colors faded.

4 /

Buson, dying. "Even being sick like this, I feel an inordinate fondness for the way and I try to make haiku." There is a natural polytheism to the life of art. Cézanne paints a bottle and some pears, a man smoking a pipe, a mountain: image after image after image. Perhaps it is the fact that he was also a painter that gave Buson this sensibility in such a pure form. He has a poem about it, of which R. H. Blyth has made this wonderful, not quite literal translation:

> The two plum trees;
> I love their blooming,
> one early, one later.

It wants to catch that sweetness of permission that the air itself gives off at the height of spring, but it also expresses a profoundly held attitude of Buson's, an inclination of his nature too deep to be called a conviction, to have even been, especially, noticed.

His work is full of the sense of turning here and turning there:

> Coolness:
> the sound of the bell
> as it leaves the bell.

> Brushing flies
> from the sick girl in the palanquin
> in summer heat.

> A snail,
> one short horn, one long,
> what's on his mind?

> Owner of the field
> goes to see how his scarecrow is,
> comes back.

That from the son of a farmer. This next one depends on one's seeing the depth and subterranean swiftness of a river in the spring thaw:

A mad girl
in the boat at midday;
spring currents.

Dew in the brambles:
one white drop
on each thorn.

Mountain temple:
the sound of a bell struck off-center
vanishes in haze.

Ricefields draining—
the long, thin legs
of the scarecrow.

Winter midnight;
the sound of a saw;
poor people.

That is also Blyth's translation.

The cut duckweed
blossoms
in the evening rain.

The chrysanthemums
lose their color
in the lantern's light.

This next poem depends on thinking of those spring nights when you just don't want to go to sleep. It is rather like his death poem, and more powerful if you remember that candles were expensive and imagine the one flame dying and the other flaring up:

Lighting one candle
with another candle—
a spring evening.

Nothing moves;
frightening!
the summer grove.

That is the Pan of panic, the old terror of the woods that somehow became for the Greeks a god of wine and sap and semen and breast milk. Birth, death, growth, madness, mistakenness, beauty, sadness, curiosity. They are all there, as one might turn from Ceres to Cybele to Apollo to Thor, each power acknowledged and given full weight. There is an amazing equanimity about this in Buson. Not that there is not horror, grief, soul-distress in his work, but that, like Bach or Picasso, he seems to find them of equal interest with dancing and nodding ironically and mild regret.

This is in some ways characteristic of the way of the haiku poet. Anthologies tended to be organized seasonally. Each poem may reach up—or in, or down—toward an absolute grasp of being but each also takes its place in the turning of the seasons, and a deep identification with natural process is the root of polytheism. One may prefer spring and summer to autumn and winter, but preference is hardly to the point. The earth turns, and we live in the grain of nature, turning with it. It is this that the spring-summer-fall-winter anthologies reflect. When the spirit becomes anguished or sickened by this cycle, by the irreversibility of time and the mutilation of choice, another impulse appears: the monotheist rage for unity, for a different order of understanding. There are works of art in which you can actually feel it rise up out of the flow of observation like the sudden jerk and twitch of the neck of a tethered horse. In Chekhov's story "The Kiss," for example:

> The river ran on, no one knew where or why, just as it had in May; from a small stream it flowed into a large river, from the river to the sea, then rose in vapor and returned in rain; and perhaps the very same water he had seen in May was flowing before his eyes. . . . For what purpose? Why?

It also arises in works of art as furious diligence. Cézanne tries a bottle, then a man, then a mountain. There is a natural polytheism to the life of art, and it is fueled often by this monotheist rage.

This is very much present in Basho's sense of the conflict between art and religion, in the focus in his late poems on the solitariness of our lives, and in his dying sense of the wandering restlessness of art. And Issa, though he is as various as Buson, was rooted in the other path toward monotheism: the desire for justice, for an explanation of suffering. His work is enormously cheerful—he resembles Whitman and Neruda in that way—but a core myth, the story of his mistreatment by his stepmother after his mother's death, runs through his prose, and the sense of injustice—and in this he is like Dickens—colors all his work. Here are somewhat free translations:

> This fucking world—
> skinny mosquitoes, skinny fleas,
> skinny children.

Approaching a village:

> Don't know about the people,
> but the scarecrows
> are crooked.

and this bitter poem written in a legal, highly formal diction:

> Child humbly
> petitioned, was spared
> punishment.

Out of this come the great poems which simply *see* suffering, like this one with the title "Hell":

Bright autumn moon;
pond snails hissing
in the saucepan.

Buson is closer to the old—it is probably as old as primitive culture—impulse of the anthologies, little temples for summer gods, little temples for winter gods. One of the things this gives his work, or so I have thought, is an interest in erotic experience that is not present in Basho and Issa, or in the haiku generally. *Mijikayo* is a seasonal phrase that refers to the short nights of late spring and early summer. Its associations are with sweetness and sharpness and brevity. Buson used it as the occasion for many poems, several of which, it seems to me, have erotic implications. They read like aubades, lovers' complaints against the brevity of the night. Each of them begins with the seasonal phrase and then modifies it. The time is early morning; the poems simply record things he sees, and there is something about the presence of water in most of them that heightens the sexual connotation. They were written over a long period of time, but taken together they make a kind of sequence:

The short night;
on the hairy caterpillar
beads of dew.

The short night;
On the outskirts of a village,
a small shop opening.

The short night;
waves beating in,
an abandoned fire.

The short night;
between the reeds
the froth of crabs.

The short night;
near the pillow
a screen silvering*.

The short night;
patrolmen
washing in the river.

The short night;
a broom thrown away
on the beach.

The short night;
the river Oi
has sunk two feet.

The short night;
broken, in the shallows,
a crescent moon.

Each of them is complete. Together they suggest his ability to live in the grain, the way he seems to give himself to the world's tides. Another poem of his—famous for the exquisiteness of its music—renders even the rhythm of this sense of things. *Haru no umi hinemosu notari notari kana*:

The spring sea
rising and falling, rising
and falling all day.

* *The dawn light is catching a white screen near a bed—and making the night shorter*

5 /

Rifling through the drawer by the telephone yesterday, trying to find a clean piece of paper to write an address on—an old man I know had died, someone was calling to tell me where the funeral was—I came across this in red pen: *You guys! I'm off to the merry-go-round. When you're up, there's coffee in.* My guess is that it occurred to her that they would already be up when they read her note. So, trying again, she hit on *sweethearts* and gave the frivolous *merry-go-round* the dignity of *work.* On the other end of the line, my friend was saying that she was going to the funeral, but drew the line there. She hated burials. This led to other considerations. It would have been a different matter in the nineteenth century; the nineteenth century was really into mortuary art. The whole difference between the nineteenth century and the twentieth century could be summed up in two words, graveyard and cemetery. I was trying to examine another drawer without pulling the phone out of the wall, thinking about how I felt about the old man, thinking that he was past revision. Imagine, my friend was saying, a Bauhaus graveyard. You can't. It's a contradiction in terms—and Bauhaus cemetery was redundant. In fact, the whole goddamn century was a cemetery.

The death was not unexpected. He grew up in San Francisco around the turn of the century. His parents were immigrants and his father left his mother almost as soon as they arrived. She had two boys to raise, and he had his first job by the time he was six, his first pair of shoes that were not his mother's high-buttons with the heels cut off or his older brother's resoled when he was fourteen. I asked him once what San Francisco was like in his childhood and he described to me playing baseball one afternoon in a vacant lot when a foul ball was hit deep into a thicket of lilac bushes. Being smallest, he crawled in to look for the ball. It lay next to the body of a dead infant wrapped in a blanket of blue felt.

"What did you do?"

"I grabbed the ball, crawled out, held it up for everybody to see, and threw it back into play."

"You didn't say anything to anybody?"

"Not to anybody."

Another time he told me another story. He quit high school after a week and went to work first in a produce warehouse lugging boxes, then in an office. He liked the office better and bought a clean shirt with his first paycheck. Later, he took bookkeeping at a night commercial high school and that led eventually to a job with an auditing firm. He did not think about his future much in those days. He did what came up and thought mostly about having a good time, which meant taking girls dancing at the hotels to the big-name bands. But he was meticulous by nature and came to be sent out of town on jobs. Once at a little bank in northern California, he was going through the books, one question led to another, and he turned up the outlines of a financial swindle, hundreds of thousands of dollars' worth, which involved the bank manager and the accountant for a combine of small lumber companies. He was young, and he tasted two things at once: power and the sense that he was unusually good at his job. He went out that afternoon into the little lumber and fishing town, five o'clock on a Friday, payday, and cabled his boss.

"Then what did you do?" The subject had been rivers, and since he had told the story and not come to a river I knew it was not over.

"I walked out of town. There was a park and a grassy bluff over the river and I just walked out there and stood on the bluff. It wasn't summer yet. The river was still high and it was running fast and clear. The surface was very calm, like a sheet, but you could tell that it was moving very fast. It was beautiful and I just looked at it for a long time. It was the first time, I think, that I ever really thought about my life."

I don't know that those images meant as much to the old man as they did to my understanding of him, but when I thought about the spring river, the dead baby in the summer tunnel of lilacs, I felt that I knew him a little. It seems to me that we all live our lives in the light of primary acts of imagination, images or sets of images that get us up in the morning and move us about our days. I do not think anybody can live without one, for very long, without suffering intensely from deadness and futility. And I think that, for most of us, those images are not only essential but dangerous because no one of them feels like the whole truth and they do not last. Either they die of themselves, dry up, are shed; or, if we are lucky, they are invisibly transformed into the next needful thing; or we act on them in a way that exposes both them and us.

Literature is a long study of instances. Stephen Dedalus growing up and into some imagination of the life of an artist. Emma Bovary's fatal imagination of herself and of the promise of her life. Gatsby and the light on the dock. Rilke and his angel. The difference between Rilke and Gatsby is something to pause over, for Gatsby is a study of an appalling literalization of the image, and Rilke with his extraordinary subtlety and dramatic quickness of imagination located the power of the image completely outside himself, as a beautiful being, absolutely real and indifferent to him. The *Duino Elegies* are a record of that face-to-face encounter with the deliteralized power of the image. The danger there is personal, spiritual: it is not Gatsby's danger or Emma Bovary's which is a danger to others as, say, Pol Pot's image of justice was dangerous to the people of Cambodia or Ronald Reagan's image of good and evil is dangerous to the people of Central America. Images are powers: it seems to me quite possible that the arsenal of nuclear weapons exists, as Armageddon has always existed, to intensify life. It is what Rilke says, that the love of death as an other is the great temptation and failure of imagination.

Speaking of Rilke and Gatsby, of course, I begin to mix up art and life, since Gatsby himself is an image—perhaps for

Fitzgerald an image created to control and deliteralize the image of the light at the end of the dock, the fatal and absolute yearning through which psychic energy that does intensify the world comes pouring into it. But that confusion of art and life, inner and outer, is the very territory of the image; it is what an image is. *And the word was made flesh and dwelt among us.* Someone defined religion as communal worship centered on a set of common images of the mystery, and it has always seemed to me a useful definition. It distinguishes religion from art on the one hand and madness on the other, from that psychotic literalization of images we glimpse in others from time to time. The young woman on the bus with a ravaged face and the intense eyes of some very beautiful species of monkey who turned to me and said, "I think I'm getting a sore throat. Can you feel it?"

Images in art, or maybe I should say images in great art, differ from religious images in that they are personal rather than communal. Though having been personal, they can become communal: some man or woman may have lived on the earth and looked at women and the rounded middenheaps out of which the human cultivation of the earth evolved and fashioned the Venus of Willendorf as an image of Ge, of the earth mother herself, and having made that image so powerfully, it may have passed into other images and entered the human imagination, in the way that some forms do, as a collective symbol; myself and my classmates in high spring carrying in procession our garlands to the statue of the Virgin in the schoolyard and singing shrilly:

> Oh Mary we crown thee with blossoms today,
> Queen of the rosary, Queen of the May.

The nuns looking on, mothers looking on as we made our adorable, brief passage through the matriarchy. But each of those successive images of the earth mother was, first of all, an individual act of imagination.

And art images differ from psychotic images in that they are both literal and not literal. Or I should say, material and not literal. They marry the world, but they do not claim to possess it, and in this they have the power and the limitations of intimate knowledge. As someone can own a piece of land and have the power to change it or dispose of it as he pleases, and someone else can use that land, walk on it, work it, know the color of it changed in gray light, when the wild radish flowers, where the deer leave imprints of their bedding down, and not own it, have no external claim to it. Some images speak to this phenomenon more profoundly than others. Vermeer's paintings, for example, are so haunting because the women in them are so intimately observed, known, and there is something peaceful and disturbing at once in the fact that they invite absolutely no claim of possession. The image in Japanese poems has that same quality. Basho's most well-known haiku is also probably a very great instance:

> An old pond,
> frog jumps in:
> sound of water.

It lays claim to the world, coming and going, whole, alert, secret, common, in the way that the image does, and it doesn't possess it, or think that it can. And so it has become a figure for that clear, deep act of acceptance and relinquishment which human beings are capable of.

Pudovkin, in a pioneering essay on film editing, tells a story about one of his teachers at the newly founded Soviet Film Institute. I think it must have been Kuleshov. Anyway, the teacher told the students he was going to talk about acting. He had taken a close-up of an actor's face, quite impassive, and glued it first between two other shots, one of a speeding train, the other of a peasant cart with a family in it crossing railroad tracks. Then the actor's face again, same shot. He also glued the close-up between two shots of a beautiful young woman running toward the camera in a white frock on a sunlit day, the seashore behind her. He showed these two film strips to the young directors and let them talk for a while about the actor's brilliant and subtle nuances of expression before he told them what he had done.

I have borrowed from that experiment from time to time when I have visited university writing programs and talked with young poets about their art. Produce an image from your day. One student wrote:

> The mound of snow
> at the corner of Broadway & 100th
> thaws and freezes,
> freezes and thaws.

Interminable city winters. We spent the next bit of time inventing titles. Here are some of the results:

THINKING THAT THE MARINES
MAY GO INTO NICARAGUA AGAIN

> The mound of snow
> at the corner of Broadway & 100th
> thaws and freezes,
> freezes and thaws.

GOOD FRIDAY,
UPPER BROADWAY, 1983

> The mound of snow
> at the corner of Broadway & 100th
> thaws and freezes,
> freezes and thaws.

NEAR DUKE ELLINGTON CIRCLE
AT THE END OF WINTER

> The mound of snow
> at the corner of Broadway & 100th

thaws and freezes,
freezes and thaws.

WAITING FOR YOUR CALL

The mound of snow
at the corner of Broadway & 100th
thaws and freezes,
freezes and thaws.

FOR THE OLD PUERTO RICAN LADY
WHO TOLD ME FURIOUSLY
THAT THERE IS NO GOD

The mound of snow
at the corner of Broadway & 100th
thaws and freezes,
freezes and thaws.

The extraordinary thing, one comes to see, about Basho's poems or Vermeer's paintings is that the world is not set against any particular loss or peril to give it intensity and importance, and so they do not will into the world any more loss or peril than all of us must suffer as a condition for being alive.

It is a truism of Japanese criticism that, of the three great poets in the haiku tradition, Basho took the way of spirituality and Issa took the way of humanity and Buson took the way of art. Which is another way of describing what I have thought of as Buson's polytheism. In many ways, Basho and Issa are more moving poets to me, but I find that there is something steadying and nourishing about the art of Buson, about his apparent interest in everything that passed before his eyes and the feeling in his work of an artist's delight in making. This does not mean that he made no discriminations, that he thought this was as good as that; it means that he acted as if he believed that any part of the world, completely seen, was the world; and behind that, of course, was another conviction which he shared with Basho and Issa. It can best be got at by looking again at a poem I quoted earlier:

> Mustard flowers,
> no whale in sight,
> the sea darkening

I suppose one of the reasons I like this poem so well is that whale-watching (unlike the more exotic cherry-blossom viewing and first-snowfall parties of Japanese culture) is also a West Coast ritual. The big mammals pass by, going south from the Bering Sea to their breeding grounds off Baja California between December and February and return north with their calves in March and April, when, as in Japan apparently, the hills develop veins of bright yellow as the wild mustard flowers. So I have seen, as Buson did, those patient parties of whale-watchers standing on a cliff and seeing no whale as the sun goes down and the sea grows dark, and watched them in their down jackets and watch caps carry their picnic baskets and binoculars and children back to the parking lot in the twilight.

I should say, I have been those people. The poem is about the opposite of what *Moby-Dick* is about. We are drawn to the sea in March for a glimpse of those huge mammal flukes rising from the cold salt in a sudden rolling motion and then disappearing again, or, on sunny days, leaping right up out of it, spuming. We go to glimpse being, or, as Robert Lowell would have it, "the whited monster IS." And of course we do see it. In Japanese, the poem does not even end with that stutter of wonder, *kanna* (!), *Nanohana ya kujira mo yorazu umi kurenu.* The tone is quite level. Buson is not surprised by the fullness and the emptiness of things.